Find Your 'It' Factor

Find Your 'It' Factor

A guide to dynamic musical theatre performance

Jacqui Hall Cuny

methuen | drama
LONDON • NEW YORK • OXFORD • NEW DELHI • SYDNEY

METHUEN DRAMA

Bloomsbury Publishing Plc, 50 Bedford Square, London, WC1B 3DP, UK
Bloomsbury Publishing Inc, 1359 Broadway, New York, NY 10018, USA
Bloomsbury Publishing Ireland, 29 Earlsfort Terrace, Dublin 2, D02 AY28, Ireland

BLOOMSBURY, METHUEN DRAMA and the Methuen Drama logo are
trademarks of Bloomsbury Publishing Plc

First published in Great Britain 2026

Copyright © Jacqui Hall Cuny, 2026

Jacqui Hall Cuny has asserted her right under the Copyright,
Designs and Patents Act, 1988, to be identified as author of this work.

For legal purposes the Gratitude on pp. 213–14 constitute
an extension of this copyright page.

Cover design by Matt Thame

All rights reserved. No part of this publication may be: i) reproduced or transmitted in any form, electronic or mechanical, including photocopying, recording or by means of any information storage or retrieval system without prior permission in writing from the publishers; or ii) used or reproduced in any way for the training, development or operation of artificial intelligence (AI) technologies, including generative AI technologies. The rights holders expressly reserve this publication from the text and data mining exception as per Article 4(3) of the Digital Single Market Directive (EU) 2019/790.

Bloomsbury Publishing Plc does not have any control over, or responsibility for, any third-party websites referred to or in this book. All internet addresses given in this book were correct at the time of going to press. The author and publisher regret any inconvenience caused if addresses have changed or sites have ceased to exist, but can accept no responsibility for any such changes.

A catalogue record for this book is available from the British Library.

A catalog record for this book is available from the Library of Congress.

ISBN: HB: 978-1-3505-5144-2
PB: 978-1-3505-5143-5
ePDF: 978-1-3505-5379-8
eBook: 978-1-3505-5145-9

Typeset by Integra Software Services Pvt. Ltd.
Printed and bound in Great Britain

For product safety related questions contact productsafety@bloomsbury.com.

To find out more about our authors and books visit www.bloomsbury.com
and sign up for our newsletters.

 Online resources to accompany this book are available at https://bloomsbury.pub/it-factor. If you experience any problems, please contact Bloomsbury at: onlineresources@bloomsbury.com

To Bailey.
You spent your life at my side,
showing me every day what 'It' looked like.
Thank you for your steadfast, unconditional love.
I miss you.

CONTENTS

List of Figures and Tables xi
'It' (from the Oxford English Dictionary) xiii
Foreword xv
Preface xvii

PART ONE: THINK 1

1 Introduction: All the world's a stage 3
　My journey of discovery 4
　How to read this book 7

2 Getting to know 'It' (Getting to know all about 'It') 9
　We crave connection 9
　A patchwork history of 'It' (aka presence and synergy) 11
　What do the experts think? 15

3 Unpacking the synergy equation: Finding the parts of the sum 19
　Let's recap our current understanding 19
　Intrinsic performative processes: Introducing the Magnificent Seven! 21
　Sensate experience 25
　Ideational cognition 27
　Intuitive cognition 29
　Emotive processes 31
　Persona processes 32
　Technical competencies 33
　Physical embodiment 34
　Putting the seven together 35
　PQ: Your unique performance quotient 36

4   Extrinsic factors: Transactional interactions making synergistic connections   39

Four transactional interactions   39
The actor   39
The work or story   40
The audience or observer   41
The environment: space and time   44
Atmosphere   47
Turning transactional interactions into synergistic connections   48

5   Constructing the sum from the parts: Ways of thinking, being, and doing   51

Actors and creatives supportive techniques   51
Ways of thinking   52
Ways of being   54
Ways of doing   57
How the pieces connect   60

6   Making synergy magic: Creating the 'greater than' aspect   63

Liquid knowledge   64
Elements that build transactional bridges   66
The role of the soul, the spirit, and the true self   74
The higher self and spirit – a part of the equation?   77

7   What 'It' is and what 'It' isn't   79

A definition of the 'It' Factor in musical theatre   79
The conceptual framework for understanding 'It'   80
Other facets of 'It' – power, charisma, sex appeal, beauty   83
Other synergy-influencing factors   86
False synergy   89

8   Where does 'It' come from, and where does 'It' go?   91

The genesis of 'It' – is it nature or nurture?   91
Where does 'It' go? The world gives and the world takes away   94
Positive psychological outlook   97
Flow   98

PART TWO: DO 101

9 Unlocking your 'It': Introducing your SASS! toolkit and play space 103
Background foundation to the toolkit 103
The SASS! toolkit design 109
Situating the toolkit 113
The 'Sandpit of Imaginative Play' 113

10 Toolkit techniques: Whole-self activation and breathing 117
Whole-self activation (aka warm-up!) 118
Stretching and breathing 121
Grounding and connecting 127
Improvising and atmosphere 130
Imaginative vocalizing 132
Finding energetic focus and readiness 135

11 Toolkit techniques: Acting and singing 137
Acting tools 137
Singing and musical tools 146

12 Toolkit techniques: Physicality and psychology 153
Physical tools 153
Psychological tools 160
The 5 'W's: The who, what, when, where, and why of you and your story 162

13 Putting 'It' together: Synergistic song study and toolkit case studies 167
Incorporating tools into song study 167
Case studies: A window into how the toolkit can work 170

PART THREE: BE 175

14 Living out your 'It' Factor: Five 'P's and eleven 'C's 177
Grounding your 'It' Factor with five 'P's 177
Some 'C's to enliven your performance processes 181

15 Give yourself permission to shine! 187
    Find your flow 188
    STOP! – Surrender, Trust, Open up, Play 190
    And above all, love 192
    Mystery and many-sidedness 193

Afterword 196
Appendix 197
Notes 202
Bibliography 209
Gratitude 213
Index 215
About the Author 221

LIST OF FIGURES AND TABLES

Figures

2.1	Still from 'It' directed by Clarence G. Badger and Josef von Sternberg © Paramount Pictures 1927	13
3.1	Performance artistry word map	20
3.2	Meet Syd Synergy!	24
4.1	Transactional interactions between actors and extrinsic factors	49
6.1	The 'It' Factor synergy equation	64
6.2	The interaction of liquid knowing, thinking, being, and doing with seven performative processes	65
6.3	Symbiotic cycle of imagination, spontaneity, discovery and curiosity	70
6.4	The subliminal transactional bridge between MT actor and observer	72
7.1	Conceptual framework for personal and MT performance synergy and the 'It' Factor	81
9.1	MT actors' keywords describing synergy	104
9.2	Creative Directors' keywords describing synergy	108
9.3	Toolkit tools empowered by psychological capital	112
9.4	The 'Sandpit of Imaginative Play'	114
11.1	What happens between stimulus and response	140
12.1	Seven energetic centres in yogic thinking	156
14.1	Personal values	178
15.1	The valence/arousal matrix for optimal performance	189
15.2	Seven Greek words for love	192
15.3	Blind Men and the Elephant	193

Tables

- **3.1** Synergy's qualities and descriptors 20
- **3.2** Keywords from data analysis 22
- **5.1** Connecting performative processes with thinking, being, and doing 61
- **8.1** Dimensions of flow from MT actors' perspectives 98
- **9.1** MT actors' preparatory techniques and tactics 105
- **9.2** Tyran Parke's techniques and modes of working 108
- **9.3** Correlating processes with keywords and toolkit techniques 110
- **10.1** Whole body activation exercises 120
- **12.1** Using the 'W' questions to gain insight 163
- **15.1** Elements contributing to performance anxiety 188

'IT' (FROM THE OXFORD ENGLISH DICTIONARY)

it, pron., adj., & n.[1]
As subject or subject complement. With reference to an inanimate thing or (where sex is not particularized) an animal or (usually young) child.

it, in thing, n.[1]
A thing (without qualifying word or expression): (in indefinite sense) anything, something. Now rare (chiefly regional in later use).

it, variant of be, v.
In progressive (chiefly non-perfect) tenses. With dynamic sense: to exist as some particular thing or as having some particular quality at a specific …

it, variant of in, prep.
Expressing the situation of something that is or appears to be enclosed by something else: within the … With determiner, especially the or a, or … with reference to an abstract thing, or a matter expressed or implied in a statement, or occupying the attention of the speaker.

E.g. See where it comes. W. Shakespeare, *Love's Labour's Lost v. ii.*

Colloquial Descriptors

Noun: Quality, feeling, energy, buzz, presence, star quality, X-Factor, charisma, flow, radiance, luminescence, beguilement, charm, odylic force, personal appeal.

Adjective: Transformative, transportive, intangible but palpable, ephemeral, heart-warming, mesmerizing, attractive, transient, magical, evanescent, seductive, overwhelming, inspiring, atmospheric, amplified, heightened, encompassing, subliminal.

FOREWORD

In 1990, while rehearsing *Sunday in the Park with George* at The National Theatre in London, Stephen Sondheim recorded an episode of The South Bank Show with Melvyn Bragg. The programme opened with him talking about the creative process and what he was trying to achieve when he wrote '*Sunday ...*' in collaboration with James Lapine.

> *I wanted to show, above all – to tell people – that Art is not an easy thing to do. There is a natural myth about the artist. I had it myself when I was a kid – that you sit in your room with your composer or a painter or a writer and wait for the muse to come ... and I've heard people say, 'Oh, So and So's so talented', as if all they had to do was get up in the morning and the painting was made or – or the song was written. And they don't understand that it's exactly as much hard work (and maybe harder) as making a shoe or anything that you make out of nothing.*

Hearing those words changed my life. Until then, I had fallen into that category of person who believed that people like Sondheim achieved greatness because they were the possessors of a natural gift. It had never occurred to me that creating something might be as difficult for him as it was for me – that it required all his acquired skills and their applications. Over the years, I came to learn that he (Stephen Sondheim) believed he could have never created anything without collaboration and, most importantly, without his craft – a craft that had been taught to him by his mentors. It had been passed on to him through lineage, as well as the lessons he learned through trial and error. He was as respectful and in awe of the skills required for someone to breed cattle, make an American quilt, or knap a stone tool as he was about the skills needed to write a lyric or compose a song.

I spent the next three decades making it my mission to hone my own rehearsal and performance skills, starting with attempting to replicate the process the writers/composers go through when they create their songs, lyrics or dialogue. I analysed every comma and full stop. I asked 'why' constantly. I questioned every rhyme. I noted every bit of alliteration and assonance. I looked for repetitions and motifs and studied what was *not* said as much as what *was* said. Though I was not a musician, I tried to understand why a certain note, chord, or key was used at any given time. I felt it was my duty to do so, knowing that the craftsperson had made deliberate and conscious choices to use certain words or notes at specific times. Gradually, I felt my insecurities lessen. I practised my craft to the point where technique was eventually transcended by instinct. In other words, I found a system of working where, when I sang or acted, I felt free – as if the words were my own and I was always saying them for the very first time.

When not performing, I devoted my life to teaching. It was where I learned the most about myself and the importance of growing and 'moving on'. I became fascinated to observe how fear, in its many guises, was the greatest hindrance to a person's growth. But, so many times, I was also witness to 'the less impressive student's' evolution into a consummate performer. Students who were regarded as stragglers and strugglers regularly had epiphanies. In an instant, things 'happened' and 'clicked' for them. In those moments, their fellow students and teachers were astounded. It wasn't that they had gained confidence so much as that they had acknowledged their fears. By doing so, they were able to 'let go' and be free. But how did this happen? What was the secret? Surely there was a key? There had to be a way of making such breakthroughs less random and more predictable, more accessible for everyone, not just an event for the occasional student. I wondered, too, how a student balances heuristic learning (creative and critical thinking) with craft and technique – especially in a world where many schools now regard the teaching of technique in film and stagecraft as old-fashioned.

Over the years, I have read every book possible on acting. I had looked for the answers in Stanislavski and his offspring – Sanford Meisner, Uta Hagen, Michael Chekhov, Lee Strasberg, and Stella Adler. For a time, Bertolt Brecht took their places along with Laban and Chubbuck. But I was always sceptical of the cult of 'methods'. None of them gave me satisfactory tools to aid me in my teachings. Musical Theatre, particularly, was devoid of recipe books. Most texts on acting seemed to be based on promoting a business – to financially renumerate the author by beguiling the reader with hope. I am not fond of *hope*. It has connotations of faith and religion. It leaves things to some divine entity to create coruscation and place stars in the constellations. I wanted something more. For me, what was always lacking in the 'how to do it' texts was LOVE. The one thing that can truly open the doors to self-discovery.

In 2024, I was performing in what I had decided was to be my last play (*The Cost of Living* by Martyna Majok) when Jacqui Hall Cuny asked me if I would be interested in writing the Foreword to this book. Jacqui had already interviewed me as part of her research project for her PhD. We had worked together as performers in my very first musical, *Candide,* in 1982. Jacqui knew of my passion for teaching *and* that I had retired from musicals. (In 2018 I had walked off stage after the last night of *Follies* at The National Theatre in London and said, 'That's it. That's as good as it gets'.) I have to confess I was a little reluctant to say yes to her request. I thought, 'That's all the world needs, another how-to-do-it book on acting!' But what I hadn't counted on was Jacqui's capacity for curiosity and her belief that everyone is capable of achieving far more than mediocrity. She has no doubt that every student has the capacity within themselves to succeed, and her work in this book, filled to the brim with her LOVE for humanity and the creative spirit, sets out a roadmap for doing so.

We had a number of discussions, and she bravely sent me what you are about to read. I was enthralled with the journey. Not since reading Melvyn Bragg's *The Adventure of English* have I read a book that fills me with such a sense of possibility. Based on her research and her enormous experience as an artist, teacher, and parent (and, of course, her LOVE for what we do), Jacqui has written a practical and common-sense book immensely useful to anybody wanting to explore their full potential.

I urge you not to 'race ahead' in your date with this book. Relish it. Start at the beginning and trust in the journey, as Jacqui leads you on the path to finding your 'It' Factor.

Have fun.
Philip Quast

PREFACE

During my writing journey, I wrestled with two questions: 'Why write about "It", and who am I writing for?' The potential answers would set the trajectory, shape, and tone of my language and style, so I wanted to nail them.

The question of 'why' took me back to my lifelong love for musicals, which began in childhood as I watched my mother play leading roles in community theatre. I loved being swept away by the power of the story, transported to fantastical times and places, and immersing myself in everything that unfolded. Later, as a young professional, I had the privilege of experiencing the magic firsthand, sharing the stage with incredible actors who inspired me and taught me so much about the world of theatre. And, as a teacher and researcher, my passion for understanding dynamic performance has only deepened, compelling me to share what I have learned.

Ultimately, my 'why' and 'who' questions are intertwined. In the early days of my doctoral studies, I looked for anything that could help my 'theatrical children' – both natural-born and adopted – find their professional feet in an oversubscribed and demanding musical theatre industry. This was a territory I knew well; I felt competent researching and writing about actors for actors. I would achieve my purpose if I could uncover some keys to help these precious, young hopefuls unlock work opportunities. And it became apparent that, maybe, my research might have a broader application.

Two events shaped my writing journey. The first was a conversation with a senior professor at a university networking event. It broadened my perspective on the 'It' Factor. After delivering my 'three-minute thesis' elevator pitch on performance synergy, the professor said, *'Please write the book. I want my 14-year-old daughter to read it.'* Subsequently, I've had many conversations with vibrant, outward-looking young people who lose their confidence in adulthood; they become anxious and suppress their creative spark. Something in the ether of their cultural community robs them of joy, and their defensive armour kicks in. I have chatted with 30-year lawyers who have never regained the bravery of youth, losing the passion and energy they once had on school debating teams or the joy they experienced when performing for family and friends. I have conversed with teachers and managers who clam up when presenting a lesson or a project, and I've talked to hundreds who have the phrases '*If only*', '*I wish I had continued*', or '*I used to, I don't know what happened*', as part of their language and story. That doesn't have to be.

The second conversation took place in London in 2023, with the highly respected theatre teacher Patsy Rodenberg. She embodies such wisdom, and her writings on acting and voice inspire me greatly. After reading her work on presence and 'the circles' in which we live and communicate, I wanted to meet her and share my nascent notions about synergy and musical theatre performance and seek her approval to move forward with my writing. Patsy was gracious yet firm in her encouragement to pursue my work, but to do it right. She emphasized the importance of continued research in this area – a pursuit that could help people unlock their ability to be fully present to themselves, to others, and to all that life can offer.

In 2022, I finished my doctoral thesis with a quote from her powerful book *Presence* (2007). I wish to start this book with that quote:

Being present is thrilling, inspiring, absorbing, surprising, and even frightening, all at the same time. It is the energy you feel when you know you are alive, the energy of those moments that writers write about, singers sing about, and the dying remember on their deathbeds. We all yearn to be present and to be met by others who are equally present. We are lonely without these encounters.

Presence enables you to honour, understand and empathize with others. A leader's presence inspires confidence in followers. A parent's presence makes children feel cherished and secure. A lover's presence thrills and satisfies the beloved. When fully present in your spiritual life, you encounter the divine.[1]

So, to answer the question, 'Who am I writing this for?' Perhaps it is you. While my observations on performance are through the lens of musical theatre, and the language and tone I've chosen are skewed towards adults, if you have read this far and feel intrigued or curious, read on. I hope to educate, enlighten, inspire and possibly challenge you to expand the boundaries of your self-expression. You don't have to want to sing, act, or dance in public, but you do need to desire to rediscover or encourage more of the best, freest, most joyous version of yourself, to know what it is to be fully present, and share that wholeheartedly with your significant others. I hope you'll join me on this journey.

PART ONE
THINK

1
INTRODUCTION: ALL THE WORLD'S A STAGE

All the world's a stage, and all the men and women merely players. They have their exits and their entrances; and one man in his time plays many parts.

– William Shakespeare, *As You Like It*, Act II, Scene VII.

I am passionate about the theatre, especially musical theatre. My senses tingle the moment the house lights dim to half and then to black, and the pre-show murmuring and rustling subside. The atmosphere palpably shifts to heightened expectations as we, the audience, take a collective breath. Often, what follows is a small hiatus, that second as the baton is raised in the pit, before the first downbeat of an overture or musical introduction. At that moment, we are suspended. Then, with the first note, we cross an invisible threshold into a world of pure imagination, and the journey begins.

I am also passionate about living life to the fullest. Shakespeare was right when he compared the life of man to the theatre. From the moment we enter this world, we are 'on stage', playing a central role in our unique story and intersecting and connecting with the people who help shape our sojourn. No matter what season of life we find ourselves in, there are entrances and exits: in and out of school, of work and family, of relationships. Each of these scenes and environments offers opportunities for self-expression and growth. Often, what happens to us may seem out of our control, but how we tell the story of our lives in those moments, in every moment, is ultimately down to us. We write the story of what our lives mean.

The ability to create, innovate, think, and dream imaginatively resides in each of us and is there for us to access at will. Whether it's maths, science or any of the performing or visual arts, playing in a sandpit, building Lego structures, planting a garden or baking a cake – the result is a form of creative expression: fashioning something new and original from other things, making something that wasn't there before. Humanity's very form of self-expression – how we choose to live, what we wear, what we listen to, and how we express ourselves in public are all creative acts. Our communication and connection to others are unique and part of our inspired individuality.

However, for some, it has become increasingly difficult to express that creative spark as today's curators of culture and the purveyors of propaganda attempt to dictate what is acceptable, good, beautiful or successful, often under the guise of trending Instagram posts or TikTok videos. We can lose sight of our individuality, refashioning ourselves to accommodate ever-changing societal or cultural norms. Trying to 'fit in' or please external influences takes a toll. The need to achieve validation or perceived 'success' overruns self-expression. Sometimes, our unique self, our personal X-Factor, our 'It', can feel diminished, hidden, forgotten or misplaced. Then, when we most need to shine and be seen – in a relationship, in a work interview, an audition or even on stage in front of hundreds or thousands – fear, lack of confidence, and self-limiting beliefs shut down our personal energy and natural glow.

If you've experienced this and think your 'It' could use a little boost, unlocking or empowering, then this book is for you. I want to help you rediscover your 'It' Factor.

'It'? What's that? Let me explain.

The 'It' Factor has been called by various names over the centuries (more on that in the next chapter), but what I'm referring to is commonly known as the X-Factor, stage presence or star quality. Those who exude it speak of 'radiating', 'flowing', 'being in the zone', 'being present in the moment', or even 'being outside yourself'. Researchers who seek to understand it describe it as 'lightning in a bottle' or 'The Holy Grail'. 'It' is perceived as something tangible yet ephemeral, impossible to grasp yet real and impactful. 'It' can appear and disappear seemingly at will, and yet has the power to profoundly affect those it touches.

We've all experienced 'It' – that attractive, encompassing energy radiating from someone who is truly present and immersed in the story they are telling. You can't take your eyes off that speaker, actor, singer, dancer or child as their luminescence draws you into their world. Whether you are watching children play in a park or standing in a stadium crowd of pop fans, that truthful, openhearted connection to the person and the action makes you feel seen, known, and understood, even if the unfolding story isn't your own. Their energy prompts you to feel empathy. It's the same energy that attracts you to a future spouse or a best friend and inspires a feeling of *joie de vivre.*

During my research, I coined a new term to describe how I understood and experienced the 'It' Factor in musical theatre: *performance synergy.* Why this term? Through years of studying this will-o'-the-wisp, it became clear that 'It' is multifaceted and alchemical. Those I interviewed referred to its dynamic attributes, describing something that forms a shapeshifting whole. 'It' didn't seem quantifiable. This phenomenon possesses a quality of 'something greater' that melds various human attributes yet is more than the sum of those parts. 'It' contains a transformational factor, creating something new and powerful. Actors, creatives and audiences are mesmerized by it and feel a touch of otherworldly energy. Yet, 'It' has eluded capture. 'It' is inherently unique. Different observers respond 'differently' to these 'different' 'It's. I needed a word that would convey this energy's metamorphic qualities and found *synergy*.

Synergy is defined as '*the interaction of elements that when combined produce a total effect that is greater than the sum of the individual elements, contributions, etc*'.[1] The term is often used in business when referring to corporate structures. In that context, it hints at the strengths that some amalgamations can achieve. Synergy is sometimes used to reference people, their ideas, and how they interact. In my research, the word refers to how we access different parts of ourselves – our human complexity – and harness them to find a dynamic energy or spark that is much more than those individual elements. People with this 'something greater' attribute appear to conjure 'It' up, amplify and send it out, and then gather it back inside to nurture and safeguard for the next time.

So, what elements constitute this 'It' and how do we access 'It'? I aim to address that in the upcoming chapters, but first, let me share how I began researching this quality.

My journey of discovery

I grew up in a family that sang and performed, and I chose this as a career that spanned decades before shifting directions to raise a family. Later, in my post-child-rearing years, I found myself trying to unravel the wonder and magic of what happens on stage, not only for myself but also for the many actors I taught and cherished, including my family members. My treasure hunt for this golden ticket to success led me through six years of postgraduate study, which helped me realize that what I was searching for, while evident in the world of theatre, can be found anywhere.

How we perceive the 'It' Factor is connected to how we, as humans, interact with one another and the struggle many of us face in living open, authentic, joyful and relational lives. To understand 'It' further, I delved deeply into the world of musical theatre, questioning those who exhibited this quality in their performances. I asked three questions:

- What are the perceived elements of musical theatre (MT) performance synergy from the perspective of both MT performers and creative directors?
- What practical strategies could encourage and enhance these elements of synergy?
- How can they be applied practically, in practice and performance?

To answer the first question, I sought the wisdom of actors and directors who regularly experience performance synergy, having direct and personal involvement with this phenomenon. I interviewed forty-two of Australia's top MT actors and the creative directors who hired them. These individuals, some of whom are well-known worldwide, consistently showcased what I was seeking. I asked these professional actors, directors, musical directors, choreographers, producers and casting directors for their thoughts on what 'It' is and how they experienced or harnessed this quality. Their responses were fascinating as they generously shared their collective training, experience and profound insights. The information they provided was vast, comprising over 800 keywords they associated with the 'It' Factor. These words formed the basis for my analysis, and during the second phase of my research, I explored whether 'It' could be effectively encouraged or harnessed through the focused application of simple, practical techniques.

I constructed a conceptual framework and a practical toolkit of synergizing exercises that might help unlock the 'It' Factor in performance. During this phase, I trialled the toolkit in an interactive workshop with talented young graduates from a tertiary musical theatre training course. To begin, I shared my research with them, and conducted group activities focusing on breath, body and mind. I then collaborated with these young actors 'on the floor', applying exercises from my toolkit of singing, acting, movement, and psychological techniques to their favourite audition repertoire. The goal was to see if we could invigorate or awaken another level of energy, or 'It', while cultivating greater focus, enjoyment, and freedom in their delivery. The workshop was recorded on video and independently assessed and analysed. The results? Synergistic performance, colloquially known as the 'It' Factor, was observed and in play!

I continued to test my ideas with other young MT professionals and later with established actors, lawyers, corporate professionals, and high school students to refine a practical training and coaching model. I expanded the toolkit with informative, accessible, adaptable, and practical tools that could be applied in various settings. I included tactics and techniques that anyone can use, individually or collaboratively, to unlock and empower their creativity.

At the end of my research, I distilled this simple truth: the 'It' Factor is a synergistic energy present in anyone, anywhere. There is no secret formula made of rare ingredients that only a blessed few possess, nor is there a skill we must strive to attain. We are all born with some kind of 'It' Factor. While some people may find it easier to shine and capture others' attention, those who exhibit 'It' share the same qualities inherent in all of us as part of this vast, motley crew we call humanity.

For MT performance to become dynamic, the 'It' Factor begins with the holistic engagement of our unique personal qualities and extends outward to those around us. 'It' transcends the integrated skills of acting, singing and dancing – distinct disciplines that each play a role in telling the musical story. 'It' is the magical, energetic light radiating from someone, even while standing completely still and simply breathing. 'It' connects the initiator to the responder, person to person, in a symbiotic, creative moment. For observers to perceive 'It', they must be open and responsive to that energy. It takes two to tango, and the performer needs a partner to dance with.

The 'greater than' aspect of 'It' is unlocked through this alchemic power I call synergy. More than just combining things, it's about transforming them. Synergized performance is not to be confused with synthesizing or integrating skills. The simplest way to describe the difference between synthesis and performance synergy is to compare it to baking a cake. If we view our competencies as butter, sugar, eggs, and flour, when these ingredients are integrated and synthesized, they combine to form cake batter. We can happily perform in 'batter' mode. However, the magic of synergy occurs when our unique, personal, inner energy is added to the equation, and we bake that batter. The result is a mouth-watering cake, warm and fresh from the oven. For that cake to be fully appreciated, the recipients must see and smell it, desire it, and taste it. The individual ingredients no longer exist independently, just warm gooeyness!

Michael Chekhov, a renowned acting teacher from the last century, expressed this process differently. He described an actor's presence, or their 'It' Factor, as 'inspiration'. He wrote:

Inspiration comes when everything is forgotten – the method, the technique, the part, the author, the audience, everything. Then a miracle happens. It happens that the play, the part, begins to exist independently of ourselves ... It is a moment of such greatness and strength that it cannot be mistaken for anything else.[2]

While my investigation into 'It' began with MT performance, the subject is now much bigger. No matter our profession or walk in life, we can learn to bake our cake, and unlock and empower personal, creative, connectional energy – that individual 'It' that is 'more than the sum of its parts'.

Some of you may say, *'But I'm no actor!'* And you might not be. However, all the world's a stage, as the Bard said. We all perform – whether on a football field, in a classroom or in a boardroom. The process of honing your craft, going for interviews, and collaborating with others is quite similar to an actor's journey of training, auditioning, rehearsing and performing. Like actors, we all strive to communicate our intentions, desires, and stories to others convincingly. If you scratch the surface, you'll find that we are not so different after all.

This book will provide multiple viewpoints on the facets that make up the 'It' Factor, drawn from those who know 'It' best. I'll show you how to combine and meld elements to create your unique personal and performative energy: your synergy or 'It' Factor. Then, I'll offer techniques to help unlock the happiest, freest, best version of yourself – tools you can access when you need to communicate what you want, when you want, and to whom you want.

This is not a 'one size fits all' how-to methodology guaranteed to garner popularity, effectiveness or professional success. Instead, this informative guidebook will help you navigate your inner world, connect it to your outer world, and suggest possible paths to move from where you are now to where you want to be. Not everyone starts from the same point or plans to arrive at the same destination. For some, this is new; others are well into their journey or just stopping for a final refuel or pit stop. The key point is that you are moving. The philosopher Alfred Korzybski succinctly stated, *'The map is not the territory.'*³ Once you begin exploring, many paths become available, and there is much to see along the way. Embrace the journey, including its twists and turns, unexpected roadblocks, mountains or valleys, or choose the scenic route. You'll get there.

How to read this book

The book aims to be informative, practical, and inspirational, and is divided into three parts. Part One: Think, comprising Chapters 1 to 8, introduces the foundational theories and concepts from my research findings. I will guide you through the synergistic aspects of the 'It' Factor and how it relates to us, regardless of who we are or what we do. You will hear from experts in the field: those who have 'It', use 'It', or work with people who possess 'It'. Their generosity and wisdom have shaped the trajectory of much of my qualitative research; their insights into this multifaceted and complex subject are invaluable. There's much to explore, so feel free to select the bits of research that resonate with you and enhance your understanding. As specific elements of 'It' are elucidated and examined, several key thoughts and questions for consideration will be highlighted in boxes throughout the pages. These will assist you in unpacking the concepts and the internal and external factors surrounding this intriguing topic.

Part Two: Do, comprises Chapters 9 to 13, and focuses on practical applications. Here, you will discover techniques, tactics, and tips that you can apply individually or in small groups with friends or colleagues. Drawn from my SASS! toolkit, these Strategies for Acting Singing Synergy encompass singing, acting, movement, and psychological techniques – some traditional, some innovative, all tried and tested. When combined and aligned with your communication goals, these strategies can ignite your personal 'It' Factor. The techniques range from straightforward approaches that free your mind and body to tactics you can apply to more challenging situations, such as auditions and public speaking. Visit the companion website linked to this text to join the actors demonstrating some of these exercises. Look for the smiling face of my cartoon character Syd Synergy, he indicates which exercises are demonstrated.

Part Three: Be (Chapters 14 and 15) aims to inspire and encourage. Some keywords and concepts are revisited. We reexamine how synergy functions in our thinking, being, and doing, and address the 'synergy blockers' – those self-sabotaging habits often hidden in plain sight. Sometimes, the solution is as simple as guided visualization, writing a journal entry, taking ten minutes to breathe deeply, or giving yourself a good talking-to.

I hope this book offers you new insights, presents challenges, and encourages you on your journey. You may rediscover hidden aspects of yourself and discover new ways to re-energize your unique, personal 'It' Factor. While it won't provide all the answers, it should point you in a positive direction. After that, it's up to you to apply what you've learned.

So, what are we waiting for? Let's dive in!

2
GETTING TO KNOW 'IT' (GETTING TO KNOW ALL ABOUT 'IT')

People recognize 'It' when they see it, but when asked to describe this energy, they can be at a loss for words. What is 'It', and why is it significant? To explore these questions, I consulted the wisdom of the world's experts through books, journals, digital media, interviews and personal conversations. I pieced together research, experiences, history and reasoned conjectures to capture its essence. This chapter will walk you through the background and critical thinking regarding this amorphous energy. We'll look at the knowledge that shapes 'It's context, informs current understanding, and positions perspective.

We crave connection

Humanity is hardwired for intimate relationships and connection with one another, our immediate environment, and the greater universe. We cannot help but discover new expressions and ways 'to know and be known'. It's in our DNA. Even in the womb, our bodies connect to the outside world, responding to sound and rhythm. Once we enter the world, vision, smell, taste, and touch combine to enrich our sensory experiences, and the ways we communicate multiply as catalytic energy binds us to significant others.

The human mind, heart and soul have always sought creative expressions of something otherworldly, something beyond. We love to celebrate our humanity, our dreams, and the imaginings that fuel our present and future lives, inspiring ourselves and future generations. For those who love telling musical stories, there is a compulsion to make the intangible tangible, conjuring the inanimate to life by embodying words and ideas. We attribute value to them, creating a heightened realism that captures, inspires and communicates with those who listen and watch. In musical theatre, performing becomes synergistic as actors use multiple skills to transport observers to a different time and place in the moment of storytelling and, in doing so, transform passive observers into active participants.

It has always been thus. Before recorded history, people gathered to listen to stories, sing songs, and dance. The inter-relational offspring of these three art forms – a theatrical style of musical acting – is the area I chose to research: musical theatre. It has been experienced by humankind and celebrated in various forms for millennia, performed on stages that are large, small and makeshift. Our lives and history have been shared in this way for generations, recorded in print and captured on tape, disc, celluloid and more recently, digital media.

Live performance has always served as a lens through which to view the culture in which it is situated. For thousands of years, bards, rhapsodes and stitchers of songs have communicated and curated culture and philosophy. In Aristotelian times, mankind's relationship with the gods and the created world was explained. During the European Middle Ages, morality, mystery and miracle plays edified and entertained the general populace. Fast forward to today's Western world, and the fundamental desire to be entertained, inspired, educated and creatively connected remains unchanged.

Over the past 120 years, the art of storytelling has evolved into new formats, and its compelling power has taken on various forms. Technological advancements in communication have come rapidly. The early twentieth century popularized the radio play, igniting listeners' minds and hearts as words, vocal timbre, music and sound effects were delivered creatively. Notably, H. G. Wells' 1897 science fiction story, *The War of the Worlds*, about a Martian invasion, was so powerfully and cleverly reimagined for a CBS radio show in 1938 that some listeners believed it was real. Orson Welles' resonant vocal timbre convincingly brought the story to life, purportedly inciting panic in some cases.

Across the Atlantic, in Paris in 1895, the Lumière brothers' first moving-picture offerings initiated a cinematic watershed that transformed Western societal entertainment forever. The 'silver screen' quickly became a global phenomenon, teeming with sights and sounds of foreign climes and larger-than-life heroes and heroines. With the advent of television in the 1950s, home video entertainment in the 1980s, the mainstream emergence of the internet in the 1990s and the twenty-first-century revolution of online viewing, storytelling has expanded and morphed to the point of no return.

Today, technology permeates our daily lives, seemingly broadening our knowledge and experiences, yet our sense of community and real connection can feel diminished. Those who control the media wield power over the masses, possessing the ability to subliminally govern us. Digital platforms filled with curated snippets of reality present a skewed view of the world and its inhabitants, prompting us to live vicariously through their content. Through the work of the camera and manipulative editing, we become enmeshed in the real and imagined narratives of others, lured into a false sense of intimacy. We relate to the triumphs and struggles of individuals we will never meet, whether they are the next vocal sensation, an aspiring master chef, an elite athlete or the 'average Joe' racing across continents, winning money on a quiz show or renovating a home in record time. These television programmes blur the lines between reality and fantasy, calling societal notions of 'truth' into question.

What fuels the immense popularity of reality TV and online viewing? I believe it stems from our deep desire to connect. We yearn to experience something immediate and extraordinary, feeling a part of someone else's story – something new, authentic, and potentially attainable. Their triumphs become our successes, and we feel uplifted, becoming part of their journey, and sometimes emotionally subsume it, making it our own. Recently, the impact of digital platforms on society has come under scrutiny. Initially designed for social connection and information sharing, these forms of personal entertainment are often monetized and leveraged for marketing purposes. Some content clutters the airwaves, affects creative freedom, and stifles originality.[1]

Regardless of the millennium or era we are born into, we all belong to a humanity that is hardwired to create and communicate. Artists who shine and illuminate the physical or digital stage are unapologetically and joyfully themselves. They invite us to join them in their storytelling. Whether on screen or live, when we observe a performer with that special spark our hormones react; we feel drawn to them and, in return, we feel known and seen. This spark, this 'It', can provoke extraordinary responses.

So, what is 'It'? Are there different types? For me, this energy was most recognizable when I watched a live performance. There were no film editors or close-ups to manipulate the reality unfolding before me. Often, in that darkened theatre, I would focus on the actors, and there would be one or two that captivated and moved me deeply. I felt their emotions and experienced a seemingly real moment through them. They had 'It'. Was it something they learned during their training?

As a passionate musical theatre practitioner and teacher, I sought to understand my experiences. During my master's studies, I explored the current tertiary training available for aspiring musical theatre actors. These hopefuls are encouraged to integrate their unique skill sets to create seamless performances. Classes in acting through song and larger student productions prepare them to portray realistic characterizations with expressive, authentic emotions that resonate with and impact the audience while advancing the dramaturgy. But how do they discover that extra spark? Can 'It' be taught?

Many graduates who have pursued successful careers in musical theatre affirm that the experience gained 'on the floor' – working in shows alongside other professional actors and creatives – teaches them how to be present on stage, fully inhabit their roles, and shine. A few still believe that you either have the 'It' Factor or you don't. However, the actors and creatives I interviewed see things differently. In the upcoming chapters, we'll explore what industry professionals consider to be the essential elements of 'It' Factor synergy and how coaching can unlock and nurture it

But first, let's examine what some historians and theorists believe is the genesis of this magic spark.

A patchwork history of 'It' (aka presence and synergy)

Early beginnings

The concept of 'It' is not new. Although the Greek philosopher Aristotle did not directly use this hybrid pronoun/noun, around 300 BCE, he wrote a book about aspects of this energy titled *Rhetoric*. He identified three modes of persuasion – *ethos, pathos* and *logos* – which impact three core communication elements: the deliverer, the audience, and the text. His treatise became a textbook for many great orators of the time. These Ancient Greeks were the equivalents of our current superstar celebrities; they had the power to sway public opinion and, at times, change the course of history. So, what did they utilize? What comprised their brand of 'It'?

Ethos relates to the trustworthiness and moral standing of the orator. Defined as *'the characteristic spirit of a culture, era or community as manifested in its attitudes and aspirations'*,[2] it is the Greek word for 'disposition' and 'character', encompassing the spirit, values, and beliefs that guide our decision-making and shape our hopes and dreams. Through ethical appeal and credibility, a person utilizing ethos in their communication conveys subliminal messages of authority and integrity, which create believability. No wonder *ethos* is a foundational tool in effective advertising.

Aristotle's second mode of persuasion, *pathos*, refers to the Greek concept of experience and suffering, as well as the connection an audience may feel with the speaker or writer.[3] This persuasive technique appeals directly to our emotions and passions. When we experience sympathy or empathy, we engage with this form of persuasion, which includes an implicit call to action.

The third, *logos*, is Greek for 'word' and serves as the factual cornerstone of the story. Through sound reasoning and a logical progression of thought, something may appear to be proven, persuading the listener to accept what they are told.[4] Left-brain energy is engaged, and truth is perceived.

The Ancient Greeks also introduced a fourth element into their version of 'It' – *kairos*.[5] This Greek word for qualitative time refers to the favourable moment to deliver the goods, that window of opportunity when communication lines connecting the giver and the receiver are open and primed to receive *ethos*, *pathos* and *logos* in varying amounts. The heady combination of these four elements create a force to be reckoned with, establishing some of the foundational qualities found in synergistic connections and how 'It' appears to function.

Moving forward several hundred years into early Christendom, two additional Greek words that express 'It's qualities can be found in biblical texts: *synergoi* and *charism*. The early Church fathers originally coined the term *synergy* to describe the collaborative relationship between God and man, which encompasses both divine grace and human freedom, as articulated by the apostle Paul: *'We are God's fellow workers (synergoi)'*.[6] Another element of synergy – that of divine phenomenological alchemy – is also reflected in the mystery surrounding the Eucharist.

Additionally, the early fathers introduced a second concept: *charisma*. This term elaborates on the idea of grace, which, in Greek, refers to favour freely given or the gift of grace.[7] In the New Testament, the term *charism*, meaning a spiritual gift endowed by the divine, is widely used. These gifts are viewed as enhanced natural abilities and supernaturally imparted powers, believed to be given for the benefit of others.

Sociologist Max Weber (1864–1920) broadened the usage of the word charisma, infusing it with social authority and acknowledging that the role of charisma in leadership is primarily recognized by those being led. Weber writes:

Charisma is a certain quality of an individual personality by which he is set apart from ordinary men and treated as endowed with supernatural, superhuman, or at least specifically exceptional powers or qualities. These, as such, are not accessible to the ordinary person but are regarded as of divine origin or as exemplary on the basis of them, the individual concerned is treated as a leader.[8]

'It' and entertainment

Jane Goodall's 2008 book, *Stage Presence: The Actor as Mesmerist*, illuminates the history and ideas surrounding another word often associated with 'It': *presence*. The earliest usages of the word indicate that it was linked to the status of pre-eminent figures – cardinals, popes, sovereigns, and royalty. In the burgeoning society of Renaissance England, dignitaries were recognized as possessing this energy; for example, in 1579, Sir Thomas More was regarded as 'a man of stately *and handsome presence*'.[9] The Elizabethan era (1558–1603) further cultivated the concept of 'larger-than-life' actors, charismatic celebrities, writers, politicians, and statesmen.

The eighteenth century saw the development of a theatre for the masses and opportunities for a different type of performance 'It' Factor to be experienced. London nurtured a hybrid form of highbrow entertainment with the political satire *The Beggar's Opera* (1728) by John Gay (1682–1732), which used popular operatic melodies and bawdy tunes interspersed with text, enthralling audiences. Actor, director, theatre manager, and producer David Garrick (1717–1779) profoundly influenced theatre practice both on stage and off with his naturalistic and emotionally powerful acting and directing. Garrick shaped much of Europe's approach to theatre, making it accessible and believable.

The trend for popular entertainment continued on the continent. In Paris, in the mid-1800s, German-born Jacques Offenbach (1819–1880), a prodigious composer and natural entrepreneur, became

GETTING TO KNOW 'IT'

the father of a new form of musical invention, the French operetta. This fun yet sophisticated form of entertainment combined elements of grand opera with social and political themes that cajoled and teased. The performing arts arena where public opinion could create stars had arrived.

In England during the Victorian era (1837–1901), Queen Victoria's reign brought significant social changes and a populace that sought entertainment in pubs and music halls, which legitimized popular songs. Gilbert and Sullivan's comedic operettas enjoyed immense popularity from 1880 to 1900 in both the UK and the US. Across the Atlantic, in the New World environment of North America, elements of Western musical theatre coalesced and found their substance and voice. With improved public transportation, theatres proliferated on Broadway and beyond. Live theatre became a primary source of entertainment, as actors brought exotic stories to life in real time. From Fanny Brice of Follies fame to Laurence Olivier or John Gielgud declaiming Shakespeare on the classical British theatre stage, actors became luminaries as impassioned audiences elevated them to the status of royalty.

But how to describe the special energy these newly minted celebrities exuded? Goodall (2008) directs the conversation to the work of Mesmer (1734–1815) and explores the notions of magic alongside the concepts of human electricity and magnetic power. She connects the concept of presence with '*the new order of scientific understanding*'.[10] She differentiates between the profound power of 'mesmerizing' and the action and connectivity of 'dazzling' and the 'magnetic' drawing power that some performers display. With the advent of the scientific use of radium in the twentieth century, a new term, radiance, was added to the descriptors. Interestingly, the growing vocabulary audiences use to describe the 'It' Factor's attractive powers signifies how it is perceived.

Now to the actual term 'It'. In 1904, Edwardian writer Rudyard Kipling first introduced the term in his short story, *Mrs Bathurst*:

'It isn't beauty, so to speak, nor good talk necessarily. It's just It. Some women will stay in a man's memory if they once walk down a street.'[11]

The 'Silver Screen'

In 1927, the term 'It' was launched into common usage when Hollywood romance writer, producer, and influencer Elinor Glyn coined the word in her novella and subsequent screenplay for the silent movie of the same name (Figure 2.1), starring the incomparable Clara Bow. Glyn makes a cameo appearance to explain the term. References in the film point to a personal power that one possesses, and the obscure shopgirl role that Bow plays is the perfect foil for advancing the notion that 'It' can be found anywhere and isn't tied to class or conventional beauty.

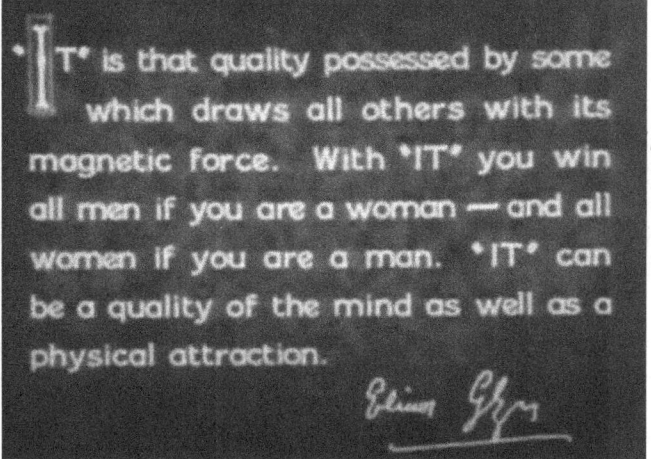

Figure 2.1 Still from 'It' directed by Clarence G. Badger and Josef von Sternberg © Paramount Pictures 1927. All rights reserved.

Note: Captured at 1:31 sec. Silver Screen Classics https://www.youtube.com/watch?v=GriikkUNalk.

Glyn first devised the phrase 'The It Girl' to refer to Clara Bow, whose meteoric rise to stardom embodied an alluring, untouchable quality. The silver screen amplified the movie star's cheeky, engaging personality, and her performance blended her natural persona with the infectiously attractive and seductive traits of her fictional character.

Glyn wrote extensively on the subject and brought her treatise to the silver screen, weaving her thoughts into the plot. She states:

To have It, the fortunate possessor must have that strange magnetism which attracts both sexes. He or she must be entirely unselfconscious and full of self-confidence, indifferent to the effect he or she is producing, and uninfluenced by others. There must be physical attraction but beauty is unnecessary. Conceit or self-consciousness destroys It immediately. In the animal world, It demonstrates itself in tigers and cats, both animals being fascinating and mysterious and quite unbiddable.[12]

Clara referred to herself as 'the real jazz baby'. Her present, 'in the moment' and unselfconscious approach to storytelling was mesmerizing. Bow was spontaneous and almost carefree while filming, wearing her heart on her sleeve, feeling, and discovering and creating moments that weren't scripted or directed. Without spoken dialogue to convey the story, her facial expressions and body language clearly communicated every thought and nuance. Her openness was extraordinary and captivating.

This style of cinematic storytelling created a confluence of the authentic and imagined. Post-war moviegoers craved this heady mix as they watched larger-than-life characters perform extraordinary feats in exotic locations on the cinema screen. It is estimated that, at that time, 50 million people visited the cinema every week – approximately half of the American population. The term began to be used more commonly to refer to those standout actors who were part of the burgeoning film industry. Those who exhibited 'It' were often seen as 'the boy or girl next door', who could be accessible and relatable yet remain transcendent.

> Take a few moments and watch Clara Bow at work in the silent movie *It* (1927). It's available on YouTube. Turn off the soundtrack and focus in on her eyes, face, body language and movement. I find her enthralling. You can read every little thought that connects her to the other characters and the advancing story. An open looseness and impulsive spontaneity keep you watching and curious. What will she do next? Many of her funny, quirky, impulsive moments were improvised during filming. There's a reason she's 'The It Girl'.
>
> Try this exercise with other dynamic actors or presenters you find online. Take words out of the equation, turn the sound off and zone in on how the other aspects of their presentation tell the real story. Now check yourself. Do your face and body tell the same story as your words?

'It' comes to the modern stage

In the same year that the movie *It* was released in Hollywood, a watershed moment occurred on Broadway: the curtain rose on the musical *Showboat* (1927) by Jerome Kern (1885–1945) and Oscar Hammerstein II (1895–1960). This musical broke from the stereotypical format of musical comedy, harnessing various musical styles while integrating vernacular song and dance. Actors were now required to be multi-skilled. Subject matter that had once been the purview of straight plays was now openly addressed through the power of song. Themes became more naturalistic, and realism emerged as a new norm. The songs within a musical were no longer merely moments for entertainment; instead, they created space for a deeper connection to the story and its themes. Musical theatre produced a new category of performer possessing the 'It' Factor: the triple-threat musical theatre actor.[13]

Many screen and stage actors and singers from the last century stand out, too numerous to mention. Some have been openly praised for epitomizing aspects of 'It'. Upon her death, opera star Maria Callas was referred to as a goddess, reflecting her luminescence. Marilyn Monroe exuded innocent sexuality in ways not previously experienced on screen, while Audrey Hepburn radiated wide-eyed innocence and tomboyish grace. Laurence Olivier, regarded as one of the finest actors of classical theatre the world has known, stated that the actor was *'the illuminator of the human heart'*.[14] The list continues: French songbird Edith Piaf, Broadway comedian Fanny Brice, belter Ethel Merman, and, more recently, Barbra Streisand. Method actor Marlon Brando created characters of extraordinary credibility on both the screen and the stage. He radiated an inner burn that inhabited his performances, yet he was continually driven by curiosity and a desire to refine his technique. He said:

> *If I can't figure somebody out, I'll follow him like a weasel with persistence until I find out what his nature is and how he functions ... I am endlessly absorbed by human motivations. How is it that we behave the way we do? What are those compulsions within us that drive us one way or another? It is my lifelong preoccupation.*[15]

Undoubtedly, the 'It' Factor is most recognized in the performing arts or public speaking arena. Twenty-first-century giants of synergy and presence continue to dazzle, electrify, and mesmerize. In a 2023 poll of movie actors, Tom Hanks, Robert De Niro, Denzil Washington, Anthony Hopkins, Heath Ledger, Cate Blanchett, Nicole Kidman, Tilda Swinton, and Charlize Theron were voted some of the most charismatic and exciting to watch.[16] These actors create lived-in, accessible, and identifiable characters filled with emotion and inner strength. They embody the essential core of synergistic performance, engendering a form of *poiesis* – calling something into existence and creating something more significant than what existed before. 'It' can be as gentle as a match to a candle wick or as powerful as nuclear fission, but either way, 'It' is synergistic.

What do the experts think?

Twenty-first-century researchers and theorists have sought to understand stage presence, and some of their ideas are worth pondering as we construct the 'It' Factor picture. Jane Goodall asks the question:

> *What is it that makes a performer compelling to watch? We might explain the fascination in terms of the performance itself as a display of exceptional talents. Still, history is full of examples of stage celebrities who gained pre-eminence despite quite obvious deficiencies in looks, technique, or discipline. Even where supremacy in skill is unquestionable, we may still find comments struggling*

to describe how there was something more than this in the performance, something experienced as uniquely powerful, perhaps even transcendent or magical. It is the 'X' Factor in the actor's art.[17]

Goodall defines stage presence as *'a coalescence of energy, mystery and discipline. The way these dimensions relate to each other is different with every exceptional performer, but there are shared traditions and inspirations for them to draw on'*.[18] She comments that stage presence lies within an actor's persona or energies, recognizing it as a gold standard of performance.

In his 2007 book, *It*, Joseph Roach calls the theatre *'the most consequential synthetic experience'* and refers to our desire to *'experience experience (by vicariously living through someone else's embodiment of it)'*.[19]

To explain the mystery of 'It', Roach writes:

It is the power of apparently effortless embodiment of contradictory qualities simultaneously: strength and vulnerability, innocence and experience, and singularity and typicality among them. The possessor of It keeps a precarious balance between such mutually exclusive alternatives, suspended at the tipping point like a tightrope dancer on one foot; and the empathic tension of waiting for the apparently inevitable fall makes for breathless spectatorship [...] a psychological contradiction with reversible polarities like egoless self-confidence or unbiddable magnetism at the source of the mysterious fascination of It.[20]

When speaking of inspired performance, two master innovators of contemporary theatre have also referred to the dichotomy of the revealed yet hidden. In his seminal work, *Towards a Poor Theatre* (2002), teacher, theatre director, and theorist Jerzy Grotowski expounds his theories of presence as a product of preparatory work and of the totalizing effect of working truthfully:

Theatre – through the actor's technique, his art in which the living organism strives for higher motives – provides an opportunity for what could be called integration, the discarding of masks, the revealing of the real substance: a totality of mental and physical reactions.[21]

Peter Brook, another theorist, director, and theatrical innovator, suggests the opposite is also in play, the hidden and the revealed. He proposes that outstanding actors *'have some mysterious psychic chemistry, half-conscious and yet three-quarters hidden, that they themselves may only define as "instinct", "hunch", "my voices", that enables them to develop their vision and their art'*.[22]

Eugenio Barba (2006), who collaborated closely with Grotowski, offers a complementary perspective. He explores the concept of presence from an anthropological standpoint, linking the manifestation of presence to the power of breath – contrasting the Latin concepts of anima, or gentle, intimate breath, with animus, a vigorous, active breath – and relates these differing energies to the actors' preparatory work in training both body and mind.[23] Barba's training approaches suggest that 'presence' carries a dual meaning: it denotes both a state of being – characterized by a captivating quality with metaphysical and spiritual implications – and an action or activity, of being 'present' or presenting something in the execution of a performance. These two states, the mystical and the practical, coexist to generate the energy we refer to as presence. Goodall endorses these notions, suggesting that presence *'must be seen as something at once scientific and uncanny, a matter of both technique and mystique'*.[24]

Performance theorist and analyst Jon Erickson believes a person's presence is a vital element that fuels human empathetic connection and relates to *'the most positive aspects of human attraction and love'*.[25] He refers to presence as: *'a kind of saturation of feeling, of sensibility, a condensation of experience that in the right circumstances emanates from the person or performer.'*[26]

Another researcher, Mark L. Latash, applies a scientific eye to synergy, suggesting that its presence relies on three conditions: a common task-driven direction that all elements work towards, an interactive flow of energy between the elements to achieve the task, and a purposeful goal.[27]

In a seminal address to mark his 100th birthday, revered voice pedagogue Arthur Lessac discussed the energy that holds all life and form together – kinetic energy, the energy of motion that is an essential part of our *'Inner Environment'* and is expressed through *'the feeling sense'*:

> … we call its workings *'the feeling process'*. It is very close to that harmonic 6th sense, and it also takes us a step closer to that elusive *'Soul' NRG*. Yes, for me, *'soul'* is the most delicate of all our body NRGs, and there are many of them, many NRG fundamentals and many NRG harmonics.[28]

Lessac explains how these 'NRG's can be felt neuro-physically. His research identified energies such as buoyancy, potency, and radiancy, and concludes: *'We can also learn to feel the energy of courage, of awareness, of curiosity, or the energies of spirit and of love. And when I feel them, I sense a bit of questing or better still, a bit of mystery.'*[29]

Research literature throws up a series of popular synonyms for the synergistic quality of the 'It' Factor, including collaboration, combined effort, teamwork, accord, concurrence and coordination symbiosis. These generalized definitions echo the actors' task as they interact with their audience and tell their story in performance. In the context of performance art, Erica Fischer-Lichte links synergy with the term *transformative aesthetics*: *'the sum total of materials, forms, devices, and means applied by an artist in bringing forth an artwork/event, and the kind of perception it enables or elicits by affecting the recipients' senses, emotions, imagination and cognition.'*[30]

These performance and academic experts provided diverse perspectives on the 'It' Factor, including philosophical, historical and social commentary, individual skills and methodologies, performance techniques, and artistry. However, as I mentioned earlier, *'the map is not the territory'*. The question remains: how do these facets of the 'It' Factor converge to create something that an everyday person can access and command at will?

> Who is on your list of 'It' Factor performers? Write down what they make you feel, and what adjectives come to mind when they perform. Are there common elements you perceive?

Others outside the performing arts arena also exhibit 'It', exuding similar qualities to an actor's stage presence. We can all think of someone who has 'It'. Sometimes, it manifests as an effortless look of public intimacy combined with an amplified personality that attracts our attention. 'It' may seem contradictory – radiating an outward-flowing aura while magnetically attracting the observer and drawing them inward to the inner sanctum of the performer's psyche and persona. Communication is open and authentic while maintaining the impression of something unrevealed or mysterious. This paradoxical description reflects just a part of 'It's ephemerality and shape-shifting qualities.

So, I went looking for more. Let me share with you what I found.

3

UNPACKING THE SYNERGY EQUATION: FINDING THE PARTS OF THE SUM

In the iconic musical and film *The Sound of Music,* the Abbey nuns endeavour to understand the will-o'-the-wisp qualities evident in the energetic, nonconforming novice Maria. *'How do you hold a moonbeam in your hand?'* they ponder.[1] That became my question, too, as I searched for 'It': what does 'It' consist of, who possesses it, how does it operate, how is it experienced by those observing, and can we unlock it or amplify it within ourselves?

Defining performance synergy was my key to understanding how various 'parts' can 'cooperate' and work together to create something tangible. To discover 'something greater than the sum of its parts', I planned to unravel 'the parts of the sum', reconstruct the equation to find 'the sum of the parts', and then unlock the 'greater than' aspect – that special something that brings 'It' to life. To accomplish this, I sought the current opinions of experts. In this chapter, you'll hear directly from those who know all about 'It' – they cast 'It', or reveal 'It', or experience 'It' daily. But first, let's recap.

Let's recap our current understanding

As noted in the last chapter, there are few books specifically written on the topic. However, there is a wealth of written and digital sources and resources that dance around the subject and its many names. Here is a summary of some of their ideas:

- There is an energy exuded or released by a performer that captures an audience's attention, engages them, and elicits recognition or response. The performer's connection to the audience can be interactive and layered.

- This energy can involve connecting to a story and being 'present in the moment', which produces an empathetic response within the audience; trust is shared between them.

- This energy is multifaceted, drawing upon a performer's internal and external processes simultaneously and costing them something.

- The engaged, embedded skills and learned techniques an actor harnesses are enhanced or assisted by other qualities, particularly a positive psychological outlook.

- This energy reflects a performer's strong connection to self and engagement of deeper personal processes connected to their soul or spirit.

Many musical theatre training books offered common thoughts on what makes up performance artistry, as illustrated in the descriptive word map, Figure 3.1.[2]

Reflecting on these, I created some generalized word groupings that collated some of performance synergy's attributes: the senses, the cognitive and instinctual mind, personality characteristics, physicality, and skill (see Table 3.1).

How do these qualities combine and function in an actor, and how do they interact with an audience? And can these keywords and ideas align with life experience offstage? I wanted to know:

- The 'who, what and how'. Who is needed for performance synergy to occur? What do actors and directors believe makes up this energy? And how does 'It' occur?

Figure 3.1 Performance artistry word map.

- The 'when, where and why'. When and where actors and directors believe synergy can be found, and why it is revealed in that time and place?

- The 'whether'. Whether an actor can create synergy or release it at will, and, if so, which techniques and frameworks can be utilized to achieve this?

Having garnered all I could from literature and digital media, I turned to the folk who knew 'It' personally. I interviewed those on the frontlines, working in the field where 'It' is most prolifically experienced. These experts were said to possess 'It' or cast performers with 'It' in the musicals they directed. Their thoughts and experiences formed a window into the world of this captivating energy.

Table 3.1 Synergy's qualities and descriptors

Qualities of presence or synergy	Keywords and descriptors from literature
Sensory or palpable	Radiant, buoyant, potent, powerful, listening, energy
Instinctive	Imagination, spontaneity, inspiration
Active cognizance	Curiosity, intention, awareness, responding, ownership, present, available
Drawing on self	Vulnerable, courage, intimacy, generous, emotion, fearless, individual, persona, soul
Physical	Psycho physicality, kinetic, connected
Skilled	Technique, acting, singing, dancing, storytelling

The Interviews

I asked some simple questions:

- What are your thoughts on performance synergy? Can you describe this, and what do you think are the elements that make this up?
- Tell us about your experience working with synergy or working with actors who display synergy in their performances.

Perspectives and expertise were shared. All the interviewees were well-established in the Australian musical theatre scene, with some possessing international experience performing or directing on Broadway or in London's West End. Their insights into what makes someone stand out from the crowd were invaluable. I accumulated over eighty hours of conversation and gathered a treasure trove of words and ideas that became my 'parts of the sum'. The result was an extensive map. It was time to begin constructing a picture of 'It'!

Intrinsic performative processes: Introducing the Magnificent Seven!

Those keywords and phrases were loosely categorized into groups before being analysed, refined, and collated. Sure enough, a pattern of thought and a conceptual framework emerged. The final dataset reflected the participants' lived experiences of the 'It' Factor, and what I termed 'performance synergy', drawing from internal, experiential perceptions and external, observational viewpoints. Actors and creatives used various metaphors and adjectives to describe what they saw, believed, intuited or felt. Their unique perspectives indicated the multiple processes they employed to create or observe synergy in performance, forming the foundation of the first overarching theme I developed: Intrinsic Performative Processes.

As I analysed their thoughts, distinctions emerged, hinting at the origins of these elements and how we experience them within ourselves. The experts identified seven human processes that we use to function and communicate, including the mind, emotions, soul, senses, and the body. These 'Magnificent Seven' are:

1. Sensate experience (*senso*) – what participants perceive through their five senses – what they see, hear, feel, and physically experience when releasing or receiving synergy.
2. Ideational cognition (*neuro*) – the actors' reasoning and creatives' considerations – what they experienced or observed and their formulated beliefs and understanding.
3. Intuitive cognition (*psycho*) – what they perceive that occurs at a subconscious or subliminal level.
4. Emotive perception (*emotio*) – what actors experience emotionally when working alone or with another actor and what actors and directors experience emotionally when observing.
5. Persona process (*persona*) – personality and character traits – an actor's understanding of themselves and others, their identity, character, and personality, issues of embodiment, and the soul. This includes innate charisma or a sense of the inexplicable, or the soul present since birth.

6 Technical competency (*technico*) – the recognized skills and training in operation that assisted actors in connecting, engaging and affecting an audience. This competency is consciously learned and then embodied.
7 Physical embodiment (*physical*) – how an actor expresses energy physiologically, including dynamism, physical freedom or flow.

Each of these seven processes presents and reflects various facets of itself, much like a well-cut diamond. The interviewees' perspectives aligned with everything I had read, experienced, and observed. Some participants had experience on both sides of the casting table; they were established actors and creative directors who sought this quality when casting others in roles. Their dual perspective proved beneficial. Table 3.2 lists some of the most frequently mentioned keywords used to describe the elements the participants believed constituted the appearance of 'It'. While this table is information-dense, it reveals the qualities that actors employ to access synergy.

Table 3.2 Keywords from data analysis

SUB-THEMES	MT ACTORS (MTA)	MTA and CD	CREATIVE DIRECTORS (CD)
PROCESSES	**Subjective:** self-generated and/or shared, internal experience or external, observational experience.	**Observed:** shared internal experience or external, observational experience.	**Objective:** external, objective observation. **C** – Choreographer **MD** – Musical Director **SD** – Stage Director
SENSATE EXPERIENCE: self-generated, experiential, observational, what is seen or experienced with the senses – *senso*.	**Self:** catapults you forward, being present, a spark, you taste it, flying, bubbling. **Working with others:** watchability, flying, shines, coming alive, draws you in, safe, welcoming.	Wall of energy, joyful energy, radiating out, fiery, mesmerizing, transportive, riveting, enormous presence, confidence energy, heightened reality, a bit of danger.	**C** – watchability, a spark, energy, unstoppable energy, armour. **MD** – fascinating, magnetic, incredible to watch, organic process. **SD** – confidence, charisma, open attitude, openness, inspiration, inner stillness, utterly beguiling, sensitivity, sit in the unsafe, a different energy.
IDEATIONAL COGNITION: concepts, beliefs, generated through thought – *neuro*.	Willing to be changed, common focus, take risks, no fear, intelligent, curious, believing you are enough, truthful, empowerment, trusting self, permission to play, laser focus, sharing energy, immersion, freedom, actual life force, unapologetic, nothing to lose.	Great perception, truthful, trust, intelligence.	**C** – access truthfully, no filter, intelligent and smart. **MD** – level of intelligence, focus. **SD** – focus, specificity, trust, intentions, true, intelligent.

SUB-THEMES	MT ACTORS (MTA)	MTA and CD	CREATIVE DIRECTORS (CD)
INTUITIVE COGNITION: instinctual, subliminal, subconscious engagement – *psycho*.	Let it happen, open, free, innately able, natural, playfulness, following instincts.	Abandon self-consciousness, simpatico energy.	**C** – sense of play, sense of coolness, ease, safety, and trust, enigmatic. **MD** – connected to the material. **SD** – make it playful, intrigue, a depth within, great freedom.
EMOTIVE PROCESSES: internal and external, perception – *emotio*.	Vulnerable, passion, excitement, always joy, happy, feel a connection.	Warmth, openness.	**C** – sense of joy, emotional connection to story, EQ important. **SD** – empathy, vulnerable, generous. **MD** – joy.
PERSONA PROCESSES: sense of self, personality, character traits – *persona*.	Bravery, authenticity, generous, buoyancy of spirit, never static, brought self, ownership, confident, comfortable, open, malleable, self-belief, respectful, giving, polite, kind, no ego, no pride, confidence, down to earth, ease, generosity of spirit, genuine.	Genuine, brave, likeability.	**C** – confidence not arrogance, effortless, charm, warmth, generosity, enigmatic. **SD** – generosity, with themselves, kind, magnetic, openness, self-confidence, humble, enigmatic. **MD** – generousness and integrity, fragility and honesty, fun, taking risks, inquisitive nature.
TECHNICAL COMPETENCIES: embedded skill base, singing, acting, dancing – *technico*.	Actively listening, responding, connection to other, focus, embedded dangerous acting, being, specificity, big, bold, connected to the moment, ownership, focus and objective, very grounded, deep concentration from deep learning, embodied.	Performance intelligence, nuance, in the moment, immersion in character, focus on text and character, secure in the material, having a viewpoint.	**C** – in tune with their own ability. **MD** – immediacy, trust in the work, take on direction, flexible, malleable, adapt, power to make decisions. **SD** – layers to peel away, positive with their training, serve the work, pulling you in, thinking inside as the character, steady security. **SD** – always a talent there, adaptability.
PHYSICAL EMBODIMENT: movement, connected, kinetic, dynamic energy – *physical*.	Your body, embodiment, freedom in the way we move, attractive, interesting.	Ease.	**C** – committed. **SD** – you expand.

A glance at Table 3.2 reveals that the many elements they identified are an integral part of our shared human experience and expression. But how could I convey this?

Introducing Syd Synergy

Meet Syd. Syd is a little character I devised to help visualize aspects of 'It' and scaffold these elements within an androgynous human frame.

Most keywords the actors and creatives used were easily assigned to one of the seven processes I identified. However, several proved challenging to categorize. These words suggested a combination of processes that occur simultaneously. For instance, 'fascinating' seemed to be experienced through the

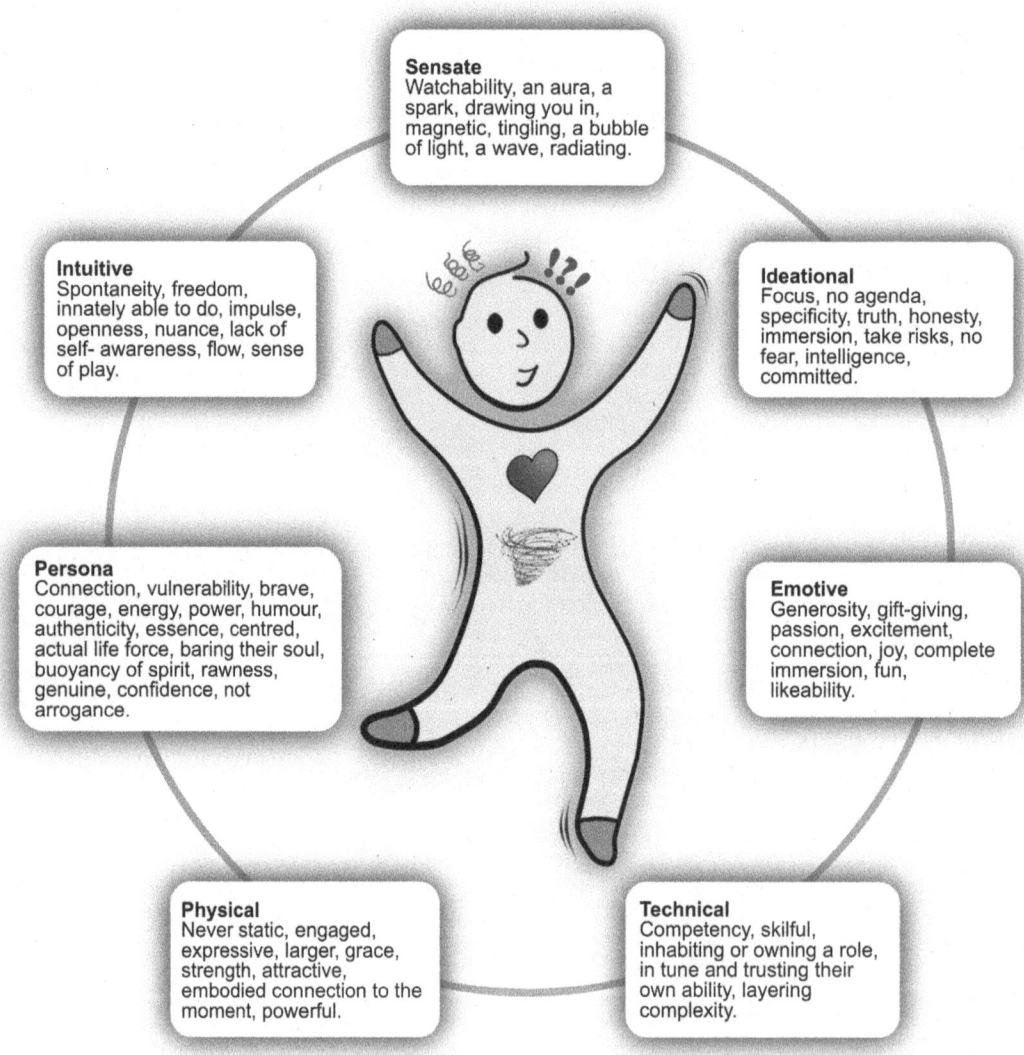

Figure 3.2 Meet Syd Synergy!

senses, examined cognitively, and felt emotionally to varying degrees at once. Words like 'freedom', 'truth' and 'connection' were more challenging to define. Freedom can incorporate 'self-belief', 'permission to act' or 'limitless imagination'. Truth, while acknowledged cognitively as thought, also appeared to access an unfiltered self or persona. Respondents frequently mentioned 'connection', which seemed to be present across multiple processes.

These abstract words revealed 'It's complexity, so I delved deeper to unpack these performative processes.

Sensate experience

The first process – sensate experience – was often used by actors and directors as they began to articulate their experience with the 'It' Factor. Their descriptors referenced four senses – sight, sound, smell and tactile sensation.

Their similes and metaphors subjectively and objectively captured their impressions on stage and offstage as they sought to describe what they were intuiting and sensing at a deeper level. Veteran actor and director, Tony Sheldon stated, '*It's that heightened physicality where the excitement becomes almost unbearable. And that just keeps building and building. And your hair starts to stand on end … I think great acting can do that.*'

Their sensory experience appeared as exchanges between actors, connecting to the story or what they witnessed as observers. Leading lady Anna O'Byrne commented:

When you're really attracted to someone, they have pheromones that kind of come off and … your smells are really good for each other. And it's almost like that kind of thing. What this becomes is, 'I love these guys. Take me on your journey.' There's that kind of buzz to it, that kind of extra level of vibration happening somewhere … it's like a smell or it's like a super high frequency that we can't hear that we're all just kind of … joining in on that vibe.

Analogies to light, heat and movement were made.

> Author Julia Cameron agrees that the senses have the power to inspire and stimulate the performer:
>
> *The artist brain cannot be reached – or triggered – effectively by words alone. The artist brain is the sensory brain: sight and sound, smell and taste, touch. These are the elements of magic, and magic is the elemental stuff of art. …Sight leads to insight.*
>
> Julia Cameron, *The Artist's Way: A Spiritual Path to Higher Creativity* (London: Profile Books, 2020), 21, Kindle edition.

Light or heat

Creative directors observed working actors in audition, rehearsal and performance and referred to the positive valence that appears as a spark, a light, an aura or a radiance. Choreographer and director Michael Ralph explained:

It's like a spark in someone's energy field or someone's aura around them when they're on stage. It's like a bubble of invisible lights that's coming off them … some kind of X-Factor light. A beacon of light on stage.

Director, actor and educator, Tyran Parke noted, *'Just add the thing that makes it light up'*. Veteran actor Natalie O'Donnell shared, *'and some people just seem to have an inner radiance or something'*, and musical theatre treasure, Marina Prior, described an actor's energy:

His stillness and his energy, he's like … a laser beam when you're watching him. And yet, he can turn on a dime and be absolutely vulnerable, open – a lost lamb. And that, to me, is extremely exciting to watch.

Movement

Actors and directors also described sensations of movement when referring to 'It', with some recounting their impressions of being moved by an energetic force. Prior said that 'It' *'feels like flying … whether it be in a dialogue, scene or a song. I'm flying … I'm transcending somewhere else, but yet, not yet.'* Experienced actor Lucy Maunder commented, *'I suppose I just feel like it's all flying and bubbling away. It's just flowing out.'*

Both creative directors and actors spoke about a quality in an actor's eyes that drew them: *'I think a lot of it has to do with the energy that's behind the eyes … that is, yet again, watchable. It's drawing people in'* (Ralph). Maunder agreed:

It's something in the eyes … it feels like there's a fire burning. And I can feel like that alone on a stage and also when you're working opposite actors as well. You can really feel that kind of chemistry with another actor when they're in that moment with you and you are both incredibly connected.

Several actors referred to an enigmatic, attractive quality that drew audiences to a performance. Anna O'Byrne said: *'It's a quality like a magnetism where you feel drawn to a person … like an attractiveness … we feel really intrigued … something where we want to sit forward and listen.'*

And leading actor Ainsley Melham commented:

The world gets really small all of a sudden. And it only includes you and the person. And that can happen on stage or if you're in the audience … So, maybe it is more about how to set that energy of welcoming. You know, bringing six hundred people into your circle and bringing them very close.

Australia's beloved musical theatre icon, Nancye Hayes, agrees: *When they first walk on stage and your eye is drawn to them, you know that there is a particular quality that this performer has that is undeniable … and it's instant.*

> The next time you experience seeing someone with the 'It' Factor, think of some 'sensing' words you would use to describe the sensation you experience – either what it feels or seems like coming from them or what you feel inside. Some words I've found myself using are magnetic, bubbly, tingly, enveloping. What is your experience?

Some actors perceived 'It' as an extreme sense of being outside your body or disappearing into the character or story. Leading lady Jemma Rix experienced this aspect of 'It' from two perspectives: watching others embodying their character, and experiencing this loss of self while performing:

There are these alignments that don't happen all the time, but that magical synergy alignment of the right place at the right time for the right role. And you see that person embody that character. It's like they're actually not there.

Rix later said of her own experience:

But the magic for me was that I'd done all of this homework and all of this work as a singer and as an actor and then on myself. And then all of a sudden I was in this zone of pure and utter listening and responding. And it ... honestly was like a spiritual experience because you are so in the moment ... I just felt like it was so instinctual because there was no pre-planning.

Simon Gleeson also explained the 'It' Factor from the actor's perspective: '*It feels like you're not there ... for me it feels like nothing, and I mean that in the nicest way, because when you're not feeling it, it feels like everything or when you're feeling it, it feels like nothing.*' Natalie O'Donnell added:

'It' just feels like every moment has the time and space that it needs ... there's a feeling between you and the other person ... and you'd have the magical moment of everything just disappearing ... you just feel like very much in the centre of something that makes sense.

Ideational cognition

Ideational cognition was the second performative process identified. Conscious cognition influences much of our spoken responses to stimuli and assists us in expressing ourselves and our worldview. Interviewees discussed the thoughtful consideration that actors bring to their performances and the reasoning that actors and directors employ when experiencing synergy. Three recurring ideational concepts emerged: self-belief, immersion and focus.

Self-belief

Self-belief and fearlessness in performance often appeared in tandem. Leading actor and composer, Alinta Chidzey spoke of confidence and surety in auditions: '*Definitely a belief in yourself – it's a really big thing,*' and Prior agreed: '*You may not be an expert in everything, but this is your field. You're an expert.*'

Creatives noted this sense of self-belief as actors presented themselves in the audition room. Stuart Maunder, a renowned opera and musical theatre director stated: '"It" *has to be something to do with one's self-belief and, and one's passions. You can tell the minute that a person walks into an audition room ... that's the most important thing that happens.*' Ralph agreed, '*A lot of it comes from the mental state of the performer.*' Musical Director Luke Hunter asserted, '*I think the thing that ties all of them in is ... no fear of failure at all ... It's almost like they think that they won't, that it's impossible [to have fear].*'

Self-belief was not seen as ego but rather as assurance and groundedness. It was sometimes expressed as bravery or confidence to explore the story or the moment: *'I think … it's some kind of personal trait, an onstage confidence that may not even be conscious,'* said Musical Director Stephen Amos.

Immersion

Immersion in the text, character and story emerged as the second recurring topic noted in the analysis of the interviews. Actor Joel Granger described it as *'just going for it and just committing one hundred percent'*. Prior added, *'All I had was my faith in my ability and my utter enjoyment and ability to immerse myself in what I was doing.'*

Focus

The experts frequently discussed the importance of specificity and clarity of thought, which can bridge the gap between the actor and the audience. Actors described their deep, focused connection to the text, enabled them to actively inhabit the story, making it feel natural. Melham said, *'When you both have the same focus … there's the ingredients for it there.'* And Gleeson added *'I think it's that feeling that it's the only thing happening in the world at that moment. Now, I know we're not idiots. We know we're in a rehearsal room or in the field, but it just is … overpowering.'*

For versatile actor Georgina Hopson, active listening and responding helped to create that level of attention:

People feel a connection with you because you are really actively listening to everyone around you and actively listening to the audience. And being with everybody – I'm with you, I'm with actors, I'm with audience … I think that is a really important part of presence … You're sort of inviting them in to share … that thing.

An actor's critical thinking process is essential in an energized rehearsal room. It helps create characterization and serves as a foundation for the next step of letting go. Director, actor, and dramaturg Jason Langley said:

The best actors are critical thinkers. They're smart, they're well-read. They work hard to understand a piece of text, they work hard on finding the humour in a moment. I say they drill into their texts, but I think the biggest thing that creates the synergy on stage is that they know how to 'let go' of that work and just … live.

Most interviewees noted employing cognitive thought to analyse the script and story, which is essential for grasping the work and their role within it. Mindful thinking was perceived as a gateway to the more intricate and layered realm of character development.

Intuitive cognition

Have you ever found yourself saying something profound before you've even registered the thought? Or felt an unexplained urge to change your direction or action, only to realize it was the right choice?

This third performative process, intuitive cognition or instinctual thinking, often referred to as 'gut responses' or 'knee-jerk reactions', can be perplexing. The human subconscious instinctively responds to simple environmental and external cues. Dr Gerd Gigerenzer, a social psychologist specializing in intuitive thought, presents intuition as a unique form of intelligence that complements rational thinking. He states, 'Intuition is an ultimate experience, beyond words: We know more than we can tell ... Intuition and reason not only go together, they depend on each other.'[3]

Gigerenzer defines it as a feeling rooted in experience that emerges swiftly in one's consciousness, although its underlying rationale remains unconscious. The brain appears to filter out cues we recognize cognitively through life experiences and habitual conditioning. It reacts swiftly and seemingly without cognitive deliberation to new information it encounters. Science suggests that certain intuitive responses can develop through practise and skill.

During the interviews, intuition was discussed in depth. Actors and directors described how establishing a strong cognition foundation and then accessing their instinctual and primal responses enabled them to operate more freely. They could then tap into their subconscious to create and embody a character, adding a natural depth to their performance.

Three recurring concepts were expressed: freedom, spontaneity or imaginative play, and instinctual flow or innate response.

Freedom

Freedom in an actor involves being open and receptive to other actors and creatives, along with a relaxed engagement with the story's content, which is expressed through text, music and physicality. Casting and resident director and producer, Natalie Gilhome, explained:

> There's always a very open attitude. And I think that comes back to the ego, knowing that being open and completely exposed, bringing other people into that scene, is, in the long run, going to be a better thing for everyone.

Actors relied on their innate abilities rather than learned techniques, gaining confidence and the freedom to access their acting needs without exclusively relying on cognitive methods. Actor Jaime Hadwen explained:

> I just try and do some sort of truth or connect in some way to what has happened to me and just tell the story. And I've always tried to find some sort of natural way to do something .... I think I just followed my instincts.

Spontaneity and imaginative play

Both actors and creatives discussed playfully engaging the imagination and creating space for spontaneity to discover character and new forms of expression. Creative directors, in particular, sought this quality in the rehearsal room. Luke Hunter put it succinctly: *'You're ready to work; you know that you're willing to play, take on direction, adapt, change, move, shift, experiment.'* This spontaneity was viewed as an instinctual response: *'The instinct of an actor is such a powerful thing. If it comes from the right place, if it comes from the text, if it comes from where they are within'* (Stuart Maunder). Creative directors applauded actors who exhibited spontaneity and authenticity consistently, in every performance: *'Some actors have the ability to do eight shows a week and make it look like it's the first time they do it every time'* (Gilhome).

> Do you have contact with any tiny people? Toddlers or young children under seven years of age? If you can, watch them bring their imaginary worlds to life when they play. There is freedom and flow in their thought processes, which are instinctual.

Several actors credited the familial encouragement they received as children to explore their imagination and trust their innate sense of play: *'They allowed me to think that my instincts were valid. I'm lucky enough to be brought up to know that working on instincts first is the best place to be.'* (Granger). They spoke of using imagination in performance to discover something new and keep the story fresh: *'And generally, it's the moments where you go – that was new'* (Melham).

Instinctual flow

Creative flow is extensively studied and practised in the visual and performing arts. When actors use the term 'flow', they describe the ease they feel as they instinctively respond to the story, while directors observe and comment on this sense of freedom. Performances appear less confined by thought or technique, even when complex cognitive and technical elements are involved. Hunter referred to one cast member:

> *She's very intelligent and very nuanced. And she's ... still breaking everything down. She knows every single thing that she's doing at every moment, but you stand at the back of the auditorium and there's this glow and just effortless ... flow. That feels as an audience member, like it's just so natural and so honest and real.*

This flowing ease may appear almost lazy. Veteran theatre director, Simon Phillips observed: *'The 'It' Factor, there's no doubt about it. And that comes through what appears to be an almost kind of casual laziness. Like you can't work out how she has it, but she has an unerring instinct for the truth.'*

Ralph spoke of dancers with a solid embedded technique who use their instincts to flow and energize their audition performances. He observed, *'The people who do exude the X Factor within that environment are the people who can absorb*

> If you enjoy singing, practise improvising and riffing on a jazz melody. Loosen up your approach to the vocal delivery of lyrics and enjoy finding freedom as you allow your intuitive approach to create something a little different every time you sing the same song. Jazz is an art form that depends on instinctual flow within structure. It helps you find your unique voice and you learn to open up and trust.

the movement as text into their being incredibly fast, and then they can start instinctively making character or energy or performance choices.'

Emotive processes

The words encoded into the fourth process, emotive processes, attest to actors' free access to their emotional core. Creative directors considered emotional depth and breadth essential traits in an actor and used their emotional response to an actor's performance to indicate its effectiveness. Two emotive processes often discussed were joy and generosity.

Joy

Joy was a significant topic. The experience of joy was both given and received in various ways: it was expressed internally as an actor performed their role and received either on stage from other actors or radiated to those watching. This joy was also linked to freedom and confidence:

> *I think empowerment for me is joy. Freedom is being able to discover something yourself because then you have ownership over it, you feel like you created it, it makes you feel confident, it makes you feel good, it makes you feel powerful, and you have control, but you are also free and not controlled.* (Hopson)

Nancye Hayes thought joy was an intrinsic part of the 'It' Factor: *'I think it's a joy, I think it's a joy of performance. I think the anticipation and the adrenaline, and the joy bring a certain aura to someone.'*

And:

> *People sing because they love the feeling that that brings when your voice soars when you tell a story, the emotional connection that comes through a sung piece of theatre that you don't get just by reciting dialogue ... There's that warmth and that joy that comes from creating that sound.* (Hunter)

Simon Philips added, *'They can be joyful in that experience. I think that if acting makes you happy, it's good, it's going to up your chance of having this ["It"] factor.'*

Generosity

Emotional generosity – openly sharing with others, combining empathy and surrender – was considered a product of a vibrant positive valence that included warmth, acceptance, buoyancy, a sense of security and magnanimity: *'Generosity in peers, a generous rehearsal room, a generous director. Yes, it's ... generosity and encouragement'* (Prior). Generosity was also linked to authenticity, openness and trust.

Highly respected actor and director Sharon Millerchip shared:

> *Generosity to other actors is just the best thing. And when you are really generous to another actor, it serves you just as much as the other person. And that's when relationships feel authentic on stage, and all sorts of things are born from that.*

Gilhome added, *'And there's a trust, there's a generosity and an openness within that person's work.'*

Persona processes

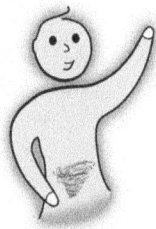

The fifth performative process is persona – an individual's innate sense of self, unique personality, character traits, natural qualities and tendencies. Actors and creative directors commonly believed that an actor's essence or soul was connected to the manifestation of dynamic performance. Directors discussed maintaining objectivity while leveraging their natural style and personality to tap into these traits within their cast. The three topics highlighted by respondents were identity, temperament and courage.

Identity

Actors brought their sense of self and their unique personality traits into auditions and rehearsals, using their innate attributes to build a character: *'I feel like it all boils down to finding what it is within yourself. You've been hired for this part because you are the character. Don't work too hard because it's all there already'* (Melham).

They had much to say from their subjective experience. *'You just present the most "you" version of you. And if you're arrogant, then be arrogant. Great. But if you're lovable, be the most lovely version of yourself,'* said Granger, while Marina Prior stated that *'There's just something incredibly attractive in the truest sense of the word about their actual life force, their essence, their spirit. And you think, oh, my gosh, you're just amazing.'*

Caroline O'Connor, a veteran of the global stage concurred, saying, *'That's ok to be a bit different. I do believe that part of "It" is accepting and really getting to know yourself – who you are, how you perform. Like really know who you are.'*

For directors, an actor's individuality was one of the most empowering and employable traits. Parke spoke of actors he's worked with, saying *' … their uniqueness isn't stopped'*. Simon Phillips added that openness and vulnerability were appealing qualities: *'You could look at her at any time and know, go straight through her eyes to her soul.'*

Musical directors brought an additional, objective perspective. Stephen Amos commented: *'Everything comes from the individual.'* Luke Hunter added, *'Yes, because there's something about what they have that I think you can't teach because it's in their personality.'*

Temperament

Keywords like easy, kind, respectful, open, and confident were frequently mentioned, indicating that a performer's personality traits were key in developing or expressing their 'It' Factor. *'I was just watching these people do what they do on stage, but also what they do behind the stage, which is grace, confidence and compassion,'* said Anna O'Byrne, while Amos remarked of one performer, *'He's one of the nicest people I've ever met … and just his warmth and connection to people, I think, made a big difference.'*

Curiosity was another important personal trait that actors and creatives identified as essential. O'Byrne remarked, *'All of those people have a complete curiosity about what it is that we're doing … they're sort of interested in the conversation of how we do what we do.'*

Courage

Courage is one of the greatest qualities found in the human spirit, exemplified in some of the world's true heroes. But like us, they too have battled fear. South African anti-apartheid activist, Nelson Mandela, learned this during his many years in prison. He stated, *'I learned that courage was not the absence of fear, but the triumph over it. I felt fear myself more times than I can remember, but I hid it behind a mask of boldness. The brave man is not he who does not feel afraid, but he who conquers that fear.'*[4]

Creatives and actors spoke candidly about the anxiety and fear of failure that actors can face while performing. For some, performance anxiety tends to escalate with age and experience. They also discussed their courage to step out of their comfort zones and onto the stage: *'There are people for whom acting is kind of torture, and they can have the "It" Factor … because, like it or not, they're at home when they're out there on stage. And that gives them that inner stillness'* Simon Philips added, *'There's an element of people giving their best, and they are going beyond safe … it's about going to the edge.'*

Courage was often tied to an actor's choice to be vulnerable and open on stage. It was referred to as 'taking risks', especially in an audition: *'And in an audition, there's expectation … to be the best version of yourself. I'm wondering … unless we're sort of risking failure, I actually don't think we have any chance of success'* (Gleeson).

Technical competencies

The sixth intrinsic process, technical competencies, is widely regarded as essential in musical theatre. A strong and ingrained technique provides a secure foundation for actors to communicate, remain present in the story and bring clarity and focus to their roles. When approaching a new work, actors employ embedded acting and singing techniques during the initial stages of character development. Some draw from a reservoir of technical experience, while others allow the role to evoke the existing skills necessary to sing, act, and physicalize the character.

Both directors and actors emphasized the importance of working with the text to unleash performance energy. For some actors, this meant allowing the text to become the primary driving force: *'Discern a lyric and to figure out how best to deliver thoughts through the lyrics that you're given … go some places and to try some things and take on board the direction that you give them'* (Millerchip). And Melham affirmed that *'the sense of story throughout all the disciplines … they really serve each other'.*

It was clear from the conversations that an actor's technique serves the heart and intention of the story, not the other way around: *'If I go in really well prepared, I really know my stuff, I've really sung whatever it is into my voice, I've really read a lot. I allow myself to become inspired and excited by it'* (Prior).

Directors' thoughts on technique and synergy confirmed their supportive role. *'So, I think it is about having an instrument that supports you,'* said Parke. Gilhome added, *'Also, people just being really positive with themselves and positive about their background, about their training, about their experience and bring that into the room.'*

Physical embodiment

The seventh intrinsic process is physical embodiment, which is considered essential for effectively communicating thoughts, emotions and the inherent self. Lorna Marshall, in her book *The Body Speaks,* captures the importance of an actor's physicality for self-expression: *'Your body can speak words in many ways, revealing countless realities through language. We know how it feels when we communicate well – vibrant, lively, true. Every part of ourselves is engaged.'*[5]

The nature of live musical theatre requires actors to create a visual impact that can engage audiences of various sizes. Actors who fully and freely gave of their physical energy were often favoured by directors. Hunter remarked, *'Eight times a week, she never left anything behind, never left anything in the tank. And that was inspiring.'*

Some directors discussed the importance of an actor embodying their character and getting on the floor during rehearsal. They believed that as the actor uses their body to connect with the character and convey the story, synergy can occur: *'You can analyse to your heart's content, but, actually, the doing is the most important thing. Being in harmony with the work they're doing'* (Stuart Maunder).

Producer and director Kris Stewart agreed:

And I think the longer you stay sitting, the more you stay the actor, not the character. You can't really inhabit a character until you're forced to take it into your body. Musical theatre is a very 'honest' sort of art form.

> People-watching is fascinating. In a crowded street or a mall, look at the way people walk – their gait and posture, rhythm and tempo. What does that tell you? What stories can the simple act of walking convey? Reflect on the many walks you have. Your body informs your mind and vice versa. And it informs those who watch you.

Veteran Musical Director Michael Tyack talked of the depth that comes with body engagement, *'It's definitely a total, whole body package connection to what you're saying that's just so much deeper than what a lot of other people bring to it.'* He went on to describe:

It's … creating a whole picture of something that goes beyond what I would imagine. It's an instant kind of transformation … Wow, where did that come from? That ability to just transform, transform in my head. I don't know that you've done that much, but you've made me do it.

Actors also discussed how their physical presence forges a connection with the story and the audience. Granger recounted observing the 'It' Factor in another actor's confident movement across the stage:

I remember seeing a production where the overture was just all these women walking across stage with nothing to do except walk. There was something I noticed about the difference between one woman to the next – one with X-Factor and one with none at all. I think it was just confidence … that they could walk across the stage with nothing to do except walk and just own it and own their space.

Others highlighted how dancers often display higher levels of connectedness to their physical bodies, that encourage the perception of synergy: *'But again, they're both great dancers too, so they're in their body, so they would have to be in tune in their physique and connected, even in their breath'* (Hadwen).

Sometimes, this synergy was described as a discernible physical strength or empowerment that seemed to envelop or attach itself to the entire actor. Ralph stated, *'There's an unstoppable energy or armour … that they know how to instinctively flick the armour on, so that it's kind of boom, I'm in it. And nothing will alter that.'* Parke elaborated:

It's kind of an empowerment … you can have all those skills. And then it is about the way you see your place inside of that, which is necessary. So, there's a different energy in the room when that happens.

Feelings of safety and a sense of physical comfort were also expressed: *'Watching someone who has "It" kind of puts you in a sense of comfort … like you trust the performer when they're exuding, it puts you in a state of trust watching them'* (Ralph).

One discussion focused on the law of attraction, and whether a performer's innate sexuality, charisma or animal magnetism could influence their stage presence. Some questioned whether an actor's physical attributes – perceived beauty, size, frailty, and strength – played a role in presenting a certain type of 'It' Factor. We'll delve into this further in Chapter 7.

Putting the seven together

Let's summarize the first overarching theme of Intrinsic Performative Processes. The numerous keywords and phrases used by actors and directors to define performance synergy testify to its phenomenological quality. Their insights established a platform for exploring the question of 'what' – what actors and creatives perceived as the elements of the 'It' Factor.

Actors discussed their use of all seven processes, suggesting that they combined and coalesced into highly individual expressions of self, with no two 'It' Factors appearing exactly the same. For those performers who knew how to discover their 'It', they had unique approaches and methods for naming and unlocking it. For instance, when discussing her technique, Georgina Hopson referred to, *'Energizing thought through embodied imagination and play'*, epitomizing how she blended her thoughts and emotions to create the internal space where synergy could occur, subsequently informing her physicality and external expression.

Actors and creatives offered their perspectives from two differing yet complementary viewpoints. Actors positioned themselves as both instigators and givers of synergistic energy, as well as engaged receivers of this quality, working alongside other actors who embody it or observing from the audience. The directors were the encouragers and beneficiaries of actors' synergy, as it manifested during auditions, rehearsals and public performances.

The consensus among all those interviewed was that the 'It' Factor represented a complex, multifaceted energy – instantly recognizable yet challenging to capture, replicate or control at will. Actor Simon Gleeson referenced a well-known anecdote about the great British actor Sir Laurence Olivier:

How many times have you've been quoted the Olivier story? ... He was doing Hamlet ... and it was amazing. This one night was just electrifying, and the audience went berserk. And it was just this extraordinary moment in theatre. And he [Olivier] came off and ... he was just really frustrated and angry, and they said, 'Why are you upset? That was just the most masterful thing.' And he said, 'Yes, I know, but I just don't know how to do it again.' ... I think that's sort of the world in which you're asking ... where you just, sometimes, have the planets align ...

As the curators of the 'story' in the rehearsal room and as observers in performance, the creative directors agreed that the elements of synergy were challenging to grasp and impossible to quantify. Yet, all agreed that actors can access this energy and flow. Here's a list of six supportive mechanisms actors use to unlock their seven performative processes:

1 Self-awareness, founded on confidence and not ego.
2 The mental and emotional space for discovery and play, finding new thoughts or emotions for audiences to connect to and to watch.
3 The desire to be authentic and bring their real self and their complete mental, emotional and physical processes to the role.
4 A passion for what they do.
5 A joyous and generous approach – seeing their performance as a gift or offering that enriched the audience.
6 A level of technical skill that could sustain and empower the rigours of the triple-threat role they are portraying.

These mechanisms are not exclusive to musical theatre; they are universal. We all possess seven performative processes, and they are similar to the concept of the seven body energy centres found in the science and art of yoga.[6] The interconnectivity of yogic chakras corresponds to how actors integrate various aspects of their unique selves in performance (more on that in Chapter 12). Although I found no scientific theory linking Indian yogic mind-body understanding with the creative power of performance synergy, the similarities between the subtle body theory of energy centres and the actors' intrinsic processes were too apparent to ignore.

The way personal performative power functions is dynamic. Varying quantities and qualities of these intrinsic processes are engaged in myriad ways, creating something unique and individual in the moment it's perceived, much like taking seven basic ingredients and baking a dozen different cakes! I coined a term to encompass how these intrinsic elements combine to create 'It' in all its various forms – *Performance Quotient* (PQ).

PQ: Your unique performance quotient

We are all familiar with the markers for intellect, IQ and emotional intelligence, EQ, so it seems fitting to embrace the concept of performance quotient, PQ, as a quotient that highlights how we combine,

UNPACKING THE SYNERGY EQUATION

synergize, and express various aspects of our intrinsic processes. Your PQ is the ability to integrate your intrinsic processes, both on stage and off. PQ is activated when multiple personal energies and essential technical skills for communication are used simultaneously. This includes:

- engagement of our senses to understand the experience (*senso*),
- cognitive understanding of self and other actors, their story and character (*neuro*),
- intuitive exploration, spontaneous expression – moment by moment (*psycho*),
- free, appropriate, emotional access (*emotio*),
- accessing our natural personality traits, combined with intrinsic, subliminal levels of personal identification (*persona*),
- our self-expression through learned and embedded techniques (*technico*),
- free, physical embodiment, play, and expression (*physical*).

Simply put, PQ requires us to:

- utilize what we think, intuit, sense, and feel in an instant – in the present moment of connection or performance,
- combine what we know with who we are, what we can do, and
- express that clearly in an uninhibited, instinctual way.

And that's achievable in performance and in everyday life.

Audiences perceived PQ's hallmarks as believable, easy, and intuitive character delivery and a dynamic story that is engaging to watch. They perceive this moment-by-moment apparent discovery of self and story as spontaneous and authentic. Several actors and directors expressed this concept of PQ as artistic intelligence:

That's somebody who gets the idea of synergy, right? That emotional, artistic intelligence that they're going to marry all of these things ... to tell this story they can put themselves in. There's some kind of talented empathy, where they can sort of transport ... I put [synergy] under the umbrella of that intelligence, that performance intelligence that incorporates great perception, nuance .... So that's why it excites me when I see somebody who I think is able to abandon self-consciousness for a moment because that is incredibly freeing. (Millerchip)

Harnessing your PQ – the energy that engages the mind, heart, soul, and body through storytelling – may sound like hard work. However, in practice, it can be the most liberating and often the most fun.

These thoughts on processes and PQ clarified the 'who, what, and how': *Who* is needed for synergy to emerge? *What* do actors and directors perceive it to be? And *how* does 'It' manifest? While I gained valuable insights into how people radiate or flow with synergy, another crucial theme emerged: the influence of extrinsic factors that shape the perception of the 'It' Factor, particularly the role of the recipient: the observer who witnesses it, experiences it, and acknowledges it. It was time to explore how actors connect to other parts of the equation.

4
EXTRINSIC FACTORS: TRANSACTIONAL INTERACTIONS MAKING SYNERGISTIC CONNECTIONS

In the last chapter, we examined the first piece of the 'It' puzzle: Intrinsic Performative Processes – what actors believe to be parts of themselves that they access to reach and inspire an audience. When combined, these internal processes radiate outward, connecting the performer to those watching, who perceive this as stage presence or 'It'. This chapter will discuss the second piece of the puzzle – Contextual Connections. Let's explore the context in which 'It' is seen and experienced, and how actors connect with various extrinsic elements to create dynamic musical theatre performances.

Four transactional interactions

'It' Factor alchemy occurs when the actors, story, onstage action, music, scenery, and production components are layered, balanced, and delivered artistically within a specific space and time. Some external factors may seem fixed, such as performing the same script or music on the same stage night after night. Yet the actors I spoke with encountered something new and different each night as they immersed themselves in their craft. Their stage presence evolved and transformed as their inner world connected with the outer world in that present moment, whether they performed something for the first or the hundredth time. The factors that encourage the presence of 'It' can be grouped into four main elements: the actor, the work, the audience, and the environment (space and time).

The actor

'It' starts with the actors, their imagination and physical energy, and what they bring of themselves to the story and the stage. Their task is to create believable characters, engage with the music, text, and meaning, and then embody that, offering it generously. As we established in the last chapter, the practices actors use to create holistic performances include:

- maintaining a state of confident self-awareness (*neuro, persona*),
- applying specificity or focus that brings clarity to thoughts and meaning (*neuro*),
- making the mental and emotional space to find something original and new: feeling free in 'the present moment' to make discoveries and to play (*psycho, emotio*),
- bringing personal honesty to their performance – fully accessing their mental, emotional, and physical processes, being vulnerable (*neuro, emotio, persona, physical*),
- being brave, passionate, and joyous about what they do (*emotio, persona*),
- offering themselves generously, recognizing the transactional quality of giving a gift as they perform (*persona, emotio*), and
- honing, maintaining, and readily accessing high-level technical competencies to sustain their contributions (*technico, physical*).

There are three external factors that profoundly influence these synergized actors every time they perform. They are:

1 the work they are engaged in and the story the actors are committed to conveying (the 'what'),
2 the audience and how they interact with the actor (the 'who' and the 'how'), and
3 the environment, atmosphere, or space surrounding the actor where communication and connection occur (the 'when' and 'where').

The work or story

In the realm of theatre, effective storytelling is paramount. While spectacle and pizzazz can amuse and entertain, identifying with a story's themes can deeply move and impact those watching. To achieve this:

- Actors engage with the story and authentically embody their characters, enabling the actor and the audience to foster a sense of ownership and connection with the material presented.
- The story arc should resonate with both the actor and the audience, igniting interest, energy or passion.
- The atmosphere in which the story and characters are presented should feel safe and secure. Actors need contextual freedom to explore fresh discoveries within the narrative.

These principles of dynamic storytelling extend beyond the realm of theatre. Effective personal communication involves sharing a part of yourself, both specifically and thoughtfully. We all have remarkable stories that deserve to

> I love watching people light up inside when they speak about something they are passionate about.
> Think of the personal stories that you are connected to, and that light you up – perhaps about a special someone, a memory, or a favourite hobby or a cause.
> Practise finding ready access to these stories and, as you retell them to family or friends, 'go there'. Relive that moment, release your emotion and enjoy being connected fully, remembering the sights and sounds and how your heart and body felt. With a safe audience, learn to be vulnerable. It gets easier with the doing!

be told. Stories serve as windows into our lives, and it's a privilege to share them, no matter how raw or painful they may be.

The audience or observer

The audience is the third element of the picture and one of the 'whys' actors perform; they are both a source of the actor's energy and the recipient of it. This often becomes clear when friends or family members attend a performance. There can be an extra 'sizzle' in the room. However, part of the audience's experience of the 'It' Factor occurs when actors subliminally add value to every audience member; the audience perceives the actors are performing just for them, regardless of personal association.

The role of 'the observer'

The role of the observer in unpacking the 'It' Factor equation is philosophically intriguing. Scientists Charles Riborg Mann and George Ransom Twiss asked the age-old question, *When a tree falls in a lonely forest, and no animal is nearby to hear it, does it make a sound?*[1] Quantum physicists continue to debate whether sound exists if it is not heard. Thus, one might wonder, if there is no one to watch or hear the synergized storyteller, does 'It' even exist?

Performance carries dual resonances. It describes an event or story and, to a large extent, also prescribes the audience's experience. To suspend disbelief and engage in a transactional relationship with the performer, audiences also engage their intrinsic processes – their senses, cognition, intuition, imagination and empathy. The watching audience can adopt various stances. As observers, they can maintain an objective distance, positioning themselves apart. Yet, once their attention is captured, viewers perceive the significance of the performance and assign a degree of care in the experience. Care and empathy have the power to transform the observer into a perceiver and then into an attentive attendee, fostering engaged cooperation in the performance. Once we care about something, we become connected. The honesty and story conveyed can swiftly shift an audience from observer to empathizer.

This shift is evident when witnessing a compelling piece of theatre. Western theatre's naturalistic acting styles showcase humanity's joys and struggles in myriad settings, from realistic re-creations to the imagined realms of futuristic fantasy. Yet regardless of the story's premise, once the audience identifies with the human condition depicted within the story's real yet imaginary world, they are captivated.

Who constitutes an audience? All of us, when we observe others and listen to their stories.

Ways audiences connect

As an entity, the audience is intriguing. Comprising of individuals with highly diverse tastes, it forms a collective whole. No audience is ever identical in size or energy, and their reactions to the actors' performances are unpredictable. Often, friends watching a musical together may have differing opinions on the 'It' Factor, as well as who are their favourite performers or moments. Nevertheless, these same viewers will collectively rise in excitement and appreciation during a curtain call.

The actors and creatives I interviewed shared three perspectives on how 'It' interacts with an audience. First, from their position as observers in the audience, they felt connected to an actor who exuded 'It' and whose energetic presence surrounded and engaged them. They also described the palpable sensation of 'It', whether alone on stage or with another actor, as 'It' moved in and through them and flowed out to the audience members. Lastly, they noted this energy's presence in the air as an atmospheric quality created either by the action on stage or the audience's engagement with the narrative.

Audience engagement is the result of the subliminal invitation actors offer. There is a tacit permission for them to experience the unfolding story. Theatre training has often emphasized the importance of the 'fourth wall', a theatrical device that has shaped performances since the eighteenth century. The esteemed acting teacher Uta Hagen explored the concept of 'public solitude', a core concept first explored by pioneer Konstantin Stanislavski. She states, *'Public solitude is being alone in the presence of others. It is the actor's ability to exist genuinely and privately in the imaginary circumstances of the play, even while being watched.'*[2]

In this environment, the audience feels as though they are witnessing something intensely personal and private being performed for them in public. Audience voyeurism fosters the illusion that what unfolds on stage is intimate or secretive. It entices the audience in, arouses their senses, and piques their interest. In the darkness of the theatre, observers spy on the action unnoticed, evoking a sense of apparent safety. This invisible, imaginary, permeable structure functions like a one-way mirror, allowing the audience to voyeuristically glimpse the unfolding drama without disrupting its flow.

However, an intriguing phenomenon occurs when we, the audience, recognize that the actors are aware of our presence while we watch from a distance. The audience is present yet not present; still, the performance is intended for them. This relationship is cyclically transactional – actors and audience initiate and respond, give and receive. Often, this symbiotic connection is only formally acknowledged when the cast takes their bows.

The creative directors I interviewed provided me with a comprehensive perspective on how large groups of people can collectively experience synergy. They spoke extensively about feeling engaged by an actor's energy, feeling a palpable connection:

As an audience member, you feel the other audience members around you …. If I'm sitting in an auditorium and someone is nailing something, that's affecting not only me. I can feel the whole group of humans kind of go 'ah'. No one breathes, you can hear the sound of people crying. (Ralph)

Luke Hunter takes this further:

There are times when actors have that natural connection to the audience, and you just have to trust them. It is about bringing the audience to you. You just know that as soon as they sing, you're in completely safe hands … we're responding to that emotional, real, primal effort that's coming through. The emotion – that's power, and that is so compelling.

He continued:

It's something about a connection that gets formed between the performer and the person watching, whether that be in an audition room or the theatre or a rehearsal … that unique magnetism or something gets drawn between the two people and the artifice of performing disappears so that there is a unique, strong connection that ties the work and the narrative and the story between those two people, or the actor and a thousand people or two thousand people. Whatever it is, it's very hard to be broken.

Millerchip spoke of this transactional relationship between actor and audience from her dual perspective as director and actor:

We perform to an audience; we perform for an audience. And I think when we open ourselves to allow them to look in and find or see that special moment, that's when we are performing for, versus to, or at, and I think it's very subtle. I'm always thinking of the audience. I'm always seeing the audience, but I don't want them to know that. I want them to think that they've caught me doing something just for me.

Actor Caroline O'Connor agreed:

You have to have three ears. You have one ear that's listening to what you're doing, one ear that's listening to what the other actor's doing and one ear to listen to what the audience is doing … how's the audience responding right now?

Nancye Hayes explained how it felt on stage, '*I can feel that moment in an audience when "that moment" occurs because its … a combined experience.*'

Actors, as audience members, also experienced a palpable connection:

When she stepped on stage and said her first line, she wasn't mic'ed. But all of a sudden, her voice felt like it was everywhere in the theatre … that was one of those moments where she just grabbed you and brought you right here, and because I was quite far back, somewhat distant and removed … somehow she was able to bridge that vast gap between the stage and the back of the theatre. All of a sudden, you were right there in her pocket. (Melham)

The timing and manner of actor-audience engagement can vary and may not depend solely on an actor's skill. Audiences are known to have certain predispositions to engage, which can depend on age or their prior connection to the work. For instance, a matinee audience typically consists of more senior patrons and children, which generate a different energy and atmosphere compared to evening performances. Granger noted the differences he observed between attendees on a Friday night and those on a Saturday night, which also reflected the energy levels of the adult audience and the impact of their working week.

Despite the audience's inconsistencies, actors recognize that their primary goal is to create an imaginary world and invite the audience to immerse themselves in it. This world can be accessed through various portals: the environment, the *mise en scène* or the audience's prior knowledge of the story. When actors blend their inner world with these external elements, an actor/audience connection can occur.

Trust and the audience

Trust is another factor that influences audience response. Audiences are encouraged to open their minds and emotions to the creative process occurring on stage. Their safety became a topic of conversation:

If you're in the audience, you feel safe to go on that journey. Be open to those energies and that synergy, but if you feel safe, then you're willing to go wherever the actor wants to take you. (Melham)

Truthfulness is a part of that safety and a trait that audiences respond to: *'I think letting the audience come to you, letting them discover it and being just really simple and truthful, is what I think people respond to … it can be the quietest, simplest song'* (Hopson). Veteran actor Philip Quast also commented on truthfulness, saying, *'The only basis that the actor has to work is to start from the basic thing of truth. I feel safe as an audience in their hands.'*

As audience members identify with the characters' truthfulness on an intrinsic level, their perception of synergy shifts. And magic happens.

The environment: space and time

A fourth transactional interaction occurs when the performer, story and audience intersect with the environment. Actors are 'on show' whenever they perform and various theatrical environments can influence how they convey their story and engage with the audience. The environment can enhance or detract from the total experience.

The performance space: Audition, rehearsal and stage

Musical theatre actors and creative directors collaborate and interact in diverse environments – auditions, rehearsals and public performances. Each presents unique scenarios with varying expectations and pressures. My investigation uncovered a wealth of information about how these three settings influence the various internal and external processes at play.

Auditions

Auditions are often viewed as some of the most stressful and emotionally intense environments for actors; here, employment decisions are made, and careers are forged. Actors shared a variety of perspectives on the presence of synergy during auditions. While some were unaware of their 'It' Factor in these high-pressure situations, many suggested they could still tap into the performative processes that energize their stage presence. Others felt a confident and bold desire to explore and experiment in that audition space, which added vitality to their performance. One actor, Ashleigh Rubenach, recounted her experience during a successful dance audition as a singer-actor. With less dance experience than others in the room, she was offered a role in a show because she embodied joyful, exuberant synergy in her audition, capturing the essence of the dance routine and the eye of the creatives.

Prior, talked of the focus and bravery she mustered in auditions to create inspiring performances:

I think performance in audition can be quite similar because really when I'm auditioning, I am performing … it's my stage. It's my space and you're my audience and you're giving the gift. That is your moment … they can't do what you can do. So, you go in there knowing that you've got the upper hand, the psychological aspect.

Jemma Rix spoke of the confidence she felt when she had prepared for the audition, and how that allowed her to take and embody direction. Speaking of a recent audition she said:

And, you know, I'd done my homework. So there was enough of a release of being able to be in the moment of what was asked. But I had a very magical audition where the musical director was giving me so much content of the character ... And so then I was just 100% in that moment I was able to deliver. And there's this energy in the room where you're like, that feels like that's what the magic is ...

MT actors also discussed how synergy can be lost when, under the pressure of auditions, they might attempt to impress or produce something they believe is expected by the creatives in the room:

Creatives ... just want somebody to walk in with an open energy ... and deliver a wonderful version of themselves through the material. And it's funny how, as an auditioner, you can shut that down so quickly with anxieties and over-analysis, how that shuts down that ... vessel for everything to flow. (Melham)

Chidzey advises:

I think the biggest thing would be to bring yourself to each role or to the work you are doing because no one can bring you into the room. No one can bring that essence that you have, so don't try to be anyone else ... you are enough.

Creative directors reported that an actor's radiance or presence influenced their decision to advance them to the next round of auditions. For many directors, audition synergy resembled generous and joyful energy, flexibility and a willingness to play and engage with the unknown, especially when auditionees were given 'cold reads' (asked to read excerpts from the show without prior preparation).

I think it's an energy thing more than anything else ... there is that element of fearlessness. I think the element of play is really important. I think that is the exciting part of performances in an audition room. From time to time, performers come in, and ... they had that 'the whole world and the room disappears' kind of thing. (Hunter)

Some directors described sensing the 'It' Factor within the first ten seconds of an auditionee entering the room. In those moments, when no specific story or character was at play, actors often presented an unguarded version of themselves, radiating energy and their own story. The actor's open persona connected with the directors who responded:

That is something that you can sense when someone walks in for the first time, and you feel engaged with them .... They immediately have something that feels like there is an open door to them ... There's something just simple and honest about it. (Stewart)

That comment highlights the element of attraction – a vibrant, authentic actor engaging with an interested observer. In this instance, neither the story nor the environment generated the 'It' Factor; it was merely two individuals giving and receiving.

We can apply these insights to other intense situations in which we live and communicate, such as the corporate world of job interviews, presentations, examinations or speaking events. How we utilize and harness our intrinsic performative processes can significantly influence how others perceive, receive and connect with us on a subliminal level. We can shape the energy we exude by tapping into what's inside. Our instinctual minds and imagination, combined with an open heart and an engaged persona, connecting with time, place and story, will allow the fullness of who we are to shine through. And it's compelling.

Rehearsals

In contrast to the intense atmosphere of the audition room, some actors favoured the rehearsal space, incorporating synergistic elements such as *'playfulness, lightness, and ease … generosity, vulnerability and courage … There is an epic rehearsal room for you'* (O'Donnell/Gleeson).

The 'It' Factor often emerges once the actors and creatives have unpacked and blocked the show. When the production's songs and scenes are stitched together, an air of excitement and expectation fills the space as actors access their performative processes:

> *I'm like a sticky ball. And then 'voom' – as all of the other elements that I pick up along the way … or thoughts that I have, or discussion I had with the director – all these little other parts attach themselves to this … through the course of rehearsals, so that by the time we're doing runs … that's when you get that continuity of it, and you fly a little bit … and flow.* (Millerchip)

Curiously, several actors noted that they lost some indicators of synergy two-thirds of the way through the rehearsal process, including joy, playfulness, and ease. They attributed this change to the negative influences of performance pressure, fear, and self-doubt. At times, these can act as a catalyst for unlocking new levels of vulnerability and synergy. Natalie O'Donnell articulated this aspect of the actor's internal journey during the rehearsal process:

> *So usually, Week One – 'I am so fortunate to be here. Isn't everyone marvellous? I just love this group of people. This is going to be so much fun.' Week Two is – 'OK, now we're getting into the nuts and bolts of it and unpicking the layers and getting serious'. Week Three – 'Why did I get cast? I am rubbish. I should never have even started this.' And it's in that week that things start happening, and maybe this is because we're just going straight back to where I'm at my most vulnerable; the barriers break at the same level as the vulnerability rises.*

We can take heart from experienced professionals who acknowledge that the 'It' Factor is not always on display. Sometimes, it requires coaxing to come out and play. Effort is needed to access and reveal those aspects of our inner selves that we protect or typically conceal in our daily lives. Still, it's worthwhile to embrace vulnerability in the pursuit of a deep connection.

Onstage Performance

Among the three environments, onstage performances offer the greatest opportunity for synergy to occur. In response to the question, *'How often do you experience synergy in performance?'* Marina Prior replied:

Quite often. And the longer I've done it, the easier I find it is to slip into it. It's easier now than it was 20 years ago. And I think that maybe even muscle memory, you know? I've psyched myself for long enough that I can actually psych myself into that moment.

Let's look at another powerful tool at the actor's disposal – atmosphere.

Atmosphere

Atmosphere feels like something in the ether or the air around us. It's fuelled by energy from within as we respond to external stimuli that trigger our instinctual reactions. A few years ago, I walked home late at night through the empty, unfamiliar streets of Brooklyn, NY. I felt safe until I became aware of a stranger walking behind me. This triggered a response that made my heart race, and suddenly, the air seemed colder and the surroundings more hostile. My fear drastically altered my perception of the atmosphere. So much so that the stranger behind me laughed oddly. Although I kept walking, he sensed my rising fear.

Our thoughts and feelings can influence the atmosphere that connects us to others and vice versa. Enter a room filled with people who are laughing or celebrating, and you can't help but smile. Alternatively, step into that same room with heavy news and observe how you can alter the atmosphere as people respond to you.

While atmosphere is often seen as a quality that occurs in a specific time and place, acting teacher Michael Chekhov believes that creating atmosphere is a skill actors can develop through their imagination. His psycho-physical exercises encourage them to explore, energize and respond to elements of their imagined atmospheres, thereby producing something that feels genuinely real.[3] In my experience, actors can tether their imagination to their senses to create moments laden with meaning. When they incorporate cognitive thoughts, which evoke an emotional response to those sensory imaginings, the atmosphere around them seems charged with energy.

A specific time and place can prescribe a type of atmospheric energy – both positive and negative. Directors discussed how actors can generate different atmospheres in all three work environments: audition, rehearsal and performance. While each setting presents its own challenges, the actors' technical skills enable them to effectively navigate potential negative emotions and change the atmosphere to their advantage.

The nature of the space in which actors perform can also support them. Environmental aesthetics combine with the subjective feelings of both the performer and the observer, creating mood and tone, the pillars of atmosphere. Actors refer to the style and size of a theatre space contributing or detracting from the atmosphere onstage. The atmosphere backstage can often intensify before a performance when unexpected elements are added, such as understudies or visiting dignitaries. Audiences also feel

> Take a moment to remember an atmosphere you have been in, e.g. a bustling commute to work, a deserted street late at night, or an awkward social gathering. What was the time and place? Were others' thoughts, emotions, or energies affecting that atmosphere? How did you feel and respond?
>
> Imagine yourself doing something different in those situations, something that could change the atmosphere. Play out that scene in your mind. You have that power.

the anticipation of what is to come and sense the elevated heart rates upon entering a theatre or concert venue. There is a sizzle in the air when powerful emotions are collectively experienced.

Atmospheres are also driven by an audience's connection to the subject matter or narrative. Two powerful, synergistic moments come to mind. The first is a scene from the 2015/2017 musical *Come from Away*, one of my favourites. Early in the show, there's a moment when the colourful inhabitants of Gander, Newfoundland, become aware of a tragedy many of us saw unfold – the 2001 reporting of the 9/11 terrorist attacks in New York. A palpable sense of shock and disbelief emanates from the actors during that recreated moment. Each time I have seen that show, the audience holds its breath, and the atmosphere shifts immediately. We are transported back in time, experiencing that story alongside them.

The second example is a masterfully crafted theatrical moment I experienced while watching the 2018 jukebox musical *Tina: The Tina Turner Musical*. Throughout both acts, we witness Tina's struggle against abuse, discrimination, misogyny, and ageism, ultimately fighting her way back to the pinnacle of her career. Near the end of the musical, her iconic 1988 concert in Brazil is recreated. The scene takes us backstage; Tina's vulnerability and fears are on display. Then she takes a breath, ascends the backstage stairs, reaches the top step, and turns. The lights and stage shift dramatically. Suddenly, we, the audience, transform into the stadium crowd and find ourselves spontaneously rising to our feet, becoming part of that crowd, singing, dancing, and championing this extraordinary artist. We are all swept up in an atmosphere that makes the recreated moment feel incredibly real.

Turning transactional interactions into synergistic connections

These extrinsic elements set the stage for the 'It' Factor to appear. So, let's briefly recap. Transactions occur between four key components:

1. the actor or instigator,
2. the work or story they are situated in,
3. the observers or audience who connect with the actor and story, and
4. the effect that the environment – the time, place, and atmosphere – have on synergy.

To commit holistically to these external factors around them, actors access their intrinsic performative processes:

- They cognitively and personally connect to the story and their character (*neuro, emotio, persona*),
- They use their senses to connect to the creatives, to other actors and to the audience in various settings (*senso, physical*),
- They physically embody their characters, bridging the theatrical space between actors and the audience (*technico, physical*), and
- They intuitively create and explore the atmosphere and environment (*neuro, psycho*).

The diagrammatic summary, Figure 4.1, presents these four components and their various elements.

EXTRINSIC FACTORS

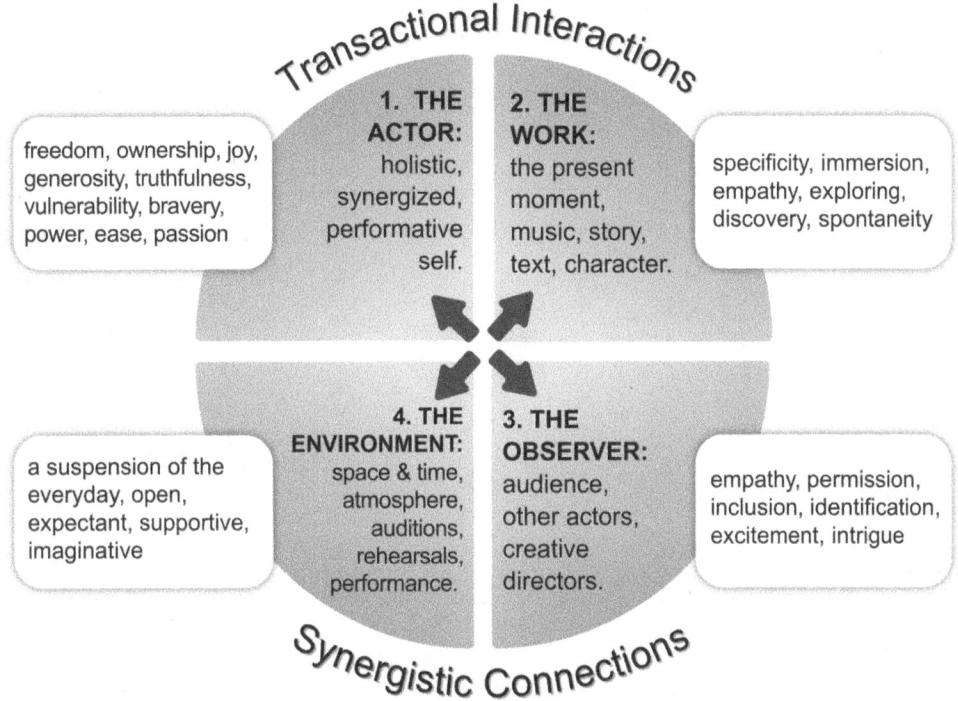

Figure 4.1 Transactional interactions between actors and extrinsic factors.

The elements in these four quadrants inform each other, creating fluid connections. Energy flows outward and inward to and from the actors in the performance. This flow is enhanced as actors embody notions of spontaneity and discovery, fostering a sense of living truthfully, even in imaginary circumstances. These symbiotic interactions create synergistic connections where initiating and responding, giving and receiving become a cyclical process, and impartiality ceases to exist. Here, there is room and energy for the 'It' Factor to flourish.

Now, let's delve into the tactics and techniques performers use and how they work to ensure this synergistic flow. It's in the next theme I uncovered – Ways of Thinking, Being, and Doing.

5
CONSTRUCTING THE SUM FROM THE PARTS: WAYS OF THINKING, BEING, AND DOING

Having established the seven intrinsic processes that performers bring to their craft and how these interact with external contexts, I looked at another 'how'. How do actors access and combine these intrinsic elements to create their personal synergy? What do performers think, feel and do when they are in flow? The third central theme – Ways of Thinking, Being, and Doing – emerged as actors and creatives shared how they nurture and express their 'It' Factor. In this chapter, we will explore the scaffolding: the learning, knowledge and skills that actors and creatives bring to their craft. These supportive structures encourage actors to engage with their intrinsic processes and deliver dynamic musical theatre performances.

Actors and creatives supportive techniques

When discussing their skills, most actors acknowledged the significance of their formative training – the singing, acting, and dancing skills they acquired during childhood or as young adults. They shared techniques they developed alongside strategies they learned from other actors and directors. These ranged from practical, thought-through exercises to broader approaches and conceptual thinking.

As expected, my data analysis revealed that the actors' techniques were often empowered by one or more of their seven performative processes, for example:

- Actors' commitment to focus, hard work and text study is primarily driven by ideational reasoning. In contrast, their use of imagination and play unlocks deeper meaning in the script and is driven by intuitive cognition.
- Actors' learned physical skills – singing, acting, and dancing – appear primarily as technical competencies, which also requires ideational and instinctual engagement.
- Acting-based skills appear to be undergirded by a holistic use of all seven performative processes.
- All singing, acting and dancing skills are individually stylized, reflecting the performers' sense of self, personality, and physicality.

Similarly, creative directors discussed the methods they employed to elicit optimal performances from actors during rehearsals and throughout the show's run. Their tactics were often broader, expanding an actor's vision, stimulating curiosity and providing signposts or personal prompts to guide actors' thoughts and enhance their awareness.

- They addressed the work's technical demands – singing, acting, dancing.
- They provided a creative, playful environment for instinctual discovery.
- They supported the actors' journey as they connected to character and story.
- They envisioned and built a cohesive, dynamic, original production.

While directors and actors work differently to fulfil their roles in production, they share three common approaches to connecting the actor to the story and character: 'Ways of Thinking', 'Ways of Being', and 'Ways of Doing'. Their methods tap into and knit together multiple elements to create a cohesive whole. Let's examine these three 'ways' a little more closely.

Ways of thinking

The first theme – Ways of Thinking – addresses the actors' use of cognitive abilities, both ideational and instinctual. For many actors, their work begins long before they enter the rehearsal room. They employ various tactics when learning scripts and songs; some even start rehearsals with their roles entirely memorized. According to Stuart Maunder: *'Almost every star that I've worked with has an incredible working knowledge of the piece they are doing before they get into the rehearsal room.'* Others prefer to learn on the job, memorizing and embedding the directors' vision along with the text and music. All actors and creatives spoke of the intensity and depth of work they apply to build characterizations and find the freedom and ease of delivery that is a signature trait of the 'It' Factor:

And it's about, as a performer, filling every moment in your brain so that you say your line and then you go there … there is never a moment of dead air when you're not in the story, actively playing something. (Millerchip)

There is extensive cognitive activity involved in reading, understanding and then embedding a role in text and song. This includes deconstructing words and music, uncovering layers of meaning in each moment and expressing those in a fresh, authentic manner. Purposeful singing is a common thread: *'No note I sing should be thrown away. "It" doesn't have to be that everything is a long note; it's more about everything is purposeful'* (Hopson).

Millerchip agreed:

Singing has to be, in a real way, thought set to melody. Otherwise, we're just reciting in front of people. 'What a lovely singer, what a tuneful singing performance that was.' But they're not going to suspend their belief for even a nanosecond. And then it will always be something that's performed at them and not something that they can immerse themselves in.

Directors advocated for thoroughly exploring the text to establish connections between thoughts, ideas and actions. Langley and Amos discussed 'mining the text' to uncover deeper meanings and nuances hidden in the lyrics. They emphasized the significance and value of every 'if', 'and', and 'but'. Amos elaborated, 'You'll get them to the stage where every *single syllable, every single note, every single moment in time, they know exactly what they're going to do.*'

The importance of hard work

Actors and creatives discussed the hard work involved in each role or production, unpacking the *raison d'être* of the work and examining the overarching themes, text, and subtext (the thought processes that lie beneath the text). These layers are woven into the piece by the writers – the composer, lyricist, and book writer – and are identified and teased out by the creative team. The context of the period and culture for which the work was written adds layers that can be explored when delving into the work and creating complex characterization. To implement the stage director's creative vision, an actor's skills and concentration are brought to the task. Hours of thought, focus, and specificity help to build a role and embed a character. Georgina Hopson spoke of the depth of background work required:

Working at such minute detail, know[ing] the intimate fabric of the piece so well that you can then forget it. Seeing something so simple, knowing that there's an iceberg underneath the water of work that person has done, to then give you that point ... that really crystal-clear point where they're clearly communicating something.

When speaking of her experience as an actor, Millerchip shared her tactic of creating a fully formed person and the world in which they operate:

Once I've got all of that base work done ... authenticity will come easily to me because they [the character] have to be a person. I can see how this person operates in society. I can [say], 'Let's see how this person is real'. I know how they stand, then I know, how they make decisions. Then, I know where the thought changes would be and what light bulb moments that person could have in that context. I just deeply invest in this person. I call on my instincts and the choices that I make and, piece by piece, it all sort of comes together.

Instinctual response

Other actors highlighted the importance of a well-developed instinctual response. Some employed a two-step process: first, doing the hard work, and then letting go of cognitive awareness to allow for a more intuitive approach to their performance on stage: '*But by doing all of that ... detailed character work, doing all of that groundwork so that the character and where I'm going is then part of my DNA ... then I'm completely able to work on instinct*' (Millerchip).

Some aspects of instinctual cognition techniques were play, immersion and freedom: '*Get off yourself and onto the other ... have fun ... and there is no going too far with this, you just play,*' said Hopson. Melham described it further:

But then it's more about just connecting with that other person on stage and really focussing on that rather than getting in your own head too much ... It's like you've done all this processing and all of this work. Now, just forget it all. Just let it happen ... Just opening that door and letting that flow a little bit more.

Quast added, *'you have to practise your technique until its transcended by instinct.'*

Several actors acknowledged that during flow moments, a percentage of objective cognition in their performance continued to manage the technical requirements of the work while they remained immersed in character. *'I am existing in that story. And there's still a part of me ... I'm still there,'* said Hopson. For Hunter, it was:

Immediacy ... she made it seem as if it's never been done before. But there was also the actor pulling the strings and another part that was stepping back and thinking and critiquing at the same time. There was a lot going on.

Other actors noted this division in cognition when performing on stage. Prior suggested that eighty per cent of her performance energy flowed instinctively through the character and story, while twenty per cent was spent managing practical aspects like lighting, staging, and the orchestra. Hopson described having a 'Jiminy Cricket' part of herself that monitored her on-stage performance to provide support. Luke Hunter explained how this cognitive duality operates and how it appeared from the audience's perspective:

Very intelligent and very nuanced. And she's ... still breaking everything down. She knows every single thing that she's doing at every moment, but you stand at the back of the auditorium and there's this glow and just effortless flow. Yes. That just feels as an audience member, like it's just so natural and so honest and real ... And immediacy ... And she made it seem as if it's never been done before.

Many actors credited their success in discovering synergistic moments to accessing their instinctual knowledge and their personality, which frequently sparked their performances and fostered flow and ease. This led me to my next theme.

Ways of being

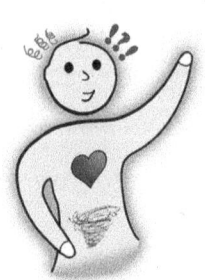

This second sub-theme amassed the elements of an actor's persona along with the techniques and tactics they brought to their work as they created and performed. The actor's thoughts, emotions, unique character traits and personality, revealed through an engaged physicality, were key ingredients in creating their sense of self. Research professor and author Brené Brown encourages us to dare greatly, saying, *'Being rather than doing requires showing up and letting ourselves be seen.'*[1] Directors observed the innate power of actors who worked in this way:

Because if you can just think and breathe a song in front of someone and live it without making a sound and I can believe that you're going through whatever you're going through, then you got me, you got me with the physical. (Millerchip)

Stuart Maunder suggested: *'Being at one with the work that they're doing ... that's the only way you can create a great piece of work ... if you are all working towards the same, to the same end.'* Simon Phillips added:

> *There is something imperturbably settled about that inner core of the person ... there are certain things you can do to work towards that being the factor in yourself ... sometimes it comes from an immense sense of self-confidence working with a hundred percent of your energy all the time ... It's really about bringing people to you in a very confident way.*

Musical Director Luke Hunter said, for him, part of the 'It' equation was the unique qualities residing in an actor's persona: *'Yes, because there's something about what they have that I think you can't teach because [it's] in their personality.'* Actor Nancye Hayes agreed, *'You're drawn to them, and your eyes never leave them and that's something that I believe is a gift.'*

Caroline O'Connor spoke of how a person can subsume a role, and make it one with themselves:

> *There's something about when you watch someone, you know they're acting, but they're being rather than acting ... So I know that everyone's acting. This is the crazy thing. But there's something about the character is so beautifully comfortable that you stop seeing the acting. They come on, they start talking and they're just ... there. And they're there for the whole night and they're in the character and you sort of get lost. I think that's when you get taken in ... you go, oh, I don't even know who that person is. I know who this character is.*

Physicality

Actors used their physical embodiment to encapsulate and express their performative processes. They spoke of being present physically as well as mentally: not manufacturing a character, but instead physically initiating, responding, giving and receiving: *'Just being free both in your body and in your intention and in your connection ... that's when those opportunities happen,'* said Melham.

Marina Prior recounts a technique that she was taught by a fellow actor, which engaged her body, thoughts, and emotions through physical specificity, focus and stillness:

> *He taught a huge amount to me about the bravery of stillness. He ... made me hold two paperweights in my hands, because he said that I was posturing with my hands, '... your voice, you're wasting it, you are dissipating your impulses through your hands and it's distracting.' And so he made me hold paperweights and do scenes ... the very intimate sort of quiet scenes, and he sat at the back of the balcony, and I stood on stage, and I had to just stand still with the paperweights and do the really intimate scene with him way up there ... the ability for you to take all your impulses and just put them into your voice ... and your face and light. Project them all the way up there and they will go there.*

Actors spoke of the power of choosing techniques that worked specifically for them internally and how ideas learned from directors helped to engender latent qualities associated with musical theatre synergy – power, freedom, joy:

I think it is a push-pull … I certainly take everything everybody says to me, and I consider it, and I roll it around, and I try it out and … sort of mutate it and make it your own and then find a way to empower it. (Hopson)

Nancye Hayes spoke of how extrinsic and physical aspects contributed to bringing her characters to life:

I feel once I see the way a designer has decided to costume you, the way you're going to look, the way you're going to move, the way you're going to sound, finding all those different areas … I find I'm much more of a person that discovers my performance in the way I present, I'm being presented as that character.

Producer Kris Stewart shared his opinion that giving actors the time and space to 'get on the floor' to work the script physically was conducive to the appearance of synergy:

Musical theatre is by its nature, it's a very physical form. 'It' exists in space and time … it encourages you to get on your feet. And I think physically you solve a lot of questions around character and storytelling.

Breath

Breath is the power that fuels a thought and conveys it to the audience. Stage directors referred to breathing as inspirational breath. It is the catalyst for a chain reaction: an actor's thought focuses their intention, which ignites the emotions needed to tell the story. Musical directors viewed breath as the foundation for vocal power and timbre that supports the dramaturgy. They alluded to the concept of primal breath – an instinctual breath that connects to an inherent acting response rather than a specific singing technique. Sharon Millerchip spoke directly about the impact of a thought-laden breath, urging actors to think on their feet: *'That split second of inhaling before you say something lets us know that you're thinking in the moment, as you say it … you think on the spot.'*

Breath also appears as a readable, observable thought or feeling: *'And … you're never thinking that you're watching an actor. They breathe. They breathe in every moment, and they respond to all outside stimuli. And they let go of ego.'* (Langley)

Simon Phillips noted, *'Then there's a lot of inspirational breath. And that's kind of a sense of breath, of breath going in, filling yourself up with the idea that you're having or with the emotional moment.'* He went on to share a powerful tactic:

I always say, put your brain in the bottom of your stomach, put it there, and take a breath to access it so that you're not calculating things in that way. You know, everything that you need to think, you access deeper … and it isn't in the frontal lobe.

Most actors saw specific breathing techniques as important preparation tools. For example, Philip Quast shared using a style of yoga breath on the side of the stage to calm the mind and energize the body before walking onto stage: *'Keep the shoulders down, relaxed stomach and you go in through the*

Many of the techniques and tactics actors mentioned are in common usage. Some noted the work of voice teachers Cicely Berry and Patsy Rodenberg, who propound vocal exercises to liberate an actor's hidden possibilities and instinctual responses. These texts encourage actors to awaken their latent performance presence through breathing and exercise. Others incorporated specific acting methods. Simon Gleeson and Natalie O'Donnell use the warm-up exercises of Michael Chekhov regularly to loosen up, connect, and explore radiance and atmosphere and bring those concepts into their work:

A playful environment, a playful rehearsal space, I just find so joyous, and again, what I said about that Chekhov thing – of lightness and ease, lightness and ease … such a revelation, even in the hardest moments, most especially. (Gleeson)

Sheldon and Quast discussed exploring the text's etymology; they loved the power they found when delving deeply into the text. Prior mentioned the 'table work' conducted in the initial stages of rehearsal: sitting with other actors and directors to read, explore subtext and talk about the layers of meaning in the story and its characters before bringing the scenes to life. Others referenced the Stanislavski-based acting techniques they had learned at university; however, most had developed their own tactics and generously shared these techniques:

I use a psychophysical objective in my mind as this character. Try and make that person hug you, or try and make them dance, or try and make them bow to you or something like that, something that is really physical, something that gets me out of my head … It's more about physicalising something and not being in my head anymore. That worked really well for me, a great technique … It's a quote or saying, 'Get off of yourself and on to the other.' It's about living in the responding. (Hopson)

Joel Granger used similar techniques adding, '*Personalisation is kind of my biggest thing, and I bring myself to everything I do.*' Quast said, '*I try to find the autobiographical parts of those words in myself,*' while Melham noted, '*I think you can feel those moments as a responder and as a listener on stage. I feel like that's a good indication that you're close to that moment of things really happening.*'

Actors spoke about learning from their peers and bringing observations from the world at large. '*I'm just talking about being curious. You're going to be slightly switched on all the time,*' observed Quast, and Granger agreed, '*You keep your brain in a state of curiosity as much as you can throughout the day; that'll help you make new and interesting and bold choices.*'

Others commented on learning through doing and how performing eight shows a week over a long run helped to expand characterization: '*A part of me loves this long run because I'm still exploring and finding new things*' (Granger). Caroline O'Connor spoke of finding musicality and rhythm in a character:

The rhythm of a character is very, very musical. Once you get an accent, a voice and a rhythm … it's the motor for the show. I noticed that … once you're on there and you start the motor, you're sort of running the show in a way.

She went on to talk about spending a lot of time in the wings, connected to the scenes, feeling the rhythmic energy, and gauging her entry based on what came before. '*I do listen a lot … I don't just turn up at the last minute*' (O'Connor).

nose and that yoga breath where you go slightly quiet with a sound on the back of your throat, without hurting the throat.'

Freedom

Feeling free in mind, body, and spirit is essential for actors to feel safe and flourish. Several creatives shared how they encouraged their cast to find freedom and engage in imaginative play to enhance the story's vision: '*Put the tool belt down for a second and just like, take a leap. But then you also don't want them to completely disregard all sense of stagecraft that they have learned*' (Ralph).

Additionally, Luke Hunter mentioned, '*This is where this song lives. This is where this role is, where this character can reside and have a sense of having the freedom to make decisions within the performance.*' Directors also talked about the need to find freedom within themselves:

> '*But what is illustrated to me is that there are no rules. You have to try different things. You have to be prepared to fail … to be vulnerable as a director in front of those people. One doesn't and can't have all the answers.*' (Maunder)

Ways of doing

Acting is not only 'being', it is also 'doing'. There is no performance without it. Actors and creatives generously shared their tactics and preferred methods for creating performance-ready characters. My third sub-theme, Ways of Doing, collated the various tactics they use when bringing a character to life. Their differing approaches highlights how all seven intrinsic processes can be engaged in 'the doing'.

> *The heights by great men reached and kept were not achieved by sudden flight, But they, while their companions slept, were toiling upward in the night.*
> – Henry W. Longfellow, 'The Ladder of St. Augustine,' Stanza 10, 1846.

Actors' personal methods and training

Everyone I interviewed acknowledged the high level of technical competencies required in singing, acting, and dancing to play musical theatre roles. Many actors practise their triple threat skills to stay 'tuned' and 'show fit'. This includes some fitness regimens or attending regular dance, movement, or yoga classes; some take singing lessons regularly to improve their skills.

Others undertake specialist coaching sessions to prepare for a specific audition or role, embedding particular technical skills into their body through repetition. Singing and musical abilities are considered essential, given the high demands that performing eight shows a week places on singing actors. Quast believed that '*few musicians are hugely successful without knowing their scales and some form of … musical structure … and technique*'. Hopson echoed this sentiment: '*Once you learn technically, you then can forget about it.*'

Rituals

Several performers referred to specific rituals they employed to focus their energies before going on stage. Visualization and breathing are two powerful tools that several actors and directors use to bring their stories to life:

Every single time before I go on stage, I find a point on the wall, a pinpoint spot, and just breathe all of my energy into that one point and visualize myself succeeding, visualize how I want my voice to sound, how my performance will be, and take two minutes of breath and stillness and focus before I go on stage. Just visualize the best version of how I will perform. and be in that very connected place ... I've been on stage when I haven't done that, and I've been all over the shop, so I really need to focus my brain before I go on. (Lucy Maunder)

Millerchip added, '*Think through the thought, visualize images.*' Philip Quast found affirmations helpful:

I do have an affirmation. Eyes closed. Sometimes I'll go, 'I own this stage, this space as mine.' I'll do that sometimes. Visualize yourself walking. I've seen my first entrance in my mind's eye before I've done it ... I can be in the audience and see me walking on and that's it.

> What are your rituals? What do they do for you? How do you focus your attention or gather your energy for a task or event? There is power in a familiar process and in repetition.

One communal ritual practised by most musical theatre casts is the company physical and vocal warm-up, typically held an hour or two before curtain up. Something changes in the atmosphere as individuals come together. Through communal physical expression, cast members find focused direction, purposeful energy and a sense of ensemble that enhances their performance.

Directors' methods

During the interviews, directors were praised for fostering a positive mental, emotional and physical space in the rehearsal room, empowering actors to explore and develop character. Hopson remarked, '*Learning from different directors has given direction that really resonates with me and given me tools that I still use to this day.*' Another added: '*I know that there are directors that we've worked with that have unlocked stuff in us. It (synergy) is not the sole work of an actor, not actually a lot of it. I think it's a really good direction*' (O'Donnell).

Several directors spoke of the importance of trust and ownership: '*Trust the process, be open to create*' explained Gilhome, while MD and vocal coach Geoffrey Castles suggested '*Finding a way to let them take ownership of the material.*' Director Tyran Parke used the simple phrase, '*What is that about?*' to provoke discovery during rehearsals and help maintain a fresh approach to the text during long runs. His process encourages actor's contributions as he works with their strengths:

I would also sit in the unknown. I think that's what's tricky ... don't try and get it right. Go, okay, we didn't quite solve that, and we don't know what 'that' means. And that's information for us. And then next time we'll build on that. That is our process. We're just going to sit in it.

Similarly, Jason Langley emphasized the importance of asking the right questions of both yourself as a director and the cast. During rehearsals he asks, *'What is this?'* He explained ... *'it takes the "it" off you, and it's on to the text, and it sets you, the performer, the director, on a path of discovery and exploration.'*

Stuart Maunder supported this collaborative approach:

You're actually treating your cast as colleagues and as people who have a major view as to what is going on the stage that you, as a director are the conduit really to let them give their best. But, just as much, that they're challenging you, you know.

Some directors employ particular tricks or processes with actors to elicit energized performances. Maunder suggested that, often, the work on the rehearsal floor is most helpful:

I think there's a grab bag of things that one has used in the past ... but there's no manual to this. You can analyse to your heart's content. But being at one with the work that they're doing is the most important thing.

Creatives agreed that an actor's technique needed to be embedded and almost invisible when used in performance, *'I think all the work is great ... but at some point, you have to, as a performer, be able to turn that off. And trust in the work'* (Hunter). All agreed that the actor's task was to find that energy eight times a week, *' ... to be able to recreate the frisson of the first time that scene happened, eight shows a week, week after week, it's really difficult'* (Gilhome).

Musical directors brought an additional perspective. Part of their brief is to encourage the appropriate timbre, vocal freedom, and storytelling authenticity that each actor is required to deliver. *'I tend to give a lot of my direction from character, motivation, point of view, or from trying to incorporate the musical elements into the wider, bigger picture'* (Hunter). They are uniquely positioned to assist the actor create the moment on stage when conducting the performance. *'There's no such thing as a solo,'* said Geoffrey Castles. *'Every solo is a duet between the person singing and the conductor; every duet is a trio between the two people singing and the conductor. So, they're never actually alone.'*

How the pieces connect

In rehearsal and performance, actors bring their unique ways of thinking and being and express that through their doing. Some found that it was when the greatest learning occurred. Hopson stated, *'I feel like my best acting training was working, was just being on stage and feeling other actors and feeling the audience and doing it all the time.'* However, when developing a character, 'doing' was considered the final step in the process, requiring integration of all the work from '*thinking*' and '*being*'. Embedded acting technique was deemed essential. Millerchip expressed it this way:

And I feel very strongly that with music theatre, you have to be an exceptional actor. You would have to be more anchored in authenticity and truth and have done your work. You have to be acting in 3D when you do musical theatre ... it's so heightened that every part of you has to be telling that same story.

How actors and creatives connect with the task at hand is summarized in Table 5.1.

Table 5.1 Connecting performative processes with thinking, being, and doing

Process	Actors	Creative Directors
Ways of Thinking	Finding and developing character and story using their own embedded acting methods (*neuro, technico*). Mining the text actively, finding objective, intention (*neuro, psycho*). Using personalization (*neuro, psycho, emotio, persona*). Embracing hard work (*neuro, persona*). Accessing their imagination, improvisational and play (*psycho*).	Creating a holistic vision and direction (*neuro, psycho*). Unlocking meaning in the work in order to bring the words and music to life (*neuro, psycho*). Understanding actors as individuals (*neuro, psycho, emotio, persona*).
Ways of Being	Bringing their own emotions, personality and intrinsic character traits to storytelling (*emotio, persona*). Utilizing their physicality to embody their sense of self, including the use of breath to fuel and to centre self (*persona, physical*).	Helping them to mine their knowledge, skills, and personality (*psycho, emotio, persona*). Connecting the cast to each other, creating ensemble thinking (*emotio, persona*).
Ways of Doing	Using learned MT competencies, particularly singing and acting (*technico, physical*). Finding and applying personal tactics, tips, and techniques while working on the floor (*technico, physical*).	Casting vison to shape and empower the story (*seven processes*). Assisting the actors' learning journey and get them working on the floor (*seven processes*). Integrating the actor, the character and the work (*seven processes*).

MT actors discussed integrating singing and acting techniques, incorporating timbre, breath, intention, action, imagination, impulse, spontaneity, truthfulness, and honesty. They emphasized the significance of curiosity and 'moment by moment' discoveries to keep the story engaging story, as well as psychological and physical freedom – staying organic, present, and energized. Lucy Maunder described how she intuitively blends these elements to create something complex and vibrant: *'I think ultimately it is instinct, and it is a presence that you may not be able to teach, but I would say that it comes directly from finding the deepest part and truth in you and the text.'*

Creative directors shared their tactics for encouraging the best work from their cast in the rehearsal room. The consensus was that it was more about creating an environment that could unlock an actor's synergistic energy than teaching them techniques. What does this look like in performance? Dr Ron Morris, a lecturer in my master's course, used to say that good singing should be 'suspiciously easy'. Similarly, when synergy and the 'It' Factor are in play, an actor's work should appear effortless.

So, where to now? We have uncovered the elements in our definition of synergy: the 'parts of the sum'. Let's construct the equation, combine the elements, and see what happens!

6
MAKING SYNERGY MAGIC: CREATING THE 'GREATER THAN' ASPECT

As observers, we've all felt or experienced that ethereal presence stirring more than simple cognition or fleeting emotion. Sometimes, we seek it; other times, it arrives unexpectedly. But we are changed as we open ourselves to receive. Our senses engage and this energy touches and permeates. Openness, vulnerability, and a willingness to participate are key. This deep, vibrational, subliminal communication, this 'something greater', this *synergy* exists – as long as we give it permission.

Even when you are not the original recipient, 'It' can profoundly affect you. The atmosphere is so energized and so palpable that those observing from a distance can also be changed – if they choose to engage. Let me give you an example.

Sitting in my lounge room in Australia, I was suddenly moved to tears as I watched Celine Dion sing *Hymne à l'Amour* at the 2024 Olympics opening ceremony in Paris.[1] Half a world away, in a magical time and space, she passionately honoured the history and heart of the French people with that iconic song, originally recorded by Edith Piaf in 1950. What made that moment 'greater than' was knowing a little of Dion's own story and her struggle to overcome crippling illness and loss of a loved one, not unlike Piaf. Watching her as she offered herself fully and triumphantly to the world in that moment was synergistic and extraordinary. Her focus and commitment, her bravery and vulnerability, her skill and utter immersion in that moment were thrilling. For me, performance synergy and the 'It' Factor were personified.

Synergy sets performers apart and makes audiences sit up and respond. This chapter is about whether we can find the 'thing' that creates the 'something greater' as we rebuild the synergy equation (Figure 6.1).

So far, we've identified the various intrinsic, performative processes that actors engage in; we've placed their different 'ways' of working within a broader context: sharing the story with an audience in a supportive environment. We have, thus far, explored 'the sum of its parts'. What makes this combination synergistic?

To delve deeper, I returned to the elements of the equation. I started with the actors' ways of thinking, being and doing – what actors use when interacting with external factors – and how these various elements, factors and approaches meld together. This led me to liquid knowledge and the 'thing' that helps connect the pieces.

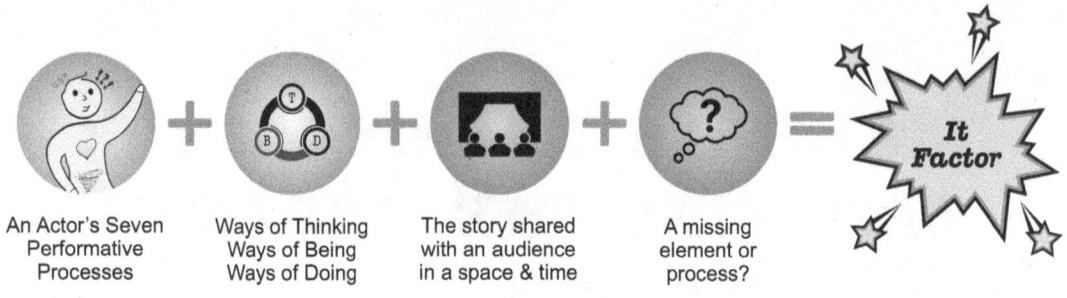

Figure 6.1 The 'It' Factor synergy equation.

Liquid knowledge

Knowing is so much more than thinking. Or factual knowledge. We all 'know' that. In practice-based research, a model exists for examining knowledge and its application in life and creativity. Robin Nelson's (2013) conceptual framework for Practice as Research[2] defines three types of knowledge, or liquid knowing, that both actors and audiences intrinsically invoke.

1. *Know-that*: an objective and learned understanding built on observation, concepts, and propositional knowledge. Know-that is what actors and creatives see, deduce, and fashion into ideas and beliefs. Know-that fuels and is fuelled by an actor's ways of thinking and doing using the processes of ideational and intuitive cognition.
2. *Know-what*: the reflective knowledge appropriated through skill-based training and articulated learning. In practice and performance, actors know what methods work and what's distinctive and impactful. This thinking empowers an actor's doing – their technical competency and physicality. This, in turn, builds more knowledge.
3. *Know-how*: embedded and embodied knowledge. Also called haptic knowing, this tacit knowledge borne of experience already working within. Know-how draws upon and is created using intuitive cognition, sensate experience, and embodied physicality.

There is a fourth type of knowledge, suggested by Australian researcher Zachary Dunbar – that of knowing oneself.[3]

4. *Know-self*: inner knowing of the unique essence of self, a fusion of an actor's personality, character, soul, and spirit. Know-self finds expression through the emotive and persona processes and outworked physically.

Figure 6.2 helps to unpack how these interconnect. I have applied these forms of knowledge to the world of theatre, the premise of liquid knowing embodies ebb and flow – one can seldom see where one form of knowledge ends and another begins. In performance, know-what, know-how, and know-that are often layered or imbricated. Actors referenced using their intrinsic knowledge – their know-self – to ignite these other forms of knowledge to create their multi-layered performances. These fluid ways of knowing

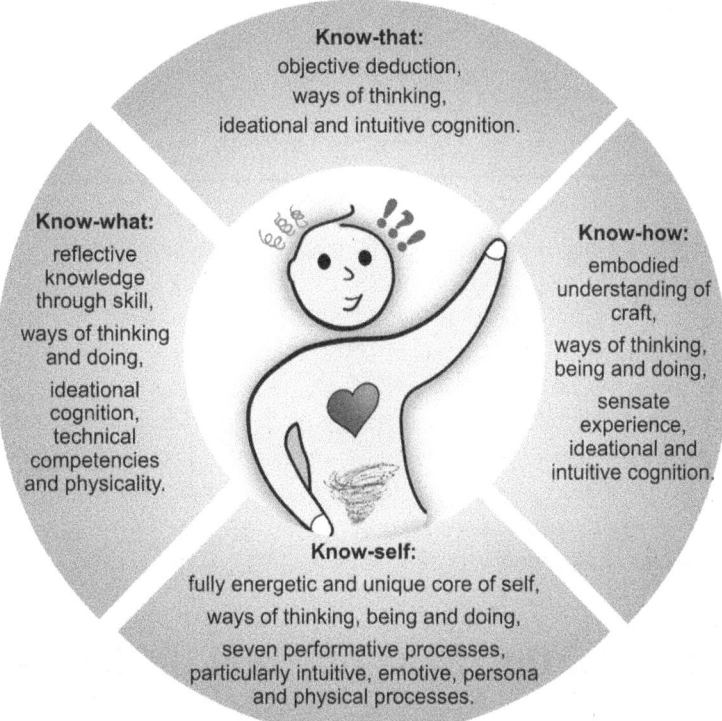

Figure 6.2 The interaction of liquid knowing, thinking, being, and doing with seven performative processes.

empower their thinking, being, and doing. Immersed in the creative act, actors evoke the impression of another level of embodiment, generating dynamism and believability. They walk on solid ground within a new existence that is, indeed, their character's world.

Much of this task remains hidden from direct sight and is often achieved as actors readily access their thoughts, emotions, and abilities, living openly and freely in the story's constructed world. The audience joins them in that world; their passport is their willing suspension of belief.

Two factors can disrupt this fragile cohabitation. The first is when the audience becomes aware of the effort happening beneath the surface of the actor's performance. In that situation, the ease is lost, and the perception of truth-telling, spontaneity, and discovery is not achieved. The second occurs when the actors do not fully immerse themselves in that fictional world, either through fear, inattention, lack of commitment, or technique. Then, the performance's believability can be brought into question, and the audience's Aladdin-like carpet ride – discovering a whole new world together – ends abruptly.

But when actors immerse themselves in their performance, they instinctively combine these four malleable forms of knowledge with their performative processes – their physical embodiment of mental cognitions, sensate experience, emotive and unique personas, and technical skills. This alchemical combination generates an observable energy that transcends the sum of its individual parts. While this may sound complex, many actors achieve this synergy with ease. The great fantasy writer J. R. R. Tolkien expresses how this combining works:

It is indeed easier to unravel a single thread – an incident, a name, a motive – than to trace the history of any picture defined by many threads. For with the picture in the tapestry a new element has come in: the picture is greater than, and not explained by, the sum of the component threads.[4]

Chekhov's psychophysical methods support this concept. He suggests that all techniques are interconnected, and once one action is initiated, others can come to life, enlivening the actor's performance.[5]

Liquid knowledge also plays a foundational role in how we function in our daily lives. When we 'know who' we are, 'know what' we understand, and 'know that' we have 'know-how' in any field we pursue or situation we face, we can confidently express more of our intrinsic selves and internal processes to others. The more we involve our whole selves in any activity, the more vibrant we feel and the more accessible we are to those around us.

A significant factor for individuals who feel insecure in communication often lies in the aspect of 'know-self'. Embracing self-knowledge can serve as a springboard for launching our unique creative expression and as a reservoir from which authentic communication can flow.

The next step in my journey to uncover the 'greater than' aspect of synergy involved revisiting the crucial role of the observer or audience – those who interact with actors and experience connectivity.

Elements that build transactional bridges

Actors spoke of constructing a subliminal bridge – a pathway where thoughts and feelings flow easily back and forth – between themselves and those watching. This nonverbal, subconscious trafficking of story and emotion creates a platform of participatory inclusion, where actors and the audience share the dramatic moment. There is something special about this liminal space: a realm where time and place become neutral territory, providing opportunities to explore, engage, and feel. There is magic in the middle, something surreal in that ether, as connections form in a deeply personal manner. With one foot on either side of the river, the audience can feel secure venturing over the bridge into uncharted territory. And there is a pathway back. What are the factors that contribute to creating this liminal bridge between actors and audience? Experts suggested several, including radiance, empathy, truth, trust, spontaneity, discovery, and mystery.

Radiant energy

Radiant energy is highly attractive. It warms and entices with a sense of otherworldliness. Audiences feel no barrier; they connect to the actor's inner core and the energy emanating from an open heart and soul. The observer is welcomed into the actor's life and world; they feel included, experiencing the actor's emotions, which are generously shared. Even if the content portrayed is dark or difficult, the performer's radiance still resonates, allowing the audience to identify with the onstage action and respond empathetically.

Their sense of knowing and being known by an actor often plays out at the stage door. I have observed some fans exuding familiarity as they greet performers after a show, affirming the subliminal recognition of the connection they formed with the actor on stage, their character, or the story.[6]

Audience empathy

The cognitive and emotional components that form empathy appear to be driving factors in the audience's positive interactions in that space.[7] Current research in neuroscience maps the functions of mirror neurons in the brain, suggesting a brain-driven correspondence between two people who engage in primal communication. From infancy, mimesis – the human tendency for mimicry – teaches us language, social skills, and emotional responses, informing much of our human development.[8] Mimesis persists into adulthood and is actively manifested when encountering a foreign culture or learning a new skill. The actors and creatives I spoke to alluded to the intuitive and emotional mimicry occurring when audiences engage in the actor's story and emotional journey. Observers feel empathy and connection as the onstage energy flows out to the audience. Hopson explained:

> *And people feel a connection with you because you are really actively listening. I think that's the same thing you can do on stage. That, when you are actively listening to everyone around you, you sort of are, in a way, actively listening to the audience. And being with everybody – I'm with you, I'm with actors, I'm with the audience. I think that is a really important part of presence.*

She added, '*Presence is being present.*'

The actors discussed how their listening and responding traverses this liminal space. Operating on multiple levels, actors and the audience connect through a shared dyadic experience. Thoughts and feelings are exchanged, binding them to a common story or cause.

Another aspect of being present for both the actor and the observer is the suspension of time. During the performance, both the performers and the audience suspend the outside world's time and space, coexisting in a shared story and creating something that feels tangible. Jaeger (2006) supports this idea, suggesting that if both parties engage in co-curating the apparent reality of this theatrical time and space, stage presence becomes apparent.[9]

Truth and trust

The term 'truth' is in common parlance in the theatre industry, where it typically refers to an actor's identification with elements of their character and an open, connected approach to the text. The concept of truthfulness in an actor's performance was highlighted as a crucial element in the equation. Subsequently, truth became an important factor in the work I conducted with young professional actors during the interactive workshop phase of my research.

Truth can be associated with several performative processes. Some interviewees described truth as a cognitive process, while others referred to emotional honesty. Still others spoke of trustworthiness or openness residing within the intrinsic persona or character of the actor. The term 'truth' was used interchangeably with authenticity, implying a sense of the genuine rather than the narrower concept of factuality. Actors referenced truth when approaching a text; they invested honest energy from their minds, hearts, and souls to bring a character and story to life. Stuart Maunder remarked, '*There's no doubt that truth is something you can't fake.*'

For an audience to engage with the narrative, they need authentic emotional connections with either the story or the actors or both. How does this happen? The key here is trust. Actors draw upon their inner selves and their skills to shape the character's narrative, which ultimately becomes the observer's story. The trials and triumphs on stage become those of the trusting viewer. As the actors convey their characters' emotions genuinely, the audience responds, engaging their own intrinsic processes. Their reactions correlate with how deeply the audience believes in the narrative or the authenticity demonstrated by the actors. They rejoice and suffer empathically alongside those on stage.

Trust, truth, and empathy coexist symbiotically. As actors reveal their souls to the audience, their perception of truth cultivates trust, prompting empathy, which, in turn, validates and reinforces the perception of truth. Musical Director Luke Hunter put it this way:

I feel it's people connecting to the material. I also feel that it's an ability to go to that vulnerable place where you actually open up and give some of yourself, but they're able to kind of go there in a way that some people perhaps connect to.

Actors spoke about connecting with their inner selves or personas, revealing themselves to their audience in a vulnerable and generous way. They described 'truth' as a tangible force:

You know, it's like truth reads to the back row. It is not about feeling that truth has to be somehow smaller to be real. Or, alternatively, that you have to act harder or bigger to reach the back row. If she's really feeling it, if I'm really buying what she's experiencing, it's like a laser beam to the back row. (Millerchip).

Rix agreed, '*You've got to have enough vulnerability. You've got to just go, "Here's my heart. Here's my offering. I release my trying." … because it needs to be open.*'

It appeared that performers with ready access to their Performance Quotient stepped into their characters easily, rendering truthful performances. Prior, a veteran of the stage shared:

I think about this a lot. I think it's authenticity. 'It' really is the truth that you're watching, in that moment …. And also that same recklessness with bravery. We know that you're watching someone who is just totally immersed, authentic, brave. You feel like they are so in touch with what they're doing that anything could happen; that actually, it's been created for the first time, in that moment rather than recreated.

Truth and trust provide feelings of safety for the observer. They sense surety in the presence of the unknown experience as conveyed by an actor. Actors also enjoy working on stage with their peers and sharing transparent, truthful, and non-manipulative dramatic moments: '*The ease and the relaxation and the joy, and the genuine. "It" is always honest and genuine, and truthful and never any ego attached … and it's simple*' (Hopson).

Spontaneity

Truthful performances often seem spontaneous as actors connect with the unfolding story. Both spontaneity and discovery help build a bridge between actors and the audience. By working spontaneously, actors bring the story to life 'in the moment' and heighten the audience's excitement by introducing a perceived level of risk. As actor Jaime Hadwen remarked, '*He was just always in it and always on the edge of … just like magic. He was just always ready to do something … that to me was something exciting'.*

Spontaneity, paired with pre-formed cognition, sparks discovery and play. When these two aspects of thought shape an actor's being and doing, the outcome is enhanced freedom in performance. This is keenly felt by the audience and fellow actors on stage. Philip Quast described what this looks like:

Watching him rehearse, he was so relaxed and open and funny and truthful and just really playful. He had such a playful energy and is probably the best actor I've ever seen. He is superb. I'd never seen anybody be so in the moment constantly and so relaxed in the moment as well that he could, just do things and make choices because he was 'existing'. He was inhabiting the character so truthfully that he was living in the world … and he was so beautiful to watch.

The onstage action, performed eight times a week for months or even years, can appear spontaneous to the audience; they believe it. Synergized actors aren't merely making impressions; they are genuinely living in the moment. That is thrilling to witness:

And it's real, and it's never been that the present moment hasn't happened before in that scene, and it creates for us as an audience, a sense that what we're seeing is spontaneous, even though we know it's not. (Gilhome)

Discovery

Actors are creative magicians who deliver a script word for word, assimilate complex stage directions, follow the conductor to remain in sync with the orchestra, collaborate in movement or dance with others, and hit their precise lighting marks on stage. They inhabit their characters in that moment as if it has never occurred before. Imagination, spontaneity, and discovery cyclically empower one another, creating momentum and dynamism. Discovery suggests that new information is uncovered or received, while spontaneity, fuelled by imagination, embodies the 'unplanned' response to it. Engaging with a sense of discovery and acting spontaneously enables performers to recreate the same fictional characters over and over.

To create the illusion of fresh discovery, some actors highlighted the use of deep focus and an immersive connection to the text, which they communicated effectively. Natalie O'Donnell explained:

When you have 'It', it's like a physical, vocal, intellectual connection to something that's all working at the same time as well … it's very grounding. And again … it looks effortless, even though it's not. But I think it's because all those things are actually connected. So, it's not that your voice is really amazing, but you're connected to the lyrics. It is like all of them are working at the same time.

Alinta Chidzey valued the power of focus and trusting instincts to '*spark something*' and create the present moment. As a strong dancer, she talked of '*understanding self*', '*keeping yourself open*', and described stage presence as '*an excitement within*', '*an energy*', and '*a connection*'. Actor and singer David Cuny also talks of using the present moment as a touchstone to stay connected. He said, '*The answer you are looking for is in the eyes of the other person.*'[10]

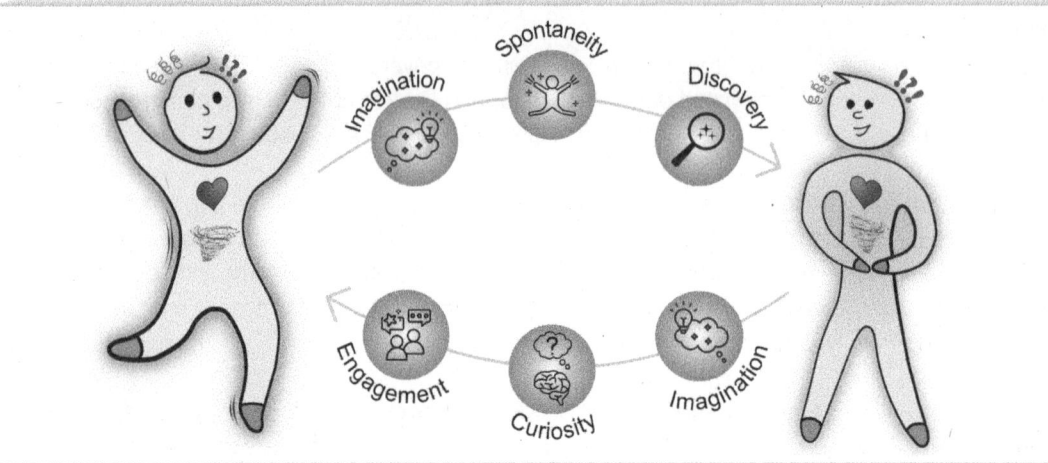

Figure 6.3 Symbiotic cycle of imagination, spontaneity, discovery and curiosity.

The perception of discovery stirs a sense of curiosity in the audience. The actors' subconscious and instinctual choices promote spontaneous play; the audience picks up on this energy and is encouraged to engage their imaginations, experiencing the performance as something fresh. When actors make discoveries on stage, that palpable energy ignites shared excitement. Choreographer, Michael Ralph, remarked on this empathetic connection:

I think there's definitely people who make you sit up ... 'Where is it going to go next?' And I've definitely felt that sense of 'I'm loving this' ... Someone can draw on your emotions as well; they're making you sit up in a different way.

The connection between actor and audience maintains a cyclical flow, with imagination, spontaneity, discovery, and curiosity encouraging audience engagement (Figure 6.3).

Mystery

Mystery, like discovery, is another facet of performance synergy that influences both the actor and the audience in complementary yet distinct ways. There is a sense of the unexpected or unknown for the duration of the performance. Theatre performances are 'live' and, while prescribed in form and content, each is unique. Sherman writes that the stage encompasses the element of mystery, stating, *'Rather than establish empirical truths, theatre asserts lived experience as the primary mode of being, one that ultimately escapes total comprehension.'*[11]

The storytelling actor embodies this sense of mystery while remaining open-hearted and vulnerable. Director Barry Kosky describes the concept of mystery as an essential element of performance, referring to it as a larger thing happening in an actor that defies explanation and fosters a sense of wonder. He states, *'The actor is, in a way, a sort of receptacle for magical forces, and that, to me, is the quintessential nature of acting.'*[12]

Veteran director Simon Phillips reiterates the importance of mystery in an actor's performance. '*They have accessed something that makes other people say, "That is my soul!"; they are extraordinary in the true sense of the word.*'[13]

How does an actor create a sense of mystery and the hidden? Creatives and actors alike discuss how performers layer their characters by adding intentions, thoughts, feelings, and personality. As actors engage their PQ, they bring intelligence, imagination, passion, identity, and embodied skill. Their characters gain dimension, situated in the time and space of an imagined world, infused with identity, history, dreams, and desires.

Sometimes, stage directors choose to discuss a character's secrets, thoughts, or backstory with an actor privately. The actor then carries that hidden knowledge as part of their given circumstances while the other actors remain unaware. Those unspoken morsels can also keep the audience attentive and guessing. Like an iceberg, much exists beneath the surface; the audience may not see the deep work that the actors and creatives do to establish a rich foundation for their character and the imaginary world in which they perform.

> Author Julia exhorts us to explore the unknown or new:
>
> *Do what intrigues you, explore what interests you; think mystery, not mastery... A mystery draws us in, leads us on, lures us. In filling the well, follow your sense of the mysterious... A mystery can be very simple: if I drive this road, not my usual road, what will I see? Changing a known route throws us into the now.*
>
> Julia Cameron, *The Artist's Way: A Spiritual Path to Higher Creativity* (London: Profile Books, 2020), 22, Kindle edition.

The work

Some aspects of the narrative can transmit radiant energy, truth, and discovery into the bridge-building space between the actor and the audience. When story writing is effective, it can be believed, no matter how far-fetched. Audiences enter the theatre and agree to an implicit contract to suspend disbelief, immerse themselves in a fictional world, and connect with the characters and the story presented.

Audience receptivity appears to increase when the story's subject matter is based on factual events. In recent years, several musicals have recreated historical events or celebrated significant lives. Successful productions like *Hamilton*, *Come from Away*, and the jukebox musicals about the lives of Michael Jackson and Tina Turner underscore the idea that reality, when presented well, is impactful. The actors' unified commitment to retelling a factual story radiates an energy that resonates profoundly with the audience. A song, a scene, or musical piece can generate a dynamic life force fuelled, in part, by the audience's prior knowledge of the facts.

Actor-driven bridge-building

So how do actors build this transactional bridge? When actors immerse themselves in a task, they draw upon radiance, connection, inhabitation, truth, empathy, spontaneity, curiosity, excitement, joy, generosity, quality of work, mystery, and beauty. These elements shape the bridge's structure, which link these intrinsic qualities with the observer's co-regulated responses, confirming the fundamental human need for authentic communication and validation. Actor/director, Sharon Millerchip, discussed the total commitment that actors make in each performance to forge a connection with the audience:

And I think that sense of the ebb and flow and connection and subliminal acknowledgment of them and working for them and with them in the storytelling is really important. That is everything for me. I'm never out there for myself. I'm always out there to craft an experience for my audience. So, for better or for worse, I'm always thinking that way. 'Are they with me? Do they feel this for me right now?', which is exhausting, but that's how I know it works. And then the trick, of course, is that I never want the audience to feel that that's what's happening. I want them to think that I am completely lost in myself. Yes, and it's so ephemeral.

Kris Stewart identified this form of connection as a transaction:

But there's something about performance that can feel transactional. You have paid a ticket and I'm going to do this thing for you. And there are some things about performance that you feel in your heart of hearts. This person would share the same thing with you if they were singing to you in their house if you saw them in a thousand-seat theatre or you saw them in a five-seat venue. And that's the thing that I think is sort of an essential part of it.

When paired with an empathetic story or character, vibrant, interconnected, and embodied performances by synergized performers can touch the audience's hearts like no other. Figure 6.4 illustrates the various components and energies that are subliminally trafficked across this transactional bridge.

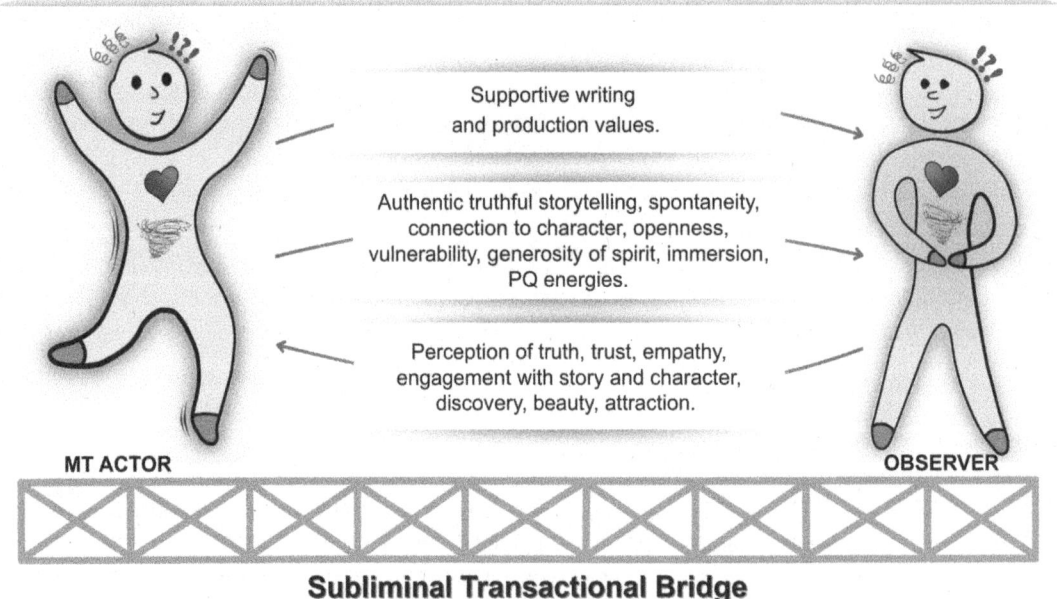

Figure 6.4 The subliminal transactional bridge between MT actor and observer.

Musical directors often conduct the orchestra in the physical liminal space between the stage and the audience. In this space, they feel the ebb and flow of this transactional energy. Hunter explained:

It is something about a connection that gets formed between the performer and the person watching ... that unique magnetism or something gets drawn between the two people, and the artifice of performing disappears so that there is a unique, strong connection that ties the work and the narrative and the story between those two people, or the actor and a thousand people or two thousand people. Whatever it is, that it's very hard to be broken. And something with the outside world, the artifice of 'We're in the theatre; we're in a rehearsal room, we're in an audition', drop away. And that character or that story or the emotional content or the thing that's being delivered, has this very solid, unbroken line between the performer and the audience. There is a part of it that's subjective. But once it's locked in, it's very hard to break.

Synergized actors can readily access their deeper processes and create dynamic performances anywhere and at any time. Sharon Millerchip recounted a powerful theatrical experience that occurred whilst directing a special review show when, in an instant, an actor's performance was 'switched on':

We were rehearsing. It was the day of the show. And it was very slapdash ... just working lights. It was fitting to have a run-through with the piano and where he [Quast] might stand. And I think I said, 'Well if you come in here ... we'll start here.' And then Michael Tyack just started to play. And he [Quast] started singing Stars, and he was five feet away from me. And it was the most mesmerizing, transportive, and ... just riveting performance I think I've ever seen. And he was able to go there – from 'Wo, to go' – in just a heartbeat. And I mean, how many times has he performed that song? And it sounds so cliché – every word he's saying, every line, it was so truthful. I hate using the word truthful because it's such a broad thing, but it was. So every thought came to him in that nanosecond that he said it, and he was there, he was transported. He was somewhere else. And yet he was aware that I was there watching him. I kind of could tell he was doing it for me. It was really amazing. And I bawled my eyes out, and he did it just on the spin of a dime. Right in front of me ...

I talk about believing. I know that he's not Javert. Yes, I know that he has sung that 500 times. And I know that's just Philip in his civvies singing in front of me, yet it touched me so authentically. And I think as humans, we crave that; we love it, and we recognize it, and it means something to us when that exchange feels of real substance because there's so much artifice in what we do.

In the moment described above, Philip Quast accessed his performative processes; he instinctively melded his thinking, being and doing with embodied knowing, and the 'It' Factor appeared instantly. It's rather like switching on the electric current to power a machine that is already primed and ready. His embodiment of character was mesmerizing, and regardless of the audience size, the bridge was built, and 'It' was instantly perceived.

The relationship between the actor and the audience relies on implicit permissions, mutually given and received. As both parties collaborate, effortless, subliminal interactions occur. Actors recounted waves of energy they could ride with a large audience cheering them on; others recalled the potent energy they received from a smaller audience that fuelled their performance.

Audience-driven bridge-building

While actors awaken their performative processes, radiating palpable energy to those of us in the audience who are willing to engage, sometimes, it may not be the actor who initiates the bridge-building.

The audience, the work, the story, the atmosphere, and the environment can also lay the groundwork and begin the transactional process. When an audience shifts from passive observers to active participants in the shared story, a connection is established, ready for the actors to utilize as they enter the stage. These transactional interactions of listening and responding to the actor, character, and story can remain open for the duration of the performance.

In his interview, actor Joel Granger spoke about listening to the audience hubbub and response during the last five minutes of a pre-show audio to gauge their receptivity. The crowd's level of excitement and anticipation created the 'performance platform' before the actors entered. However, those extrinsic factors alone cannot sustain the synergistic bridge; without the actor's efforts to authentically bring the story to life, 'It' cannot exist. Once again, the performers who open themselves to an expectant audience and ride the energy wave ultimately create dynamic performances.

The role of the soul, the spirit, and the true self

Having fully examined both the intrinsic and extrinsic aspects of the synergy equation (see Figure 6.1), I questioned whether there was yet some other unexplored element or process – something that 'baked the synergistic cake' and caused the 'It' Factor to flourish. I was reminded of one area not yet investigated.

During the interviews, another subject arose: the role of the soul, spirit, and higher or true self in the emergence of the 'It' Factor. Several actors and creatives spoke about connecting with something profound and internal. Some acknowledged the presence of a higher or greater energy that might exist beyond themselves, which they could tap into.

The soul

Associated with the intrinsic process of persona, the soul is typically regarded as a part of our inner self and a facet of our unique identity. Along with the heart and mind, performers spoke of drawing from a deep inner well as they connected with a character or narrative. The phrase 'baring one's soul' captures this idea. Within the soul lie the seeds of creativity expressed through our cognition, personality, talent, and skill.

Actors and creatives sometimes expressed being profoundly touched by an actor's soul, as if that actor knew them personally or was reaching out to them. Prior discussed this feeling while speaking about a fellow actor she worked with:

> *Absolute authenticity, bravery, and ability to command a moment and a space is ... thrilling. And he also has that fabulous 'trust' thing where ... he'd bare his soul; I'd bare my soul. And there was a nakedness, you know, not literally, but between us that it was very, very thrilling and inspirational.*

When describing attributes of the soul, actors generally identified combinations of virtues, including transparency, vulnerability, courage, joy, generosity, and truthfulness.

Although the terms soul and spirit are commonly used today, how do they relate to the 'It' Factor? Acting teacher and pioneer Jerzy Grotowski theorized that actors cultivate the quality of stage presence by assuming a state of readiness. They subsequently open themselves up and tap into their inner being or soul, sacrificing a part of their inner self. In his book *Towards a Poor Theatre* (2002), Grotowski states:

> If I were to express all this in one sentence, I would say that it is all a question of giving oneself. One must give oneself totally, in one's deepest intimacy, with confidence, as when one gives oneself in love.[14]

Offering the deepest parts of ourselves is more effective than any formulaic approach. This creates interest and excitement for both the performer and the audience.

The soul and its role in creating artistic performance are part of a greater ongoing conversation. Jemma Rix muses:

> And that's how I've taken this life; these opportunities have come up and they've come up for a reason. And so I've got this kind of openness to knowing that there's a bigger plan for me. And, I've just got to work on the little Jemma who has her fears and insecurities.

Respected performers across all genres speak of harnessing a deep passion and purpose in their work. For screen actor Bradley Cooper, giving of himself seems vital. In an interview with SAG-AFTRA, he discussed baring his soul and the state of vulnerability and humility that grant the observer access to the performer. He states:

> You show your soul in what we do – and it is a privilege to do what we do – it calls upon us to be naked for the audience – for them, we're doing it for them ... You mirror the world back to itself, and you allow people to feel things and look at this in such a different way than they would have done before ... The only way to do it is to be honest, and that is what's so hard and what people react to, and that's what takes a piece of our flesh.[15]

His perspective reinforces the idea that an actor's deep vulnerability elicits a powerful response from the audience, enhancing the transactional relationship.

The spirit

In my research, the concept of spirit was also less easy to define. When the word spirit was used in the interviews, it was often coupled with a qualifier; for instance, actors referred to a '*spirit of generosity*' (Hopson). Several participants seemed to associate the concept of their spirit with personal attributes they deemed were part of their energetic selves rather than something separate. They also spoke of altruistic or universal spiritual qualities such as truth, grace, and joy.

Schwartz (2012) reminds us that, in the scientific language of physics, the word spirit and the word energy are not dissimilar. He writes:

> In physics, energy refers to the capacity to do work and overcome resistance. Energy reflects power, force, vibration, vitality. Interestingly, the term spirit is often associated with life, vitality, passion, strength, conviction ... Taken together, the terms spirit and energy both share an implicit (i.e. inferred) sense of the capacity to act upon and have effects on things.[16]

How they connect

Research has also provided context for the terms 'soul' and 'spirit'. Weger and Wagemann view the 'soul' and 'spirit' as the experiential and non-material aspects of psychological phenomena, stating:

> ... the soul is the individualizing element in our relationship to the world, the individual configuration of thoughts, feelings, and will impulses in their experiential, non-material dimension; the spirit, on the other hand, is the bridge to universal principles (including the conceptual) that do not remain isolated entities but unfold into the other realms and can be accessed through thinking.[17]

Their research further explores the trichotomy of body, soul, and spirit as individual elements inextricably linked, overlapping, and empowering each other.

A holistic approach to the body, mind, soul, and spirit – each informing and contributing to a powerful, unified self – has strong roots in South-Asian, Eastern, and Middle Eastern traditions. For millennia, yogic thinking has explored the connections between the body, soul, and spirit, as well as their impact on performance. Yogic theory asserts that the energy-based self, often referred to as the 'subtle body', functions best when the central regulating system, composed of seven internal energy centres or chakras located at ascending points along the spine and skull, is unified and balanced. Carman (2004) proposes a relationship between chakras and our creative expression, stating: '*Singing comes from the soul through the mind to the body. Yoga is a practice to develop and discipline the body for the mind's use, the mind for the soul's use, and the soul for its creative life.*'[18] The concept of chakras has gained further scientific credibility, with studies suggesting a connection to our central nervous system.[19]

The concepts of the soul and spirit have always featured in writings about theatre performance and have inspired artistry. The father of Western acting, Stanislavski, wrote about his experiences with performance energy, suggesting a connection with the mind, heart, will, and body. Despite writing in repressive Soviet Russia, Stanislavski used the terms 'soul' and 'spirit' nearly fifty times in his treatise, *An Actor Prepares* (1980). He stated, '*The essence of art is not in its external forms but in its spiritual content.*'[20] He later said, '*An actor must have full use of his own spiritual, human matter because that is the only stuff from which he can fashion a living soul for his part.*'[21]

Other acting teachers share the idea of the human spirit working through an actor's body to create character and inspired performances. These include Zinder (2009), Balk (1985) and Chekhov ([1953] 2014), who distinguishes between the Lower Self or Ego, whose horizons are confined to everyday experiences, and the Higher Ego, which arises through artistic activity, becoming visible onstage during performance:

> *In everyday life, we identify ourselves as 'I'; we are the protagonists of 'I wish, I feel, I think.' This 'I' we associate with our bodies, habits, mode of life, family, social standing, and everything else that comprises normal existence. But in moments of inspiration, the I of an artist undergoes a metamorphosis. 'It' is a higher level I; it enriches and expands the consciousness.*[22]

Although the notion of spirituality in performance seems less emphasized in the fast-paced twenty-first-century theatre industry, these acting pioneers highlighted the importance of seeking inspiration and connecting to deeper processes to access the inner creative mindset.

The true self

Performing arts literature also proposes another concept: the 'true self' or 'inner man': a unique essence that defines our humanity and individuality. Marshall (2008) challenges our understanding of this amorphous core within an actor's personality:

This situation arises through unclear thinking. When we talk about our 'self', we are generally pretty fuzzy. What is our 'true' self? Is it our conscious idea of who we are? Or is it our persona (the self that enables successful functioning in a particular social context)? In fact, there are many aspects to the self: the persona (social presentation), the intimate self (shared with close friends and family), and the private self (what we know and think but do not expose to anyone). The sum of these three aspects is the personality – the person we know exists. But there is one further aspect; the self that we do not know exists. This is our hidden unconscious, which makes itself most evident when we dream at night. In fact, your actual, true self is the sum of all the public, private, and unconscious processes. And it is with this self we work as creative beings.[23]

In many Western societies, the true self is viewed as a moral essence – a source of creativity and purity that remains untainted by the shadows and temptations of daily life. It serves as an anchor of stability amidst the more fluid traits of our personality and is often perceived as a lasting kernel of truth that endures beyond the more volatile aspects of our character. While this idea is prevalent among many in Western civilization, the terminology differs; the true self is sometimes referred to as the real, authentic or essential self, among other designations.[24]

What became clear in my research is that when actors engage their deepest processes, striking and captivating work emerges. Their inner selves, unveiled through performance, foster dynamic artistic expressions.

The higher self and spirit – a part of the equation?

Some actors and directors suggested the involvement of a higher self or a spiritual element that influences their perception of 'It'. Words such as transcendence, magical, and miracle emerged during the interviews. Although this topic was not openly explored, it was suggested that there might be another intangible, perceivable, external quality empowering the actors' performance. A stage director stated:

Synergy, to me, infers that you can make it, that you can put two things together, and it can happen. In contrast, something that's intangible, transcendent, or charismatic, that kind of presence to me, infers something less make-able. (Gilhome)

A question remains: could the performance synergy that actors experience be linked to other, higher, external aspects? For actors, the 'unmakeable' part of the equation could be what lies at the deepest levels of human communication, involving surrender and transparency. Perhaps, it is tapping into something outside and letting go of ego or cognitive self to inhabit a role authentically. Either way, there is an implicit acknowledgement that the body's experiential cognition serves as the outward expression of two other non-material dimensions: the soul's behavioural expression and the spirit's conceptual realm.

Some actors experienced a temporary loss of their identity while narrating their character's story. Others described a feeling of being outside themselves. These sensations can also be attributed to a 'flow state', as identified by researcher Csikszentmihalyi.[25] Time can stand still; there is effortless absorption, freedom from judgement, and a post-performance autotelic experience of satisfaction and enjoyment for all who partake in this union. Studies in flow theory indicate a correlation between heightened concentration, skill, and an 'out of body and time' state of being.[26] As actors harness their conscious mind and allow space for their subconscious selves to find expression, audiences are touched and respond intuitively to this deeper level of engagement with empathy.

Several key qualities identified as elements of synergy are also regarded as valuable and desirable human attributes in Christian and Buddhist traditions. Joy, generosity, kindness, truth, specificity, immersion, absence of agenda, freedom, strength, passion, and being fully present are discussed in their sacred texts. Is a synergized person someone who lives life as their best, fullest, freest self, uninhibited by preconceptions or expectations and who believes and values something greater? Perhaps the journey to discovering the missing piece of the 'It' Factor equation is simply about rediscovering the essence of who we are – our deepest and our highest selves – and relearning to express our unique humanity, freely, honestly, and lovingly with one another. Is the 'greater than' part of the equation as simple and profound as that?

7
WHAT 'IT' IS AND WHAT 'IT' ISN'T

What we know is a drop, what we don't know is an ocean.
—Unknown (Occasionally attributed to Isaac Newton).

The vastness of the 'It' Factor became quite clear. My research, conducted through the lens of musical theatre, had only scratched the surface. However, let me share what I learned. From my analysis of 800 keywords and phrases gathered from experts, along with the practical knowledge gleaned from the application and independent assessment of my synergizing toolkit, essential elements were illuminated. Based on these findings, I developed a definition of 'It' as it applies to the realm of dynamic musical theatre performance and extrapolated a conceptual framework that outlines how this energy can be prompted, accessed, and encouraged in various situations and contexts.

A definition of the 'It' Factor in musical theatre

To summarize: for 'It' to occur, two agents are fundamental – the instigator and the responder – or, in the context of theatre, the actors and their audience. In its most primal state, an actor can simply stand on stage and radiate an energy or quality that attracts an audience member and connects with them. The performer and audience also engage with production elements – the *mise en scène*, the genre and storyline, music, lyrics, other actors on stage, the environment, and their own expectations. These extrinsic elements can influence the perception of 'It'. The audience's transactional response to the synergized actor and the external elements surrounding them remains individual and personal.

> *Your body can speak words in many ways, revealing countless realities through language. We know how it feels when we communicate well – vibrant, lively, true. Every part of ourselves is engaged.*
>
> Lorna Marshall,
> *The Body Speaks: Performance and Physical Expression,* rev. edn (London: Methuen Drama, 2008), 92.

My working definition for the 'It' Factor, and musical theatre performance synergy, sums this up:

> *The 'It' Factor or performance synergy is a unique, dynamic, palpable, experiential energy generated by the cooperation between two individuals – an instigator or performer and a participatory observer*

or respondent. The product of several elements, how it presents itself, and how it is experienced is highly individual and multi-faceted.

In musical theatre, for 'It' to occur, the actor relinquishes, ego and inhibition, tapping into their individual performative processes by combining singing, acting, and physicality to authentically embody their role. Aspects of the actor's entire self are synthesized – including their energy, persona, passion, and openness, as well as their singing and acting techniques, physicality, and sound. When these elements merge with the story and character they portray in a specific time and space, something individual and unique emerges. The integrated sum of these components surpasses the individual elements, creating synergy or the cooperation of parts within the actor. This connects to and engages with the willing observer – actor, director, audience – who responds empathetically and transactionally, absorbing this energy and story while recognizing the presence of something 'greater than'.

The 'who' of the actor, the 'what' they are telling, combined with the 'when', 'where' and 'how' this is given and received, creates the interaction known as the 'It' Factor.

For the audience to experience the 'It' Factor, two things must occur. The first involves the actor: intrinsically, their acting stops, and through ownership and habitation, they transcend into the character, becoming one with the story. The actor taps into their physical ease and awareness, mental spontaneity, and emotional availability, all wrapped up in technical mastery yet hidden from the observer. They utilize their voice and physicality to express themselves; in an instant, one side of a transactional bridge is created from the stage to the auditorium. Others sharing the stage can feel this connection. Their shared story and emotions generate an atmosphere and a readable, dimensional world.

The second step occurs when audience members enter this world, connect to and interact with it completing this interactive bridge. Their primary senses of sight and hearing become highly engaged, leading observers to feel a quickening that can be described as excitement, expectancy, empathy, or sensual arousal. When these two forms of cooperation transpire, the energy felt by both the actor and the audience is palpable, dynamic, and memorable.

'It', experienced as performance synergy, is like electricity flowing from and through us, connecting us to others, revealing our inner selves, and enlivening the story we are outliving and delivering to those who join us, in that present moment. This factor inhabits the space between the performer and observer as both parties give and receive, listen and respond. 'It' is individual, allowing for differences in audience perception of who has 'It' or whether a performance is imbued with 'It' or not.

The conceptual framework for understanding 'It'

How can this look? My conceptual framework for how this synergy works is illustrated in Figure 7.1.

Personal versus performance synergy

Can we unlock ourselves and empower 'It' in our everyday lives? What is the difference between personal and performance synergy? Are they merely different buckets drawing from the same well? Based on

WHAT 'IT' IS AND WHAT 'IT' ISN'T

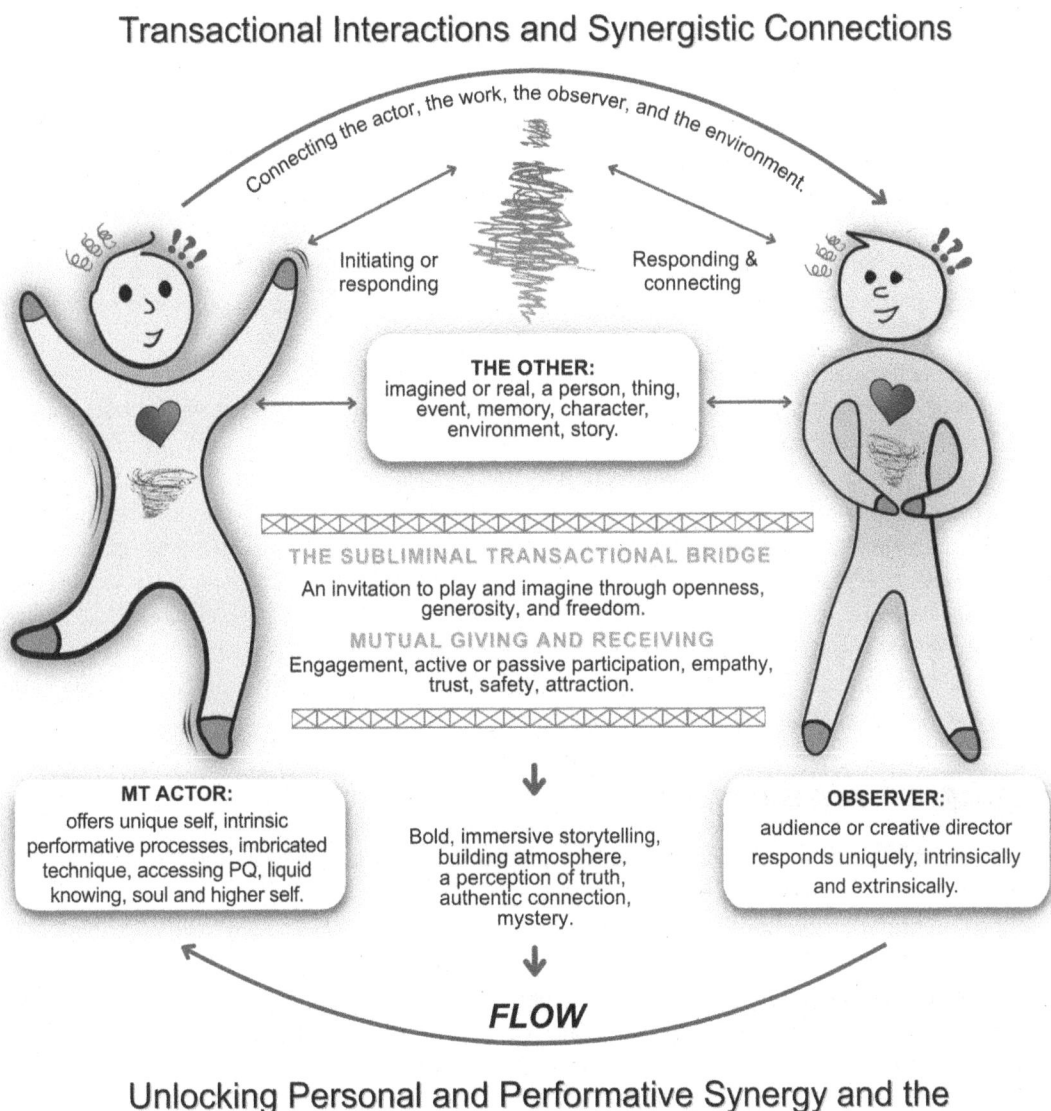

Figure 7.1 Conceptual framework for personal and MT performance synergy and the 'It' Factor.

my research, I believe, in part, yes. The environment in which we radiate our 'It' Factor and where it's perceived – whether a sandpit, a kitchen, a workplace, a bedroom, a concert hall or a stadium – will contribute specific nuances to what this energy looks like and how it's given and received. However, the basis for 'It' remains the same; there are some common denominators.

Personal 'It'

To understand our personal 'It', let's examine how we connect with ourselves and others. In her insightful book, *Presence* (2007), Rodenberg outlines three circles of energy in which we, as humans, operate. Her framework for understanding 'presence' is remarkable. The first circle describes our connection to our internal life. We operate in this circle when we gather our energy inwardly, disengage from others, withdraw from conversation or take time for private reflection. We use second circle energy when we connect to someone or something outside ourselves through giving and receiving. The number of people we connect with doesn't change the circle; we may relate intimately in a one-on-one situation or perform for one thousand. Finally, we use third circle energy when communication flows outward from us and doesn't seek interactive feedback. Examples include expressing an immoveable opinion or imparting specific instructions.

We navigate between all three circles every day, in various ways – mentally, emotionally, physically, and socially. Our personal 'It' Factor can be released when we openly interact with others, utilizing second circle energy. When we communicate through our *ethos*, *pathos*, and *logos* at the appropriate *kairos* moment (see Chapter 2), that's when our personal synergy, something greater than our individual parts, can emerge, fostering a deep connection with our inner life, with others, and the wider world.

My firm belief is that 'It' can be found anywhere. We can all engage our intrinsic processes in various ways to create and express our personal 'It' – our fully free, unfettered, dynamic, energized self. Remember, some creatives I interviewed mentioned experiencing that actor's quality when they entered the audition room. The actor didn't even need to say a word or connect to a character for 'It' to do the work of making them stand out. Their open willingness to fully engage at that moment, with the panel, generated a magnetic, attractive energy that signalled success.

Finding 'It' in performance

In some respects, performance synergy or stage presence resembles personal synergy, just amplified and magnified. In the context of a theatre performance, the connection occurs between the actor, the story, the environment, and the observer. Viewed through a specific character and story arc, supported by production values – music, sets, lighting, costumes and enhanced by the combined synergy of other actors on stage, that 'larger than life' experiential energy is intensified. 'It's essence feels enlarged and powerful yet accessible to the audience, personal, and real – partly because 'It' is.

What we, the audience, respond to is not something phoney. Acting teacher Sanford Meisner describes the acting process as '*living truthfully in imaginary circumstances*'.[1] Some of the magic occurs in the apparent honesty of sharing our inner selves and audiences experience empathetic connections with the human condition portrayed. I recently had this experience while watching veteran actor Philip Quast portray a struggling, unemployed truck driver named Eddie in the Pulitzer Prize-winning play *The Cost of Living*, which highlighted the need to care and be cared for. His character's deep sense of pain and hopelessness was so skilfully represented on stage that it profoundly impacted the audience. There was a palpable sigh of relief when Eddie was offered a redemptive lifeline.

The term *performance synergy* refers to any situation where you find yourself in a more public setting, aiming to connect with multiple people to share specific information or achieve a particular goal. That same energy can also be harnessed to empower our interactions across various work contexts. For teachers, it might be the classroom; for lawyers, the boardroom; for actors, the audition room; or for corporate management, the office. The job essentially remains the same – creating transformative connections with one person or many.

But is 'It' always the work of an individual, or can 'It' be perceived in other ways? Let's take a look.

Ensemble synergy

Performance synergy can appear to an audience as emanating from an ensemble or group that creates a unified impression through collaboration. One choreographer discussed the concept of ensemble synergy:

The 'Ensemble X ['It'] Factor', in my eyes, is a different kind of X ['It'] Factor … a different kind of ability. And it draws on others as a group, and when those X Factors each come together, then it can be magic in watching 10 people move and sing and act in a way that is so cohesive. Yet each individual person is sparkling on their own. You know, the lights are all aligned in a row, and they're all pointing in the same direction. And their spotlight can go wherever the hell it wants, but they all have their own X Factor, too; it's just a different kind of thing. (Ralph)

Flow and the elusive 'It' Factor are often evident during group activities, particularly in professional team sports. In football, basketball, or hockey, collaboration is essential for scoring a goal. The audience witnesses the seamless connections among players as they focus on a shared intention and task, creating a thrilling dynamic energy. Conversely, when the team's play feels disjointed, the crowd can sense it, flow ceases, and 'It' dissipates.

Other facets of 'It' – power, charisma, sex appeal, beauty

There is no doubt that 'It' can look different and appear differently to different people. In the interviews, actors and creatives referenced other physical, personality, or character traits they believed were part of the magnetic or attractive qualities that actors bring to the stage. Power, charisma, sex appeal, and beauty were traits that seemed to resonate with different observers. This led me to question:

- Do perceived power, charisma, sexual energy, or beauty contribute to the appearance of synergy, or can they create a false impression?
- What part does genre or musical style play in the perception of synergy?
- Are there various types of performance synergy, each created by different factors within an actor, the performance itself, or the production?

Power

We have all encountered personality types that exude strength and confidence, whether in themselves or their skills. Several actors mentioned others whose commanding stage presence impacts an audience with what I call the *Pow-Factor*. These actors resonate with power in their performances and this energy appears to bridge the gap between the stage and the audience. However, actors indicated that power alone does not create that frisson of response or foster an interactive connection with those watching. While observers may be impressed, they can remain detached. This third circle energy is unidirectional and non-specific. The Pow-Factor can also seem unfocused and lacking in precision. Performances by actors who primarily rely on power to engage their audience are sometimes perceived as limited; the actor's energy flows outward to the audience, capturing their attention but failing to foster an interactive, two-way connection that invites intimacy and deep engagement. The difference between the Pow-Factor and the 'It' Factor was articulated this way:

There are performers where you just go, 'Oh my God, they are impressive'. But then there are performers who actually give you a moving experience, and that can be in a Broadway tap dancing kind of thing, or it can be an intimate drama. Whatever it is, there's a difference. (O'Donnell)

While entertaining to watch, actors working in the third circle can seem to listen less to their fellow actors or the audience, which can diminish their impact. Emerging professionals may mistakenly adopt the habit of telling the story through generic gestures and trying to make their thoughts heard or understood, rather than trusting in the subtle power of intimacy and focused interaction. Sometimes, these novice actors channel this third circle energy in their quest to impress, oblivious to the fact that creating a good impression differs from establishing a meaningful connection.

Charm and Charisma

The C-Factor – the charm or charisma factor – is another form of energy that can exist independently from the actor's other performative processes. At its most superficial, it can be easily recognized as an affectation. However, when combined with elements of their genuine inner selves and presented generously and humbly, charisma becomes incredibly disarming and can enhance the 'It' Factor.

Directors often recognized this form of charisma, with some perceiving it as a facet of the actor's personality. Originating from the Greek verb *charizesthai*, which means favour, and the noun *charis*, meaning grace,[2] this alluring and magnetic charm awakens the creatives' senses. It captures their attention, drawing them irresistibly to that actor. Upon reflection, two directors analysed this appeal into several key elements that embody the essence of charisma. '*And then the word charisma – what is charisma?*' '*It's an energy that someone possesses because they're confident; they know who they are. They're very self-aware,*' said Gilhome. Stephen Amos added:

I'm quite sensitive to people's energies and them as people. He's one of the nicest people I've ever met. And I think that made it just added that element of 'Ah', to the charisma that he sort of naturally has. And just his kind of warmth and connection to people, I think, made a big difference. And a lot of the people I've worked with who have 'that', they do have that warmth and generosity to other performers.

This confidence, self-awareness, natural strength, generosity, and genuine warmth cultivate a connection that enhances the impression of charismatic synergy.

What is interesting about on-stage charisma is that it can be developed and used to connect with others. While not necessarily an innate trait, charisma draws people in, with hallmarks of genuine warmth and care. Some creatives noted that certain actors' charismatic qualities are less evident in their off-stage personas but become apparent when they light up on stage:

You can kind of feel that they're going to give you that ['It']. But it's not like they're this amazingly charismatic person you meet in real life. But then, when they get on stage, that does translate. (Amos)

I have spoken to many actors after seeing them perform on stage. They can be unrecognizable at the stage door, not only because of their attire and lack of makeup but also due to a significant shift in their energy levels. At times, these actors appeared less vibrant and seemed smaller. The transition from on stage to offstage, this change in charisma suggests that it may reflect aspects of their 'It'.

Sex appeal

Charisma and sex appeal reside on the same street. There is undeniable power in the sizzle of sexual energy that can pass between two actors on stage. In interviews, several actors and directors discussed this type of 'It' Factor, or *Sex-Factor* – a visceral power of attraction sometimes felt in the audition room. While partly triggered by an actor's physical appearance, it is not necessarily linked to conventional beauty. My experts believe that looks alone will not unlock the multi-faceted qualities found in a synergized performance. However, some acknowledged that a degree of sexual appeal could help certain actors establish a connection with their audience. One actor reflected: *'Charisma ... every time I'm thinking of examples of X Factor, I think there's an element of sex appeal to it ... the more I talk about it, the more I do think it has to do with attraction'* (Granger).

Several creatives proposed that sex appeal or charisma when paired with performance attributes, can ignite the emergence of 'It':

I think sex appeal and charisma are something you lock into a personality attribute that's not necessarily a performer's X-Factor ['It' Factor] .... But the people who have that in their personality, I think, are more likely to access a point of X-Factor sometimes, just because they're so in their personality. They're very laid back or relaxed in their effortless way. They use their body and or voice and or expression. (Ralph)

After considering whether sex appeal plays a role in my synergy equation, I concluded that sexual energy and its effects act as a form of currency. It can establish the initial connection between the actor and the observer. However, without elements of PQ to support it, an actor will find it challenging to sustain the synergistic relationship with the audience, the story, and the character for the duration of the performance.

Beauty

Some interviewees discussed a sense of beauty when considering the elements of synergy. The allure of the 'halo effect' has been extensively researched and documented; it plays a role in Western society's perception of success.[3] There exists an ubiquitous and unfortunate bias that equates beauty with intelligence and other performance strengths. In theatre, certain roles have a required aesthetic, and an actor's appearance may enhance the authentic portrayal of that character; however, it was suggested that the attractiveness halo may also influence a creative director's perception of performance synergy.

And then also some people ... they're also just gifted with beauty ... And I do think that does, unfortunately, have something to do with the X-Factor. But it comes down to what you were wanting for that character, or what that character needs, and what is aesthetically important. (Ralph)

Audience members are sometimes drawn to specific actors due to their perceived beauty. This extrinsic trait can foster an empathetic connection with viewers who then identify with the actor's character or aspire to emulate them.

Later, Michael Ralph added:

I don't want to expect it to be attached to the way people look. I think someone could be a very ordinary-looking person who you would never guess would be on a stage. And yet the moment they move their mouth and their shoulder and their eyes, and then all of a sudden you are like, 'Oh, my God'. So, I think it's appealing in a handsome sort of or beautiful sense. But also, I feel if the physicality or the aesthetic is slightly awkward or non-traditional or unique, then that also can fuel the X-Factor in a whole other way. That's really special.

Two adages spring to mind. The first is *'Beauty is in the eye of the beholder.'* The observer's perception of beauty is subjective; the variety of opinions shared by creatives highlighted the inherent variability of personal taste. The second, *'Beauty is only skin deep',* has dual resonances. Actors can be appreciated for their outer beauty, and they can also create the perception of this quality by engaging their intrinsic performative processes and emanating their true beauty from within, transforming their appearance.

Other synergy-influencing factors

Numerous elements beyond the actor's control can shape an audience's perception of the 'It' Factor. The work – music, lyrics, and book – is one such contextual factor.

The power of supportive music and lyrics

The quality of the text and music can also foster a vitality that contributes to the emergence of synergy. While stage directors mentioned mining the text for gold, musical directors highlighted the beauty and power of a well-crafted song, noting how the arc of a lovely melody enables singers to express the actor's vocal timbre, convey emotion, and bring the lyrics to life. Actors and directors discussed the strength and depth of a well-written text, which serves as a rich source of inspiration and supports characterization. Although quality writing alone isn't essential for synergy to develop, actors spoke of the ease they felt when working with a piece that elevated them, while directors reflected on the joys of discovery.

I want to know what the playwright's giving us in order to create character, in order to honour their story. I will always mine the text for all the clues that the playwright has given us. You know, I teach classes on detective work for actors. (Langley)

Let's circle back to the 2013 musical *Come from Away* where the impact of good writing on an audience is evident. Thoughtfully constructed around accounts of events stemming from the 9/11 terrorist attacks in the US in 2001, the foundation of truth and the rich stories depicted in the musical resonate deeply with the audience. In the performances I attended, there was a palpable sense of connection and anticipation in the auditorium, even before the actors stepped on stage. The musical showcases ensemble writing as a powerful compositional device. Twelve actors work in sync to guide us through the compelling narrative. Based on the collective viewpoints of individuals and how the 9/11 tragedy affected them, the writing requires the actors to play multiple parts; this dynamic ensemble work draws the audience into the heart of the story, celebrating the goodness of humanity and the importance of community. This musical exemplifies how three contextual factors – vibrant, innovative writing, a truthful work, and an atmosphere created by the harmonious ensemble – connect with the audience and contribute to a sense of synergy.

The work, its style, and content provide the essential material that actors share; however, no story exists on stage without its human expression. Composers and writers dream, conceive, write, and value their creations as worthy. Once formed and committed to the page, directors, actors, and musicians bring it to life each time it is performed. Ultimately, it is the actor's work that embodies the story in an authentic and accessible manner. Audiences have an implicit understanding that once the curtain falls, that moment is over; it can never be experienced again in the same way. You can never step in the same river twice.

A tale of five synergies

The concept of different synergies shaped my evolving understanding of this energy. As a researcher gathering data and developing a theory on the constructs of performance synergy, I decided to experience firsthand how this synergy could manifest, look, sound, and feel in its various forms.

In January and February 2022, I tested my findings and analysis by attending five different musical theatre performances in Sydney and Brisbane, Australia. These productions – four musicals and one cabaret concert – showcased some of Australia's finest talents, including several actors and directors I had previously interviewed. The performances occurred over eight days and provided me with a snapshot of Australia's professional musical theatre industry. I enjoyed five distinct performances. Multiple elements – the actor, the story, the environment, and the audience – converged to foster five differing forms of performance synergy.

The first musical was an Australian premiere, acclaimed in London and on Broadway. A jukebox musical with a twist, its subject matter was bleak, and the ensemble cast vividly depicted the struggles associated with the time period in which it was set. The songs interwoven into this narrative often served as objectively detached commentary. Several outstanding actors shone through, but one in particular delivered a song as an internal monologue. With her back to the audience during the first section of the song, she entered her private world, allowing us to glimpse and hear her inner thoughts and feelings. The depth of her character and the intense drama she conveyed were heightened by her strong vocal technique, physical freedom, and complete immersion in the story, which brought the song to life. This actress's unique skill generated the *story-driven performance synergy* I experienced. Vulnerability and strength intertwined with her other performative processes, genuinely connecting the audience with the character's struggles. In that moment, we believed her.

I found myself seated in the back row of a large auditorium for the second musical. Although not an ideal spot to view a performance, the visceral energy of the show captivated me from the moment the actors stepped onto the stage. The ensemble's physicality was striking, and their vocal work was exhilarating; twenty-two actors conveyed the same story with a shared timbre, purpose, and focus. Their solidarity embodied *ensemble synergy* in action: one voice, one story.

I also sensed that I was witnessing something iconic and unique. The show's reputation amplified my perception of synergy – it was innovative in many ways and had garnered significant acclaim. The pathway to the synergistic bridge connecting me to the action on stage felt easily accessible. Expectations can be two-faced as the potential for disappointment is heightened; however, the collective dynamism of these actors, the staging, and this work itself triumphed.

The third musical, a contemporary rock cult phenomenon featured a small but dynamic cast. Even before the house lights dimmed, there was a palpable air of excitement. The enthusiastic audience cheered loudly and clapped during the show's opening bars, exhibiting classic *audience-driven synergy*.

Initially, I felt this musical exhibited more *Pow Factor* or *Wow Factor* than true connectivity to the simple storyline. The costuming, on-stage band, and pop-diva musical style delivered an explosive burst of energy to the enthusiastic audience. The fourth wall was lowered during the performance; the audience was addressed directly and invited to participate in the unfolding scenario. The musical incorporated hybrid, quasi-cabaret elements throughout much of its presentation. However, as each performer conveyed their story through individual songs, the characters they portrayed resonated with the audience, resulting in moments of genuine engagement.

The cast brought a varying array of performance experience, yet each delivered their story powerfully. The youngest member of that cast was a recent college graduate, but her performance exuded an intensity beyond her years. I had interviewed her directors earlier; they suggested she was an actress with a natural ability to connect with aspects of her persona and share them intimately, which had further developed in rehearsal. In their view, she exhibited the hallmarks of skill and a natural affinity – *innate synergy*.

The fourth musical was from the Golden Age and stood in stark contrast to the other performances. Based on an iconic orchestral work, this musical features beautiful melodies, soaring arrangements, and a classic Hollywood-style aesthetic. Presented as a dance musical, the breathtaking choreography served as the primary means of conveying the story's inner life. This piece is a quintessential example of *genre-driven synergy*. The performers displayed exceptional skill and physicality, and the show's classic subject matter and writing style were well-received by the audience.

My fifth musical theatre experience was a concert: an evening with one of Australia's leading musical theatre stars, celebrated for his outstanding singing talent and charisma. Although not strictly classified as a musical, it featured significant elements of theatrical production, with a storyline linking the songs and on-stage performers to help set the scenes. Because of this performer's extraordinary musical talent and reputation, the audience was receptive and eager to engage. What we witnessed was a *personal performance synergy*.

The night was filled with magical moments. I witnessed mastery at work – a veteran who connected effortlessly with his audience in a warm, personable manner. He invited us into his world and created an intimate connection while maintaining an air of ineffability. He selected iconic songs from his repertoire that immediately sparked reactions from the audience – our memories of his past performances, along with the characters and stories behind the songs, deepened the strong rapport we felt as we listened.

Interestingly, when this artist performed songs from roles he created and played on stage, he transported me directly to that character's time, place, and journey with just a look, a breath, a shrug, or a hand gesture. There was focus and power in the simplicity of his delivery. I watched him deeply immersed in the moment, seamlessly tapping into his PQ. However, at times, he sang pieces he hadn't previously performed on stage. While these songs were wonderfully crafted and highly entertaining,

> Think of the times you've experienced that dynamic 'It' Factor energy as an audience member. What was it that connected you to an actor, the stage action and the story? What are your 'It' Factor experiences?

they didn't create the same synergistic connection for me. The familiarity of the character he portrayed seemed to have a subliminal effect on me and possibly him.

The ephemeral and shape-shifting qualities of the 'It' Factor contribute to the unexpected wonder that audiences experience in live theatre, regardless of genre or venue. The five musical events mentioned earlier varied significantly in terms of venue size, production and staging elements, genre, music, storyline, content, required skills, and the reputation of the shows or performers. Yet, as the curtain fell on each performance, the audience responded positively. Reflecting on the different types of synergy I encountered, I realized that within each production, the levels and intensity of engagement I felt with an actor, the stage, the song, or the dance were not static; they fluctuated. At times, the synergy felt intensely personal as I connected with an actor's expression, a shared thought, or a sung moment. At other times, it was the anticipation and atmosphere fuelled by the audience, the power of the music, the visual imagery, or the collective energy of a powerful, well-crafted ensemble that projected from the stage and pressed me into my seat, no matter where I was in the audience. Multiple intrinsic and extrinsic aspects of performance combined to create diverse synergistic bridges that resonated with me. Whether simple, like a solo line sung with sincerity, or the impactful intensity of high production values and a 22-voice ensemble, these performers crafted subliminal pathways that welcomed me into their stories and made me feel included in the unfolding events.

Elements of the 'It' *Factor* were demonstrated clearly in those five shows. There was a two-step process at work: internal and external, synergy within and synergy without. Actors empowered their 'It' as they open-heartedly, creatively, and unashamedly connected with us, the ready audience.

False synergy

During the interviews, an unexpected topic emerged: that of 'false synergy'. Two types were talked about. First, creative directors shared their observations of actors who initially exuded a spark of energy that ultimately failed to materialize in subsequent rehearsals. These actors performed admirably in the audition room, however their perceived expertise did not develop as they collaborated with other actors and directors. Instead, their delivery of lines and songs stagnated, their energy diminished during rehearsals, and they flatlined during performances. Creatives considered these actors as professional auditioners – a term used by several creatives to describe an actor who creates the illusion of performance synergy that ultimately proves misleading.

Both actors and directors discussed a second type of 'false synergy' and referred to performers cast for their celebrity status rather than their performance expertise. These actors are lauded for their identity, and producers book these performers as attractions, leveraging their reputation as a marketing tool. A starstruck audience will often overlook a celebrity's lack of technical competence or their inability to inhabit their role and deliver an immersive experience.

This type of energy is experienced as the *Wow* Factor or *Star* Factor. While entertaining, this factor doesn't necessarily foster depth or complexity of character. Fortunately, some famous actors possess both. Their celebrity status or Wow Factor attracts audiences to the theatre, while their fully embodied performances genuinely engage them. Several years ago, I witnessed the incomparable Bernadette Peters make her first entrance on stage in the Broadway production of *Hello, Dolly!* Because of her celebrity status, the show was halted for a solid two minutes due to the extended applause from an adoring audience. Thankfully, once it resumed, her portrayal of Dolly Levi earned every accolade.

Stage director Stuart Maunder referred to the word 'star' in a different way, reclaiming the term when describing a performer who achieves the pinnacle of their career through talent and hard work rather than fame. He reflected on his experience, noting a 'true star' who gave her all for her craft and her audience:

> Do you have a performer that easily draws you to themselves? What do you find appealing? Are there commonalities in your instinctual personal preferences?
>
> Is it their intense focus, or their radiating joy? Their unpredictable, risky edge, their effortless freedom, or their flamboyant physicality? The intrinsic processes you access easily may influence your personal synergistic connections to others.

This singer … what a glorious performer. And I saw her one night before one of the shows she was doing, and I remember thinking, 'This is costing you greatly doing this … always at the service of the audience and the piece that she was doing', and she would never give anything other than the most riveting of performances. A true star is the one who will serve the piece and the ensemble that you are doing. There are some people that I will never employ again and there are a few I will because they are a beacon in the middle of the stage of an extraordinary performance … But you know, nothing is exciting as being in the presence of a great performer.

Is the 'It' Factor in the eye of the beholder?

The short answer to that question is yes – absolutely. The beholder's needs, desires, and personal preferences determine whether they connect with the actor. Audiences consist of individuals who make instinctive, subconscious choices as they respond to the energy that actors provide. For instance, when observing Clara Bow, some viewers are captivated by her vulnerability, while others may be moved by her tomboyish abandon. However, there will always be those who look at that actress and fail to find a point of connection. And that's what keeps the ephemerality of the 'It' Factor alive.

Next, let's look at the age-old question of 'nature versus nurture'.

8

WHERE DOES 'IT' COME FROM, AND WHERE DOES 'IT' GO?

'She has it. After all, her grandmother was (insert here the name of an iconic Australian actor), *so it's in her genes.'* In 2017, I found myself sitting before the head of one of Australia's most prestigious musical theatre programmes, discussing the abilities and potential of the current cohort of university students for my master's research. One final-year student stood out in particular; she always seemed to be lit from within. The director believed her heritage was a contributing factor.

Later that week, I interviewed that vibrant young woman. Over the following years, I've watched her launch and build her career – sometimes standing in the wings, waiting for her chance to shine, and other times successfully taking on leading roles. We've had conversations about her acting journey in this volatile and often unforgiving industry during the half-dozen occasions we've met since that initial discussion. She has always appeared positive, upbeat, and grateful for every performance opportunity. So, is her 'It' Factor the result of a positive upbringing and her studies, or was she simply born this way?

Young actors work hard to build their skill sets, and it can seem unfair that a few individuals may possess 'It' while others do not. However, I have observed some members of a tertiary cohort, seemingly endowed with this 'presence', lose their radiance and light. In contrast, others who flew under the radar during their early training have grown, flourished, and shone by the time they reached the professional stage. How much of 'It' is determined by nature or nurture?

The genesis of 'It' – is it nature or nurture?

This question was frequently discussed during my PhD interviews. The diverse perspectives of the interviewees on this topic supported the concept that while 'It' can appear to be a natural gift, this unique inner energy can be nurtured and encouraged in all. My position, gleaned from teaching and performing experiences, and supported by other pedagogues, agrees. It is both: all performers possess an inherent ability to radiate self and engage with the outside world.

Nature

Most directors and actors expressed the belief that an actor's natural abilities and tendencies can significantly contribute to creating performance synergy. Directors occupy a privileged position; they regularly observe the manifestation of synergy in the actors they audition and cast for their productions.

Some creatives noted that a few auditionees arrived as a complete package, possessing that innate quality.

Several actors supported these insights: *I do think there are performers who are fully formed; I think people walk in, and you go, 'Well, I have nothing to teach you' ... Some people are born performers who sort of know everything instinctively.* (Sheldon)

Prior remarked:

Singing was a very natural thing ... I already had that innate ability. And I think I caught it really early ... so that my training just enhanced what I could naturally do. And acting ... I always had a great desire to do it, funnily enough. All I had was my faith in my ability and my utter enjoyment and sort of ability to immerse myself in what I was doing. Sometimes, it takes all that technique to realize that, actually, you do it innately.

Some of the actors I interviewed showed this quality, instinctively demonstrating a high PQ, and effortlessly navigating various performance processes to convey their story.

Interestingly, the most obvious and intuitive 'It' Factor moments that some creatives encountered in the audition room originated with children. While discussing casting for the lead role in the musical *Matilda,* Millerchip remarked:

She had a natural ... she just kind of got it ... that is such a relief for me because now what I do is I feed little ideas, and she will bounce off them, and things are going to go ping, ping, ping, ping, ping, ping. And she's going to come at this performance and make some discoveries. (Millerchip).

Stephen Amos also shared his experience working with child actors. Several of those he had cast seemed to radiate a captivating natural energy that was a pleasure to watch. The assumption was that this ability was, in fact, an innate talent or propensity:

But we had one girl in particular ... who definitely has The X Factor ['It' Factor]. She kind of always had it. And then, when I look back now, I can sort of see that. But they all get exactly the same rehearsal process. But for whatever reason, she partly came with some of those skills.

These young performers made instinctive choices, unshaped by years of training. Their unfettered performances flowed naturally from within.

When given permission and space, children will often reveal their natural 'It' Factor. I vividly remember sitting at a bus stop in Paris, observing three French children passing the time playing an imaginary game. I didn't understand their conversation, but they were mesmerizing as they chattered, laughed, ducked, and weaved. Other adults around me smiled discreetly at their enjoyment while maintaining polite decorum. The moment was synergistic.

Nurture

Most actors and directors I interviewed believed that dynamic performance energy can be cultivated and developed in an actor. Comprehensive technical training can equip actors with the necessary skills to connect with the audience and effectively portray their roles.

A seasoned actor, Simon Gleeson, spoke of using his performative skills to engage and influence the audience:

And as you get older, I think you do start to learn how to manipulate those moments a little bit. You do know how to make things land. You learn those things. So even when you're not feeling it, you've got the skill set to still be able to create those moments. We learn how an audience responds ... through experience.

The interviewees' stance and my own growing understanding of the source of synergy is supported by performance researcher Jon Sherman, who stated,

Actors may be born with it, they may study to acquire more of it, but actors are the ones who have it and 'it' is 'of' the actors. Which is also to say that in some way it relates to them as persons; 'their' stage presence is a function of their specific being placed in front of other beings.[1]

Being and doing

It became apparent that the 'It' Factor's appearance may not simply involve being *versus* doing but rather being *and* doing together. Actors suggested that both could create a perception of synergy: the innate ability to express oneself freely in public solitude, and the learned techniques that deliver that same energy. Some directors further suggested that nature and nurture can interact within the same actor at the same time. Luke Hunter suggested:

I think there might be two different types of performers that have this sparkle, this X-Factor, because ... I've worked with a couple of leading performers that are solely intuitive. If you ask them to break it down, what they're doing, they actually can't do it, and they are fascinating and they are magnetic and incredible to watch. Then, there's another kind of performer that I've worked with ... that, as an audience member, you are equally drawn to ... equally special, but they are very cognizant of what's happening around them. They over-analyse every single element that happens to them on every performance, like a lot of performers do, but there's something about them that, from the outside, you can't see all of that work going on. They know everything that they're doing; we, as an audience, can't tell.

He spoke of one actor as:

Very intelligent and very nuanced. And she's still breaking everything down. She knows every single thing that she's doing at every moment, but you stand at the back of the auditorium, and there's this glow and just effortless ... flow ... just so natural and so honest and real. And immediacy – she made it seem as if it's never been done before.

Familial and formative influences

I pondered whether familial or genetic advantages contribute to the synergy equation. Several actors and directors shared their views that their home environment, which valued and encouraged creative expression, played a significant role in their success. Some hailed from a lineage who performed professionally on stage and modelled this behaviour. Tyran Parke remarked that this background did not diminish the necessity for hard work:

> But you know ... ['It'] comes from the experiences of her life, actually combined with very hard work, singing, acting, and dancing, but it doesn't come from a cognizant thought of how you pull those things together. 'It' comes from her hoofing it. So, I feel like there are two versions. We get those people like [actor's name], again, who come from a theatre family. You see them when they come in, you see them when they arrive, and you go, alright. They've come from something that values this thing.

This director believed that, in addition to this actor's dedication to work, a supportive and creative family background could improve their confidence and comfort, which might, in turn, contribute to the perception of synergy.

While some actors benefitted from family encouragement during their formative years, it didn't seem essential for developing the 'It' Factor. Several participants recounted stories from their family backgrounds that presented different perspectives. These included broken homes, family tragedies, and issues of rejection; nonetheless, these actors learned to overcome those early experiences. Despite and sometimes fuelled by their challenges, they moved forward to achieve success as actors and creatives in the commercial industry in Australia and beyond.

My verdict? Both nature and nurture influence various aspects of performance synergy. Some actors effortlessly tap into their personas, infusing their performances with a unique quality. Others navigate their journeys, cultivating and releasing synergistic energy through a more intentional approach. In both cases, a dynamic exchange occurs.

Personality types and learned behaviour can play a part. As I began working with the young actors in my interactive workshops, some participants were naturally open, discovering their performance energy organically and creatively. Others in the group needed encouragement to unlock their minds, hearts, personalities, and skill sets. It seemed they required permission to play. Once these participants started to experiment and enjoyed making discoveries with the character, text, and music, the interactive connection between the audience and the actor was activated. Both nature and nurture were at play.

Where does 'It' go? The world gives and the world takes away

The first decade of this millennium introduced us to 'technological intimacy' and instant gratification through social media. The tectonic shift in the way we communicate has reignited and redefined the anxiety that accompanied this advancement. In 1947, W. H. Auden wrote a poem titled *The Age of Anxiety,* which won a Pulitzer Prize in 1948. The poem addressed the disillusionment, isolation, and uncertainty felt by the Western world in the aftermath of a world war, partly due to the loss of tradition and religious belief. Ironically, it is not a world war, but rather the increasing pace of our lifestyles and societal expectations in this current age – the Digital Age – that brings this term back into focus. Pop troubadour John Mayer sings about *The Age of Worry,* as more young people struggle with anxiety and related mental health issues. It appears that the median age of sufferers is getting younger. The growing pressures on the population to perform at work, in school, on stage, and at home, combined with feelings of isolation, create a cocktail of stress and insecurity that harms cognitive perception, inhibits self-expression, and undermines self-belief.

On one hand, TV and social media suggest that we have the 'permission to shine': we, too, can experience a TikTok moment of fame or 'influence' the masses, finding significance and financial gain through the attention of many followers. Aspirational marketing subtly alters our perception of what is genuinely important or valuable, manipulating aspects of human desire and creating false emotional connections with consumers. Deception and inauthenticity are prevalent. The very foundations of Western societal structures appear unstable. We wonder whether we can trust our environment, our relationships, our ability to discern, and even our competence, which puts us on guard. Our posture becomes defensive or detached.

Over the years, some actors have openly shared their feelings of fear and anxiety offstage. Well-established and highly respected, they experienced the 'bravery of youth', which instilled a sense of invincibility in their early careers, but this diminished as they aged and became vulnerable to society's foibles. The reasons they cited were varied: striving to maintain a presence in a fickle industry, dealing with sporadic unemployment or unkind criticism, facing unjust remarks from peers, or simply fearing the onset of age or being viewed as 'past their prime'.

However, I have witnessed these remarkable performers in action. When the lights dim before each show, they enter the performance space and set aside any debilitating feelings. These dynamic actors believe in their craft – in the significance of the story or character they embody, their love for the art of theatre, and their genuine passion for storytelling. They immerse themselves in the moment of performance, rediscovering the childlike joy of play. This requires immense courage and intention from them. Even if actors silently question their abilities, they never lose sight of the importance of that moment, that story, or the ultimate reason for performing – that is, to generously offer a performance, a narrative, and something valuable to their audience. Meanwhile, the audience remains unaware of their private struggles.

The creative directors I spoke with also noted how an actor's inherent stage presence can be hindered by fear or ego, often masked as bravado. Resident director and choreographer Michael Ralph elucidates:

I would categorize 'It' into three categories of performer. I think that there are people who have 'It'. And know how to use it and trust it. Then the second category would be some people who might have 'It', all the natural ability of 'It', but don't trust it, so they're stopping it. And then there are people who don't have 'It' but have natural ability. And don't quite know how to unlock 'It' … I think a mental state is a big part of unlocking this.

How is 'It' lost? Or sometimes never found? What happens between childhood and adulthood that impacts our personal 'It' Factor? I believe there are several factors. Here are my subjective and incomplete thoughts.

In humans, a coherent self-view forms during childhood; we establish our sense of self through continuous inner congruity. Our childhood experiences contribute to the development of personality, learned values, and a growing concept of self. Then, as we mature, layers of life experiences, values, attitudes, and beliefs shape our internal views. However, for some children, patterns of behaviour learned in their early years from well-meaning yet limiting instruction can inhibit the natural expression of 'It'. *'Don't* be such a show-off!' and 'You are making too much noise!' are just two unhelpful comments that adults use which smother a creative or expressive spirit. The damage done early in life can have lasting effects.

The voices that stifle the 'It' Factor can also emerge from peers. My experience working in a private studio with teens and young adults has been enlightening. For many, the tumultuous early to mid-teen years are challenging to navigate, leading to questions about identity and personal values as they develop. I've observed bright, young communicators who, six months prior, led the debating team or performed in front of others, beginning to retreat; they feared standing out. Some succumb to peer pressure and ridicule, forsaking previously held desires or dreams. The external voices in their high school environment begin to shape their identity and sense of acceptance, and in their pursuit to conform and 'fit in', their inner creative spark becomes dampened or extinguished. Suddenly, during a week-long holiday break, these young individuals can swiftly transform from confident, radiant people into withdrawn, insecure ones.

Unless louder voices affirm their individuality and uplift these delicate souls, many choose to retreat and safeguard themselves. Those individuals with a strong sense of self, or those cheered on by supportive voices – family, friends, or fellow performers – often succeed in carving their paths through these formative years and discover their *raison d'être* and means of self-expression.

Debilitating self-image is not solely an issue for the young. As adults, our self-perception, identity, and self-worth require a reliable infrastructure to endure societal pressures. We humans need three supportive elements: security in all its forms (mental, emotional, physical, financial, and societal), significance and purpose, and authentic connections with others through meaningful relationships. Without these pillars, our inner congruity can become unstable and difficult to navigate. Imposter syndrome, fuelled by a lack of self-belief can undermine our sense of security and significance; doubt becomes real and lurks in the wings.

Fighting your demons!

During an episode of *The Graham Norton Show*, actor Hugh Jackman shared a story about his first meeting with the extraordinary actress Dame Judi Dench, who was on the programme with him. It took place at a Royal Charity Gala Concert 'Hey, Mr. Producer' in London in 1998. It was early in Jackman's career, and he felt nervous about singing in front of the Queen at such a prestigious event. Judi was on the programme to sing the iconic Sondheim song 'Send in the Clowns' just before him. As he approached the stage, she was waiting in the wings, ready to go on, but muttering to herself, 'Why did I say yes? Why did I say yes? I'm not a singer. I can't sing.'[2]

> Dame Judi's performance of that Sondheim song can be seen on YouTube. If you haven't seen it, I urge you to watch it. For me, it is one of the most powerful examples of immersive acting through song. A masterclass in the 'It' Factor. And knowing her private journey prior to the song makes it all the more thrilling.
> https://www.youtube.com/watch?v=yE3dLzIYKs8

Even the most talented and experienced performers experience insecurities and fears – it's a natural response to the pressures of their work. One effective way to overcome these disabling emotions is to step onto that stage, approach that mic or enter that boardroom with a compelling reason and a story worth sharing. Instead of making the moment about yourself, concentrate on the message. Focus outwardly on the reason and the story; they will guide you through.

Positive psychological outlook

Our sense of identity, attitudes, and behaviours stem from our foundational beliefs and values. In the early 2000s, social science researcher Fred Luthans developed a concept he termed positive psychological outlook, or 'psychological capital' – PsyCap.[3] Considered essential for successful work performance outcomes, PsyCap continues to be utilized in the competitive workplace. Its core construct revolves around a sense of well-being, built on four pillars: hope, efficacy, resilience, and optimism (HERO).[4]

Hope, the first element, is a forward-looking belief that often manifests as a positive emotion. This process stimulates our willpower to pursue a desired goal and the way-power, or strategic planning, to achieve a favourable outcome. Hope fuels us when the goal or direction of our endeavour seems attainable. In acting terms, hope in action involves a genuine appraisal of the task at hand – whether it's an audition, rehearsal or performance – owning our skills and feeling confident to 'go for it'. Creating a mental movie of a desired outcome, or goal visualization, is one effective way to actively nurture hope. Try imagining confidently walking onto the stage, or, as one actor I interviewed does every night, visualize yourself in the audience watching your character enter the story.

The second aspect, efficacy, revolves around the self-belief we cultivate in our abilities, motivating us to push forward and explore new possibilities. Positive energy radiates as we engage with our tasks and approach them confidently. Create opportunities to experiment, play, and learn new skills while rehearsing a song or scene without any agenda other than, 'Let's see where this goes or what we discover.' Each morning, rise with your affirmations and dedicate time each week to developing your technical skills, whether in a class, lesson, or on your own.

The third quality is resilience: the ability to bounce back from adversity or setbacks and grow despite negative experiences. In the ever-changing landscape of the theatre industry, securing a role is often more of an exception than the rule. Staying 'show fit' and auditioning are central to the work that performers engage in. How actors perceive positive or negative experiences cannot be framed in the same context as corporate employment. Resilient actors typically possess a core belief that creativity and the arts are essential to human expression, and every opportunity to share that gift with others is considered a success. Seek out opportunities to perform!

The fourth pillar of PsyCap is optimism, which involves believing in the universe's inherent ability to produce positive outcomes. Like hope, optimism is future-oriented and based on the belief that both the present and the future are filled with possibilities and opportunities. Practise optimism!

Actors' perceptions of well-being are also positively influenced by the discipline of learning, mastering, and curating essential skills for musical theatre performance. While some performance theorists argue that technique can inhibit the flow of performance energy, others present a contrasting perspective. They propose that strong techniques can lead to beneficial psychological changes for an actor, shifting their self-perception as they learn and develop various disciplines. For instance, as a performer acquires new dance skills, their body image transforms both physically and psychologically.

The qualities found in PsyCap reflect those found in an actor's PQ: self-belief, confidence, boldness, freedom, and courage. Actors who harness these traits develop a robust mental attitude, which is an asset in the potentially stressful environments of auditions, rehearsals, and performances. Our intrinsic reserves grow as we cultivate a positive self-image and commit to our beliefs and values. This acts as a reservoir from which we can draw when working hard or under pressure. Ultimately, we are left with ourselves and our foundational self-belief in our worth as human beings, with a rightful place on this planet and something valuable to contribute or share.

Flow

As mentioned in Chapter 6, the concepts of flow and 'presence' or being 'in the moment' share some common elements. Mihaly Csikszentmihalyi (1990) identified nine traits that characterize a flow state, enabling access to higher levels of creativity and expanding various dimensions of consciousness. He explains that a flow state:

> ... provided a sense of discovery, a creative feeling of transporting the person into a new reality. It pushed the person to higher performance levels and led to previously undreamed-of states of consciousness. In short, it transformed the self by making it more complex. In this growth of the self lies the key to flow activities.[5]

Many actors and creatives acknowledged these similarities, highlighting how finding flow in performance has been beneficial to them. Table 8.1 aligns their perspectives with Csikszentmihalyi's nine dimensions of flow.

Csikszentmihalyi questions whether a flow state can be summoned at will; however, actors have discovered that certain supportive structures can encourage them to induce a form of flow. Those who possess a strong sense of self-worth find they can concentrate effectively; they are unafraid of challenges, are intrinsically motivated, and their performance can be intrinsically rewarding. Furthermore, a high level of emotional well-being appears to promote the presence of flow.

Table 8.1 Dimensions of flow from MT actors' perspectives

Dimensions of Flow	Actors' Perceptions of Flow in Performance
Challenge to skill balance	Harnessing competency and skills to match the challenge at hand; motivation to face the challenge, belief in skillset.
Action and awareness	Effortless absorption, complete immersion in the music and story, and merging with the task; an ecstatic state; correcting and adjusting without thinking.
Clear goals	Knowledge of objectives and intentions as the character; connection to the task, awareness.
Unambiguous feedback	Transactional interactions with actors and audience, that positively influence but not impede. No need to stop to reflect on their progression.
Total concentration	Total focus, intense concentration and connection to the specifics of the story; working in the here and now, being present.
Sense of control	Easy personal control is maintained, while environmental control may not be. Challenges exist but are met securely.
Loss of self-consciousness	Freedom from inner self judgement, and negative inner voices; feeling of harmony and union, intrinsically and extrinsically.
Transformation of time	Changed perception of time: it can speed up, slow down, be at a standstill or disappear altogether.
Autotelic experience	Post flow feelings of happiness; enjoyable achievement and reward.

Flow is also examined in Bonfitto's book, *The Kinetics of the Invisible* (2016), which offers a detailed analysis of twentieth-century avant-garde theatre pioneer Peter Brook's work while juxtaposing the concepts of possession, flow, and connection.[6] Brook views actors as 'carriers' of these three qualities. During his experiments with his performance troupe in Paris and Africa, Brook developed a unique physical and improvisational theatre style. He deepened the understanding of how flow operates within the framework of theatre, emphasizing the crucial interactive connection with the audience. Bonfitto explores the flow states achieved between audiences and Brook's actors, quoting Csikszentmihalyi: '*A person who pays attention to an interaction instead of worrying about the self obtains a paradoxical result. She no longer feels like a separate individual, yet herself becomes stronger.*'[7]

The traits that cultivate a flow state in artists, actors, or musical theatre performers are similar to those experienced by individuals involved in non-performance projects. Indeed, anecdotal evidence suggests that people from all walks of life report encountering remarkably similar states, characterized by a distortion of time and a cyclical connection of energy with those around them or the tasks they are engaged in. Flow in performance and positive PsyCap are interconnected. In other words, if you believe in and trust yourself, let go, flow, and enjoy yourself, your 'It' Factor can emerge and resonate with others.

Time to play

In the first eight chapters, we have been baking our 'synergistic cake'. With the aid of historical perspectives, insightful theorists, performance teachers, and highly experienced creatives and actors, we've dissected existing knowledge on stage presence, deconstructed and reconstructed the performance synergy equation, and uncovered some characteristics of the magical 'greater than' aspect. We've connected this ephemeral quality to those who experience it – the audience. Furthermore, we've examined what it is and what it isn't. Now, it's time to begin to play and start creating our own magic. Join me in Part Two, where we will unveil practical ways to release, foster, encourage, or reignite the 'It' Factor within each of us.

PART TWO
DO

9
UNLOCKING YOUR 'IT': INTRODUCING YOUR SASS! TOOLKIT AND PLAY SPACE

The soul desires to dwell with the body because without the members of that body, it can neither act nor feel.

–Leonardo da Vinci *Notebooks*, Ed. Irma A. Richter
(Oxford: Oxford University Press, 1980), 43.

Observing an actor flowing synergistically is akin to witnessing a magician's conjuring trick – effortless and captivating. Can we learn to harness and exude this energy? I wanted to make the seemingly inscrutable perceptible, then marry this newfound knowledge with my imagination and create something attainable – something that could unlock or cultivate 'It'. So, I took what I learned during the interviews about Intrinsic Performative Processes, Contextual Connections, and Ways of Thinking, Being, and Doing and using a practice-based methodology, I developed and tested a synergy-forming toolkit, which I call SASS! (Strategies for Acting Singing Synergy).

Background foundation to the toolkit

My belief was that the right tools would cultivate the appropriate mental and emotional mindset that would enable performers to express their Performance Quotient freely when observed – whether entering an audition, developing a character in rehearsal or sharing a story on stage. But what tools?

Existing literature and online resources abound with acting and singing techniques. While certain established approaches provide exercises that can build an actor's skill base, I was looking for more. The interview keywords used by my expert actors and creatives had opened my eyes to another way of thinking. The strategies they employed embodied the essence of synergy. Their perspectives pointed the way.

I sorted through the available techniques and tips gleaned from the interviews with my experts and added the exercises from literature they referenced – those that aligned with their practices. I then added tactics I had learned from my own performance experiences, the professional development I'd pursued in various acting and singing disciplines, the decades spent trialling ideas, and the pedagogical approaches I'd developed in my teaching studio. My criteria was that these exercises would relate to the concept of synergy and open up the ways actors think and embody their craft on stage.

I knew for the toolkit to be effective, it needed to be:

- Adaptable: suitable for use at home, individually, in a group setting or in the studio with a coach or teacher.
- Stimulating: both the intrinsic and extrinsic aspects of the synergy equation.
- Inspirational: a variety of techniques and tactics for actors to tease and entice.
- Safe: with a dedicated space for spontaneous play, singing, acting and experimentation.

Actors' keywords and techniques

The keywords I had garnered from the interviews were invaluable. Over many years I'd witnessed these experts' skills as they performed on stage or creatively envisioned the shows I attended. I vividly remember specific moments when I felt tangibly connected to the synergized performances they crafted; I trusted their perspectives and ideas.

Actors described a deep connection they often felt with their characters and the audience (see Chapter 3). They referred to being immersed in the 'present moment' of the narrative they were portraying. Some of their keywords can be seen in Figure 9.1.

Several actors were aware of entering that experiential zone at various moments during nearly every performance, while others felt that they truly embraced their synergistic journey only a few times each week. They all recognized

Figure 9.1 MT actors' keywords describing synergy.

how their inherent skills helped them access that state of ease and joy. The methods they employed included visualizations, centring and focusing the mind, accessing intentions, personalization, psychophysical character development, and warming up their bodies and voices. These specific techniques facilitated their immersion into the character's world. Table 9.1 provides a great snapshot of some of their ideas and summarizes some of the key strategies and tactics referenced by MT actors in their performance preparation.

Let me share some additional insights from four other dynamic actors, currently working around the globe. To begin, Ainsley Melham explains his process using intention and personalization:

You know how you can bring your experience closer to the character. It's just your body embodiment. The most important thing is, try not to recreate it. Because you have to acknowledge that you can't recreate that. More often than not, those synergies are the result of the infinitesimal, just little things that have stacked up to create that moment. And you can't do a lot of those factors, they are external,

Table 9.1 MT actors' preparatory techniques and tactics

MT Actor	Tactic or Technique
Joel Granger	Singing: story-focused; not just about beauty; belt from a place of heightened emotion. Acting informs the breath. Acting: identify intentions and objectives, and how you affect your acting partners. Use of personalization for characterization, be curious, make interesting, bold choices. Ask, *'What else? What else?'* Stay in a state of curiosity. Stay open and free.
Jaime Hadwen	Acting: centre yourself, find calm. Listen, be bold, make choices, get into your body, let go, listen and connect.
Ashleigh Rubenach	Acting: build connections.
Tony Sheldon	Acting: 'mine' the text. Make decisions about who you are, and who the character is, and inhabit that person for the show. Never stop playing and thinking. Be adventurous. *'That allows you to then experiment on a nightly basis because you're so solid with your research and your character and that you can just play.'* *'Think through the thoughts, visualize images.'*
Alinta Chidzey	Singing: warm-up, embody technique, free the voice. Acting: meditate, focus energy, give without looking to receive.
Georgina Hopson	Singing: maintain a really structured singing technique. Build it from the ground up, then forget about it. Acting: use psycho-physical objectives. Choose what you take on. Mutate it, make it your own.
Philip Quast	Singing: know your scales and musical structure. Acting: explore etymology and deep work with text. Find autobiographical parts of self in character. Be curious. Be switched on all the time. *'Be very present'* and *'It is surprising, a sense of discovery, spontaneity.'*
Sharon Millerchip	Acting: listen, learn, trust yourself and instincts, be authentically yourself.
Lucy Maunder	Acting: use low deep breathing, visualization, focus, living in the moment, find the new.
Ainsley Melham	Acting: use listening and responding techniques (Meisner).
Simon Gleeson	Acting: practise Chekhov's psycho-physical exercises and warm-ups, with lightness and ease. Bookwork, repetition to build embodiment.
Natalie O'Donnell	Acting: get out of your head – receiving and responding. Use Chekhov exercises – tempo and Psychological Gesture. *'Just be brave enough to bring the audience to you.'*
Marina Prior	Acting: text driven, use of 'table work' in early rehearsals. Working with other actors and directors to explore character and subtext. Journal. Be brave, take risks, layer it up.
Jemma Rix	Singing: do the work, match your warm-up to the character's needs. Breathwork to focus. Acting: meditation, to set up the mental space you need and let go.

and you can't replicate those. And if you obsess about replicating them, then that starts to hinder your performance. So, you do have to be surprised and moved by it when it comes and just be ready for that to surface.

It's about taste testing, I guess, you know, like trying a little bit. And I feel that's where synergy comes back into it. When you get the right thing, when you taste the right thing, all of a sudden, you're like, 'Oh, that's what you can feel like.' A little spark that's working. And, so, then you allow yourself to go further with that option or, in that direction. But yes, certainly, in the beginning, particularly in rehearsals, it is about pushing into those areas and giving yourself permission to try and experiment with those. But not necessarily having to fully immerse yourself in it. Only then when you go, OK, yes, that's the one. Then, you can go further and really do the work.

Ainsley offered an exercise he used that was similar in concept to Meisner's listening and responding exercise:

And basically, the exercise is, you know, you'll improvise the scene, and whatever the other actor gives you, you go, 'Yes.' And then you bring another offer. And it's always about accepting that person's offer and sending out a new one and never shutting it down, you know. And if you're in that process of shutting things down, then it's not going to work. If you're in that vibe of bringing generous contributions that build on what the other actors are giving you and never judging what the other actors are giving you, then that all feeds into that, into what you're talking about, I think. (Melham)

Our second veteran, Marina Prior, discussed her methods for approaching a role and how she collects material to inspire her imagination:

I'm about the character, the plot, the thoughts, the big ideas, the small ideas, and the text work that allows the character to come off the page. Then, I just intrinsically and instinctually immerse myself. 'It' seeps in. And then I kind of just get inspired to try things.

So, I want to just feel really present in my body, too. Confident. My body is just in touch, and then I just play. Do it a million different ways. Then there is this funny thing where I just like to let it sit; I just let it simmer. And there's stuff going on. I don't even know that it's going on. But then, when I revisit it, it's stewed a bit. For me, it really is instinctive.

I just sort of get the sense that if I read and absorb, I watch a lot of different people doing it and all that sort of thing. But then I just steal a bit from here and there, but ultimately, I just find my own truth with that particular character … It's really interesting. I know I tend to just get an impulse and jump in and take it from there and try … I do write notes, I journal a bit about a character, I get a mood board, and I will collect ideas …

That's been kind of how it seeps in. And then I get inspired to try things, I guess. Well, I think the most valuable thing I have learned in doing straight plays, as well as musicals, is to be brave enough to look foolish and take risks basically in rehearsal and make terrible mistakes and have massive, spectacular failures. (Prior)

The third, Sharon Millerchip, had worked a lot as a resident director in recent years, and brought her wisdom from both sides of the table. As an actor, she stated:

I see story and song as a 'mountain graph'. It's got so many peaks and valleys and sometimes I visualize it. I can see it like that. I could see where the valleys are, and I can see where I'm going to pull back and where I'm going to take them somewhere they didn't know they were going to go at the beginning of the song and where this bit is going to lead to. And it's going to go here, and then we're going to finish somewhere, do you know what I mean?

I just deeply invest in this person [my character]. And then again, I think I call on my instincts and the choices that I make and piece by piece, it all sort of comes together. It comes together in the fact that before I, get to the rehearsal room, I read, I read a script three or four, three, four, five times. Maybe I just read it like I'm reading a novel. I read the whole [script], and so that it sorts of gets in there by osmosis. And I kind of get to know my character and all the other characters around me, which when you know all the other characters around you, they deeply inform me.

I guess that it is that breath, that split second of an intake of breath before you say something, which lets us know that you're thinking at the moment coming to you as you say it. And you know, I say this to kids in music theatre all the time. Think on the spot, think on the spot, you know.

The fourth, Caroline O'Connor, a veteran with over 40 years of experience, shared:

I think you really can't move forward unless you look back. I love looking back at all the great performers … to get greatness and to get gems. I've learned a lot of my work from watching those great performers from the 40s, 50s, 60s, 70s. That's the first thing I would say to them is that please, please look at performers that have gone before you … because they did it. They did it without fireworks … they created magic.

She continued, '*Do not be afraid to be yourself because you people will love it. They love the fact that you are exactly what's on the label. There's nothing stands out more than someone because of who they are.*'

Creatives keywords and techniques

The creatives brought additional perspective. When asked whether the presence of synergy influenced their decision to hire or collaborate with an actor, the directors unanimously responded, 'Yes.' They discussed what they typically look for in a singing actor's audition performance and emphasized the importance of the energy emanating from an actor who demonstrates openness and availability.

Creatives described the auditionees' personal energy, which sometimes manifested as passion, excitement, joy, commitment or strength. They mentioned actors who appeared free, fearless, unfettered, selfless, spontaneous, authentic, and true to themselves. The word cloud (Figure 9.2) illustrates the characteristics of personal energy that creatives often seek in actors.

The directors noted that when the 'It' Factor was present, actors appeared to rely on instinctual responses to stimuli, moment by moment, cultivating a sense of discovery, even while repeating the same material. Those performances felt intuitive and authentic, deeply connected to the actors' unique personas as well as distinctly linked to the audience. The frameworks and techniques creatives shared included:

- Directing actors by focusing on character and motivation. Discovering the depth of the character and the story and exploring the territory in which the character resides.

- Incorporating musical elements into a broader context and thinking beyond just technique and music. Guiding actors to understand where the goalposts are – where the role and the song reside – and then making choices within those goalposts: *'Serve the piece, the character, the motivation, and the actor'* (Hunter).
- Working individually to determine *'what that personality is going to respond to'* (Amos), and similarly,
- Working instinctively to *'find the thing that taps into individual'* (Ralph).
- Centring the thought and breath lower in the body to engage a genuine, physical, breath-driven connection to the story: *'What I think I do as a director is that I try to, you know, make the physicality of what people have to achieve. The kind of nuts and bolts of what people have to achieve very clear for them'* (Phillips).

Figure 9.2 Creative Directors' keywords describing synergy.

Other creatives supported a hands-on approach. Langley captured the concept of melding self and character together:

And let go of self … and just embrace this other character. And of course, we all know as performers, a great percentage of our character comes from ourselves as well as all the clues the playwright has left us. So a sense of ourselves is still in there.

Tyran Parke was particularly instructional, showcasing several tactics he employs in rehearsals. Table 9.2 summarizes some of his approaches. His techniques highlighted how creatives tap into and encourage an actor's intrinsic performative processes.

Table 9.2 Tyran Parke's techniques and modes of working

Techniques and Modes of Working	MT Actor's Process
Find out where this text exists inside of actors, to communicate quite clearly.	neuro/physical.
Holding play and focus together, and going, 'How do these things live alongside each other and what gets in the way of your instrument being released?'	neuro/psycho/physical.
Allow them great freedom to play and feel like they are creating it.	psycho/emotio/physical.
A lot of it is just about keeping them playful and not locking down.	psycho/physical.
You are trying to go with impulse, instinct and energy – Chekhov is the way in for me.	psycho/physical.

Other creatives illuminated the process of building and layering a character. As both actor and creative director, Millerchip saw the transactional and interactional relationship of the actor and audience very clearly:

Every single person is different. There is a need for finding something new in the moment to create a sense of real – when your audience look and they go, 'I think I just caught something there. I think I just saw her. She had a real moment.' And for that to happen, we kind of have to believe that the person who is performing is having an authentic experience as well. That's why I kept saying the other day as an audience member. I want the audience to feel like they're witnessing me having a genuine experience, not just watching me perform at them. It's that suspension of reality, even when you're singing, even when you're dancing, it's that moment of suspension where they buy it. And that's when some 'frisson' happens, and that is the difference between someone saying, 'Oh, that was great' and 'that was amazing'.

Millerchip encouraged in-depth study to understand the complexity of character and story. Working with the cast of the musical *Six*, she explained:

The girls had a clear idea about who they thought these women were, and then they married their instincts of how they felt about that person's journey and the material. And we kind of married it together. We did a lot of improv and sort of built them, and it was quite a thorough process.

The insights and generous sharing from these creatives and actors affirmed my toolkit design.

The SASS! toolkit design

To accommodate those features discussed by my experts, I chose skill-specific strategies that would assist performers in awakening their intrinsic performative processes and integrating singing, acting, and movement into a cohesive whole. While not prescriptive or fixed, these exercises aim to unlock and release synergy.

Two important parts of the synergy equation are addressed: first, opening actors to their fully energetic self, and second, helping them connect to the surrounding extrinsic factors – audience, story, and environment – where the 'It' Factor is actively observed and experienced.

Easy to understand, the exercises can be adapted to suit a person's natural abilities and incorporated into both general warm-ups and specific performance preparations. The various 'tools' have multiple uses, much like a general hardware toolkit that includes a hammer, screwdriver, pliers, saw, and more. They can be used differently by performers or their directors, teachers or coaches, who can adjust them to meet their needs.

Tools to unlock intrinsic processes

Firstly, the chosen tools specifically correlate to the discoveries discussed in Chapters 3 and 5. Synergistic actors instinctively connect their performative processes to their liquid knowledge and skills displaying confident individuality, specificity and focus, spontaneous discovery, open-hearted empathy, joyous generosity, and physical, emotional, and mental freedom. When practised, integrated and activated, they form an actor's developed PQ.

These exercises will encourage actors to:

- engage both cognitive and intuitive aspects of *thinking*, including stimulating the imagination and promoting free, spontaneous play,
- be genuinely present in the moment of *being*, engaging their senses, creating and generously sharing their emotions and unique selves to tell authentic stories, and
- synthesize the diverse and sometimes oppositional skills required in the *doing*: to perform while singing, acting, and dancing simultaneously.

Take a look at Table 9.3 – Correlating processes with keywords and toolkit techniques. It connects our intrinsic processes and the keywords and elements of performance synergy with the exercises that may promote and encourage them. Column 1 – 'Ways of thinking, being and doing' lists some of the concepts and strategies that actors use to open themselves up and forge synergistic connections with other actors, the narrative and the audience. These are grouped under the performative processes they activate. Column 2 – Keywords from interviews showcases the concepts that actors and creatives employed when discussing synergy, along with terms sourced from the research literature. Column 3 – 'Potential toolkit techniques' lists exercises that could align with both the actors' processes and their modes of 'thinking, being, and doing', as well as the keyword concepts presented in the research.

Table 9.3 Correlating processes with keywords and toolkit techniques

Study 1: Processual Ways of Thinking, Being and Doing	Keywords from Interviews	Potential Toolkit Techniques
THINKING		
Cognitive thinking (*neuro*):		
hard work, skill, commitment, character work, repetition, mining the text, memorizing, building layers of meaning, finding details, specificity.	focus, specificity, awareness, direction, intention, open, no agenda, trusting, self-belief, fearlessness, inspiration, bravery, boldness, thought connected to moment, self-knowing.	text work, subtext work, given circumstances, monologuing, actioning, intention work, targeting and referencing (Donnellan).
Intuitive thinking (*psycho*):		
instinctual, immersion, have fun, ease, just connecting, transcend, let it flow, effortless, immediacy.	playfulness, spontaneously connecting, new discovery, curiosity, exploring, flowing, open, imagination intuition, available, new, responding.	improvisation (Spolin), atmospheres (Chekhov), psycho-physical exercises, Seidenstein's clown work, listening and responding (Meisner), atmospheric walks, primal sound (Chapman), primal breath.

Study 1: Processual Ways of Thinking, Being and Doing	Keywords from Interviews	Potential Toolkit Techniques
BEING		
The senses (*senso*):		
visualize, engage senses, use breath.	experiential, interesting, tangible, palpable, excitement, radiating, watchable, riveting authentic, honesty of self.	listening and responding, five senses stimulation, visualization, music monologuing.
Intrinsic self (*persona*):		
sense of self, being present, focused stillness, breathing, put your brain in the bottom of your stomach.	unique self, ownership, confidence, strength of convictions, potent, powerful, truthfully connected to story, unique self, love of performing, generosity of spirit, openness, vulnerability.	Crossing the Threshold (Chekhov).
The emotions (*emotio*):		
joy, empowerment, affirmations, being at one with the work.	energetic, buoyant, passion, joy, rich emotion, love, freedom of expression.	energetic centres, guided meditation.
DOING		
Technical Competencies (*technico*):		
singing techniques, acting techniques – actioning, finding intention, listening and responding, being curious.	powerful, vibrant, focused energy, embedded skill, competent, understanding words, meaning, in the present moment, telling a story.	Chekhov's psycho-physical exercises including qualities of movement, breath work (Rodenberg), outside-in.
Body (*physical*):		
lightness and ease, physical freedom.	kinetic, freedom to move, physical looseness, physically connected, strength, embodying story, psycho-physicality, physical presence.	Clown Secret mechanisms (Seidenstein), Eight Efforts (Laban), Moulding a Character (Chekhov).

These exercises aim to stimulate and engage the mind, heart, soul, and body through improvisational, imagination-building, discovery, and confidence-enhancing techniques.

Many of the tools listed will help to integrate and empower the actor's performative processes and their triple threat skills. For instance, at a given moment, an actor's cognitive (*neuro*) or intuitive (*psycho*) thought triggers a breath (*physical*) that informs a sung note or a dance movement (*technico*) to convey an emotion (*emotio*) in a unique way (*persona*) incorporating the body's expression (*physical*). Often, these processes fire together almost instantaneously.

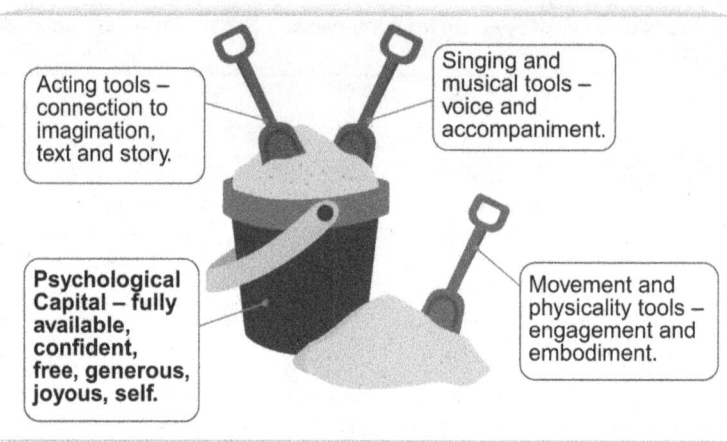

Figure 9.3 Toolkit tools empowered by psychological capital.

Most actors noted that having a positive mental attitude significantly influenced their ability to access synergistic energy. So I included exercises to promote a fourth competency: positive psychological capital, which supports other technical competencies and enhances their performance.

Tools to encourage extrinsic connections

Secondly, the toolkit contains exercises that encourage the synergistic connections that link the audience to an actor and the story. These activities help to foster the relationship between an actor's open-hearted vulnerability and the audience's positive receptivity, allowing energy to flow in a cyclical manner. It is vital for actors to build those transactional interactions mentioned in Chapter 4. The toolkit promotes:

- the identification and connections an actor initiates with the character or story,
- the subliminal interactive bridge between observer or audience, and
- the atmosphere or environment in which the storytelling occurs.

My objective with these exercises is to inspire actors to immerse themselves in a vibrant world of their own creation. I want them to enjoy exploring what their characters might experience within that space. Traditional tertiary acting training often focuses on building the character – deconstructing text, establishing acting intentions and objectives and creating specific thought processes and actions to investigate. To broaden perspective and enhance acting choices, I included various exercises to explore different forms of psycho-physicality and harness the power of improvisation and imaginative play to stimulate other aspects of an actor's thinking and doing, enriching their existing skills. My goal is to encourage fresh discoveries in performance moments, including harnessing radiant energy to create atmosphere and opening pathways to the audience (Figure 9.3).

Situating the toolkit

The time and place where actors and coaches train and rehearse can significantly influence their effectiveness. If actors are glancing over their shoulders, concerned about who is judging their work, mental and emotional freedom can easily slip away. Having witnessed and experienced the master/apprentice model used in traditional conservatory teaching, along with the limiting and sometimes detrimental constraints that a more formal coaching environment can impose on self-expression, I felt it essential to establish a creative, theatre-style work environment where actors can utilize my toolkit. I wanted to create the ideal cognitive, emotional, and physical play space, free from judgement and filled with encouragement to experiment and play.

This specific, symbolic, user-friendly 'space' needed to be engaging, adaptable, with room for growth and an invitation for others to join and participate. It would encourage playful moments and allow for multiple iterations, each unique and fresh every time the song is sung, or a scene is played. Here, every iteration could be dismantled and reconstructed as the actor wishes, without unwarranted judgement. In this space, actors are encouraged to tap into their innate processes to create imaginary environments. As actors apply their singing, acting, physical, and psychological tools in a safe and supportive environment, moments of imaginative exploration and discovery can occur.

The 'Sandpit of Imaginative Play'

My inspiration for the perfect context for the toolkit came one day when I observed a young child engaging in imaginative play without a hint of pretence. Several years ago, I spent time caring for the young daughter of a friend. My babysitting duties at their house invariably ended with a session in her sandpit. I watched her delight each time she knocked down the sand structures we built together before starting anew. Our play was filled with tales of castles, mermaids, and crocodiles – the creativity was boundless. Each time we finished a story, she joyfully let her last sandy creation go and embarked on another adventure. She was onto something.

A metaphorical sandpit is the ideal space for actors to play. It is a place where there are no mistakes, only opportunities to explore and enjoy the adventure. So I positioned my toolkit exercises within a framework that I call 'The Sandpit of Imaginative Play'. This practice-based environment enables actors to experiment with techniques, delve into their inner processes, and apply concepts that resonate or function, enlivening their performances. It serves as a transactional space where stories can be shared, emotions can be experienced, and various explorations can be pursued safely.

I first experienced the joy and adventure that can be found in this sandpit as a nineteen-year-old when I attended a national Christian arts conference in the Snowy Mountains of Australia. Hundreds of musicians, singers, actors, dancers, and visionaries gathered to explore all things creative. It was a week-long event filled with extraordinary opportunities. In that rarefied atmosphere, the sky was the limit. Each day, a small team of us would dream, scheme, devise, and implement the evening concert-like events featuring music, bands, drama, and dance – all connected by a common narrative or theme. While the physical resources were limited, the human resources were remarkable. Night after night, something unique would unfold, blaze, and then vanish. I learned so much creating a fantastic story for one night; when it was over, we'd start anew.

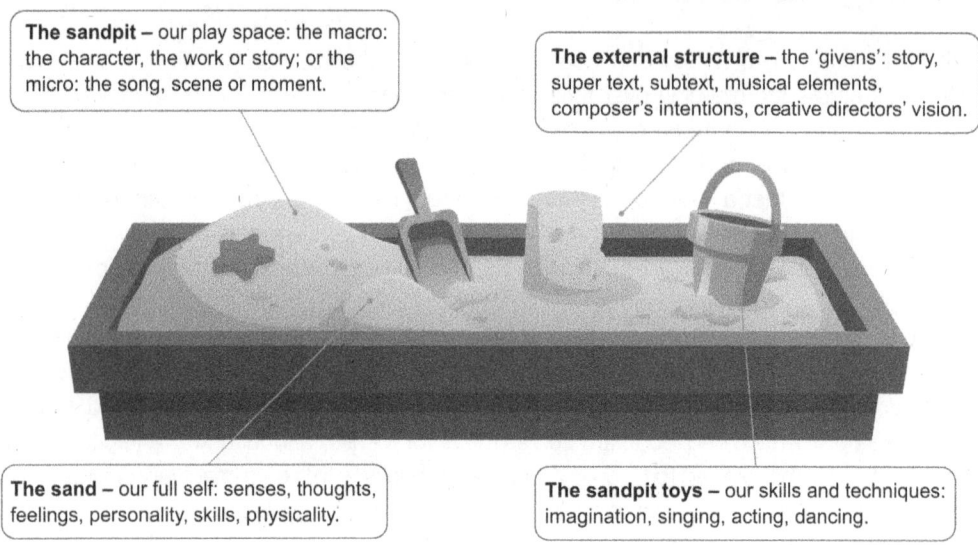

Figure 9.4 The 'Sandpit of Imaginative Play'.

My philosophy on how this sandpit can benefit singers and actors has evolved over the years as I've witnessed both young and old flourish when given the freedom to have fun and explore. Young children can often be our best teachers. Unfettered by unnecessary rules and regulations, they fully tap into their boundless imaginations. As I write this, my two-year-old great-nephew reminds me of the sandpit's significance and the need to let go of my rule-laden perspectives on how to play when I enter it.

Let's unpack the components of this sandpit as they correlate to actors and their work (see Figure 9.4).

The sandpit is a place for personal, unfettered play and can be tailored to individual needs. Here you can explore, make discoveries, imagine scenarios, travel to different lands, and become other people. Close your eyes for a moment and recall a sandpit and the freedom you felt while playing as a child.

Aspects of a physical sandpit correlate to our metaphorical one. The external structure or physical space can represent 'the macro' – the entire story, or your character – or perhaps it is 'the micro' – a song, scene, or 'a moment'. During my workshops, participants are encouraged to visualize their sandpit, examine its external structure, and determine what shapes and defines the play space. For instance, the 'givens' that actors work with are:

- the story, super-text, the written text,
- the musical elements, including melodic contour and harmony,
- the composer/writer's intentions – lyrics, story, book, and
- the creative directors' vision.

While certain boundaries of the external structure exist, within that, the sandpit serves as a free space for exploration, and we – the actors and coaches – come as children, ready to play.

The sand symbolizes our cognitive and instinctual thoughts, feelings, personality, and essence. Our physical expression can shape and sculpt this rich resource to tell stories and create new imaginative worlds. By drawing on our senso-neuro-psycho-emotio-persona-technico-physical processes, countless opportunities for creativity emerge.

The sandpit toys are the skills and techniques we bring into the sandpit and can be picked up or discarded at will. Applied in various combinations, they help us transform the sand into something new and fresh. Each playtime adds layers and nuances to the story; previous iterations leave impressions that are easily accessed, built upon, or discarded with every play.

By inviting actors to step into this open space with a sense of freedom, empowerment, passion, and curiosity, I encourage some simple questions: 'Who are you? What is happening, and what do you want to do? When and where are you? And why are you there?' This approach sparks their discoveries. If the answer is 'I don't know' or 'I'm not sure', that's okay. These questions shouldn't create pressure; instead, actors can enjoy resting in the unknown and observing what unfolds. I advise them to sit in the unknown and allow the context of the text and the musical elements to guide them and reveal the hidden aspects of the story.

There is no single way to play in the Sandpit of Imaginative Play; there is no right or wrong approach. Immersion is the key to having an exciting time. When all endeavours in that imaginative space communicate the same story, it becomes engaging, watchable, and authentic. Similarly, in musical theatre, when actors focus on conveying the story in its entirety and connecting with the music and lyrics, their use of breath, thought processes, vocal timbre, and physical expression delivers a specific, coherent narrative that is believable.

As mentioned earlier, the sandpit toys used by musical theatre actors in this play space fall into four broad categories: singing, acting, physical, and psychological. These tools can be employed to unlock an actor's seven performative processes. The tools I selected for the toolkit were tested privately before being assigned. Although categorized separately in the following chapters, many toolkit exercises combine elements of music-making, acting, movement, and psychology, synthesizing these four skills.

Getting ready to play

None of the exercises in the SASS! toolkit require advanced technical skills; however, some may need practise before achieving effortless proficiency. The toolkit encourages experimentation and discovery, allowing you to explore and utilize various tools in your preferred way. Cultivate those you find most valuable. Remember, there are no strict rules for using these tools. The techniques aim to stimulate and inspire creative thinking, ignite the imagination, open hearts, and promote uninhibited physicality.

I often use this paradigm – the safe space of the sandpit and toolkit exercises – when I coach musical theatre actors. Each session varies based on their objectives and whether I am working one-on-one or with a group. To start, we warm-up, using a simple set of loosening and freeing exercises that prepare actors for playful exploration. These include breathing exercises, physical loosening and connecting activities, psycho-physical work, physical clowning techniques, imaginative walks, energetic centres, and radiance exercises. Together, we activate and loosen our bodies and minds during warm-ups before focusing on repertoire.

Although I have taught this way for years, recently I discovered my pedagogical approach aligns with Michael Chekhov's 'five guiding principles for actors,'[1] summarized here:

1. **The mind and body are one. Use movement to evoke emotions.** This principle reminds me to incorporate psycho-physical exercises, whether by conducting or dancing to the song's musical accompaniment, or through other 'outside-in' techniques to establish an emotional connection.
2. **Utilize the landscape of your imagination to create a powerful sense of tangibility.** This principle inspires me to incorporate exercises such as atmospheric walks, and physical expansion and contraction.
3. **The work is spiritual, not religious. Discover something greater than yourself – higher or unconscious intellect.** This principle motivates me to cultivate energetic centres and tap into the 'larger' something or self that radiates outward to the world.
4. **One engaged technique will trigger others.** This principle encourages me to incorporate cross-training exercises that combine singing with acting or music with movement, such as primal sound and breath or music and text monologuing.
5. **Artistic freedom is essential.** This principle shaped the foundational guidelines I developed for the sandpit and for fostering an environment that encourages the exploration of various exercises within the same song. The actor possesses the power to create moments through free expression and creativity during play. There are no right or wrong answers, only opportunities for exploration.

Beyond the acting arena

SASS! can stimulate communication and connectivity skills regardless of the arena the user lives and works in. Interestingly, in recent years, I have collaborated with people from other professions in workshops, productions, conferences, and performances. As they explored the toolkit in a safe play space, their experimentation created wonderful moments of personal and artistic expression. For some I worked with, the key to unlocking intrinsic processes was remembering how to be a child again. The 'who of us' that forms our essential core – our cognitive mind, intuition, emotions, personality, soul, and physicality – is a resource ready and waiting to be explored and enjoyed.

In today's volatile social climate, personal and professional circumstances, along with cultural strictures, can shape our internal landscape and hinder easy access to those processes. Take time to reconnect with your inner child and explore new avenues of communication. Use this toolkit to enrich that journey, moment by moment.

Let's begin with the warm-up; it reminds us to breathe, take time to vocalize, imagine, and play.

10
TOOLKIT TECHNIQUES: WHOLE-SELF ACTIVATION AND BREATHING

The following three chapters will introduce you to the SASS! toolkit: the techniques, tactics, and tips I have used to unlock and foster synergistic performances. Many of these exercises were tested during the masterclasses and workshops I conducted with young theatre professionals, all who were just beginning their careers. Our work on their audition songs focused on merging and integrating their skills with their other intrinsic processes to enhance their performances, awaken personal synergy, and create new connections with the audience.

This chapter focuses on whole-self activation – known colloquially as a warm-up – and breathwork. The next chapter details acting and singing/music techniques applicable to songs and text. Chapter 12 explores physical movement and addresses some of the psychological components that enhance stage presence or the 'It' Factor.

As you exercise, remember to stay flexible and adaptable. This isn't a strict, step-by-step methodical approach, but rather, a collection of ideas and practices that you can integrate into your routine and self-expression. Stay curious about these strategies, and discover which ones resonate with you as you experiment. Even better, find your own additions and modifications! Your needs will vary based on yourself, the day, and the task at hand. If you're working alone, without a coach, it might be helpful to record your discoveries as you work or record your reflections in a journal afterward. This simple act will help you perceive how your efforts connect with a potential audience.

Although the exercises are categorized under specific headings, such as breathing, singing, and acting, it is essential to view whole-self activation as part of a complex, multifaceted whole. For instance, as you breathe, stretch, lunge, or walk, allow your imagination and physicality to narrate the story simultaneously.

How often have you watched a performance or spoken with someone and thought, 'I don't believe them'? Perhaps their eyes, voice, or words don't align with their physical presence, inner energy, or emotions. When there is a disconnect between a person's inner processes and what they convey, their presence diminishes. We know that synergy emerges when an actor's performative processes converge.

Construct that equation. The more foundational components you integrate and layer, the more they blend together, yielding something new and organic – a dynamic, exciting performance. As you practise, if one area feels restricted or lacking – such as expressing your thoughts physically, sparking your imagination, or focusing intently on listening and responding – seek out exercises that will help you develop that aspect. Then, continue layering and integrating them with other parts of yourself. If you're experienced in musical theatre, you may have all the tools you need to create dynamic and exciting performances. Let these chapters inspire you to explore what you already know and do and perhaps discover new ways to ignite your creativity.

Whole-self activation (aka warm-up!)

Actors share many similarities with elite athletes. Our bodies serve as our instruments. As performers, we require holistic activation – our entire being must be engaged. When traditional skill-based warm-ups for singing, acting or movement are done in isolation, sometimes the critical connection between the whole-self and body may be overlooked. When you practise, how often do you notice that the skill level attained in one exercise doesn't always transfer to the repertoire you perform? Integrating singing, acting, physicality, and psychology can turn your physical or vocal warm-up into a comprehensive form of self-activation.

The power of a good warm-up should never be underestimated. Simon Gleeson, a seasoned actor who has portrayed Jean Valjean in major productions of *Les Misérables,* emphasized the importance of warming up, stating:

Your instrument and your body and your mind are properly prepared to go into that show, and that's where warming up comes into it, that's where your acting technique comes into it – perhaps taking a moment before the show to just centre yourself and focus in on your job and zero in on the character and try and leave behind whatever's happened during your day, warming up your voice to make sure it's in the right pocket and marrying that with warming up your body because we know how the voice works from the body and vice versa. So, if you're really adhering to those preparations, then that's creating an environment where that synergy can happen more often.

The term 'warm-up' typically indicates that the body needs gentle stretching and mobilizing to enhance flexibility and perform at peak efficiency and strength. Ten to fifteen minutes of low to moderate intensity is generally regarded as ideal before engaging in strenuous activities. Various sports utilize highly personalized stretching routines. Often, sports and dance warm-ups incorporate cardiovascular activities to improve blood flow and increase energy throughout the body. Mobility and stretching also stimulate the nervous system and engage large muscle groups. This occurs through any exercise that contracts and lengthens muscles while also challenging balance.

In the realm of musical theatre, warm-ups take various forms. Before a show, the dance captain may lead a ten-minute session of physical stretching and cardio on stage. These exercises engage and warm the body, but we must also activate the mind beyond the movements. Another valuable tool that actors use privately is yoga. Participants stretch, focus on their breath, and settle into each pose, which fosters bodily flexibility and mental tranquillity. However, physical exercise alone does not connect multiple processes.

Theatre performance activation/warm-up

What might an activation entail for the holistic theatre performer? In a physical sense, what is presented here resembles aspects of an athlete's, dancer's, or yoga warm-up; specific physical elements must be awakened. However, during an activation warm-up, the synergized performer focuses on awakening and enlivening their seven performative processes. This entails:

- activating learned and embedded singing/acting/movement techniques (*neuro*),
- activating the breath and warming up the voice and the body (*technico*),
- energizing thought through physicalized imagination and play (*senso, psycho, physical*),
- finding psychological freedom: being organic, present, spontaneous, in the moment, connected to thought but not bound by it (*psycho*),
- maintaining free emotional access and freedom of expression in their physical body and the voice (*emotio*),
- accessing vocal timbre, intention, action, imagination, impulse, spontaneity, truthfulness and honesty (*all seven processes*), and
- being bold and immersing themselves in the character, utilizing personality (*persona*).

The warm-up below provides physical stimulation as well as the mental and emotional space for the actor to engage their intrinsic performative processes in clear and simple ways. When technical competency is embedded and easily accessible, other processes can be activated without difficulty. Layers are incorporated, including thoughts and intentions, imaginings, feelings, and connections to others or the imagined environment.

Let's begin

Performance activation involves awakening, opening up, and letting go – energizing your breath, body, mind, imagination, and heart through physical and vocal self-expression. The duration of your warm-up is entirely up to you, depending on how you choose to prepare and the time you allocate to each phase. Some physical warm-up routines can last as long as an hour. The process detailed below can take anywhere from twenty to forty-five minutes based on the exercises you select and how many you choose to execute. My activation outlines five components: Stretching and Breathing, Grounding and Connecting, Improvising and Atmospheres, Explorative Vocalizing, and Focus and Readiness.

Table 10.1 provides a quick list of activation exercises and some possible ideas to engage your imagination. The basic exercises are listed in Column 2, while some additional creative ideas for expanding each exercise can be found in Column 3 – Imagination Activation. Choose one or more exercise from each category to tailor the warm-up to your needs. Many of these activation exercises have also been videoed and narrated and may be accessed through the book's companion website.

As you work, engage your imagination and memory through your senses. You will discover another level of activation if you allow your thoughts to find emotional expression. Empower each activity with your unique persona. Pay attention to the thoughts and feelings that arise during the exercises. Don't try to suppress them – instead, let them connect with you and influence your physical expression. Even thoughts such as '*This is stupid*', '*This is not working*', or '*Am I doing this right?*' are valid. Acknowledge your emotions and let them guide your next move, linking those feelings – whatever they may be – to your actions. Nothing is wrong or should be repressed unless it is unsafe.

Table 10.1 Whole body activation exercises

Aspect	Exercise	Imagination Activation
Stretching and Breathing	Say hello to you	Body-based imagination
	Child's pose yoga breathing	
	Stretch your breath	
	Squat breath	
	Feeling full	
	Rhythmic breathing	Travel the world
	Yoga – breath in a square	
	Singer's and actor's breath	
	Primal breath	Instinctual response to thought
		Word and subtext triggers
Grounding and Connecting	Finding engaged neutral	Ocean, Butterfly
	Puppet play	Add intention, change the stakes
	Front foot rocks	
	Walk run stop	Connect to a scenario and respond
	Ball work	Give and receive physically
	Partnering work	Find teamwork and unison
	See-saw	
Improvising and Atmosphere	Isolations with meaning	Discover something new each time
	Creative twisting	
	Nothing exercise	
	Atmospheric walks	
Imaginative Vocalizing	Exploring resonance	Be Tarzan
	Swiss army knife exercise	Be imaginary characters
	Loaded SOVT sounds	Be imaginary animals
	Vowels with attitude	Add thought that brings emotion
Focus and Readiness	Energizing meditation	Create space and fill yourself with radiance
	Crossing the threshold	

For additional help, look for Syd Synergy's friendly face, positioned next to the exercises that are demonstrated and supported on the book's companion website: http://bloomsbury.pub/it-factor

You may find yourself vocalizing or using your breath to express your feelings, so feel free to do so. A movement or stretch might spark a memory or a metaphor; are you arching like a cat or reaching for a balloon that's floating out of reach? Follow where your body leads you, safely. If you're in a group, avoid trying to imitate anyone else; just be yourself. Remember that when you activate your imagination, your movements on the floor may appear childlike, but set aside any preconceptions about what defines appropriate adult behaviour. Instead, imagine yourself in a sandbox, having fun. Keep in mind, the goal is free, unrestricted, wholehearted, joyous, and spontaneous play.

Stretching and breathing

As you begin, take a few moments to familiarize yourself with the space around you. This area is your Sandpit of Imaginative Play for today. Move about, observing the light, colours, textures, and qualities surrounding you. Feel its edges; sit, lie, or roll on the floor. You might take a brisk walk, run around the space, or do a few skips or jumps to connect with the ground beneath you. This will help clear your mind and elevate your heart rate a bit. Take deep breaths; inhale the air. Get comfortable here and establish your safe space within this area. Settle into a relaxed position, whether sitting or standing.

Say 'Hello' to you

Let's reacquaint ourselves with our bodies through meaningful isolation work. Many of us have experienced isolation exercises in dance or movement classes. This time, as you connect with each part of your body, greet it, check in, and observe what it needs – whether it's more loosening, increased blood flow, or simply an acknowledgment of its role in your overall connectedness. Each session will feel different, as the body's needs are always changing.

- Begin with your head; say, '*Hello*' and gently touch, massage or stroke your scalp and face. Your skull rests atop your vertebral column; acknowledge its weight and balance. Use incremental movements: up, down, forward, backwards, and side to side. Wake up your face. Frown, then raise your eyebrows high, blink or flutter your eyelids, scrunch your nose, drop and wiggle your jaw, stretch and pout your lips, and say hello. Wake up your neck: massage your posterior neck muscles (there are three layers – superficial, middle and deep), and then gently stretch them. Softly stroke the front of your throat, greeting and thanking your larynx for providing you with voice. Gently rotate your head; make gentle circles, nod up and down, and gently drop it from side to side. Let the weight of it gently stretch your opposing neck muscles.

- Continue down your body, massaging, touching, moving, or rotating as you greet your shoulders, ribcage, tummy, spine, hips, pelvis, buttocks, legs, feet, toes, and finally, your arms, hands, and fingers. Acknowledge any stiffness or tension you feel, and offer those areas some tender, loving care. Once you've attended to each body part, connect them all with fluid movements of your choice – this could be a Mexican wave, a cat-like stretch, a snake-like undulation, or a spiral twist. Let your imagination guide you. Then, take a deep breath and give your whole body a jelly-like shake for about fifteen seconds, saying '*Hello!*' to yourself. If you find yourself spontaneously vocalizing as you move, feel free to add sounds or words, though it's not necessary.

Breathwork

Just as your mind serves as a springboard for storytelling, your breathwork provides the foundation for your physicality – whether singing, acting, or dancing. Breath prepares and energizes both the body and mind for action, supplying the power necessary to accomplish the task at hand. Patsy Rodenberg describes it succinctly:

All human energy is breath. The body houses you and breath powers you. It's the first act you perform and it is the last. Breath powers your body, your voice, your mind, your heart and your spirit. In fact, if you examine words like inspiration and respiration you notice the presence of spirit embedded in the word.[1]

Breathwork is an integral part of warm-ups. It focuses on reminding the body how deeply and freely we can breathe, how to expand the ribs and back, and how to engage the diaphragm to support the lungs. Many of us spend most of our day simply maintaining our existence, inhaling the minimum amount of air necessary, which leads to a lot of shallow breathing.

Gently stretch while you breathe. This quiets the mind and connects us to the life force of our breath. Stretching expands the ribcage and back muscles, releasing tension in the torso, which allows for a deep, connected breath that fills the body. It also loosens the neck, shoulders, back, and hips.

Here are some breathing and stretching exercises that you can incorporate into your warm-up routine or practise independently. None of what I'm sharing here is new; these methods have been tried and tested. These exercises can help you cultivate a strong intercostal diaphragmatic breathing technique, which has served as the foundation of bel canto, classical, and 'legit' musical theatre singing for hundreds of years. I've also included two yoga breathing techniques to enhance oxygen and energy flow, stimulate your brain, and improve physical fluidity and balance. Once you grasp the physical movements of each exercise, begin to integrate your imagination and the feelings that naturally accompany your thoughts.

Child's pose yoga breathing

One quick and easy stretching and breathing technique is to spend several minutes embracing a state of repose while taking deep, centred breaths in yoga's child's pose. Stretching as you breathe helps to open up spaces in the torso. Once you feel comfortable, add another layer by engaging the senses and imagination; create a story or atmosphere.

- Start on your hands and knees, kneeling on the floor. If needed, place something soft, like a mat or towel, beneath you for comfort. Relax your buttocks back onto your calves and stretch your body and arms forward, resting your head on the ground with your palms flat in front. Feel the stretch extend through your spine down into your pelvis, deeply relaxing as you release your shoulders and neck. Breathe gently but deeply into your back and softened belly. Remain in this position for a minute, continuing to breathe deeply. What can you envision in this space? Are you a cat stretching in the sunshine? A devoted worshipper before an ancient deity? Or perhaps another type of creature? How does that make you feel? Slowly rise, transitioning through all fours into a neutral standing position. Retain the deep breath you found in that pose as you continue your warm-up.

Stretch your breath

This exercise is all about releasing muscles, especially your intercostals and your back. Begin this breath by integrating it with movement and stretches.

- Lift one arm up and over, allowing that arm to gently flop over your head, thereby opening up the intercostal muscles on that side. From your hips, gently twist forward into a diagonally flat back to enhance the side intercostal stretch. Ensure that your shoulders remain relaxed; do not lift them. Breathe in and out into that stretch, which should extend down your side. Then ease out with a gentle release. Swing up and over as you paint the ceiling with your fingers and return that arm to your side. Repeat on the other side.

- Back breath: start with your feet shoulder-width apart, wrap your arms around yourself, and give yourself a hug. Feel your back open up between your shoulder blades as you breathe into that space. Who are you hugging? An old friend? Why? Allow your thoughts to add meaning to these stretches.
- Allow your body to relax from the waist while maintaining a hug around yourself. Keep your neck, shoulders, knees, and hips loose; let the weight stretch and release your spine and neck. Hang in this position for twenty seconds. Sway gently from the hips, feeling your breath opening up your back muscles.
- In that flop position, imagine you are an underwater diver filling air tanks on your back with oxygen. As you breathe in, feel the air travel down your spine toward your buttocks. You can sense your pelvic muscles relaxing as you breathe deeply and gently. Let go of your core and belly muscles as you inhale in this flop position. Release your arms from their hug and allow them to dangle toward the floor. Then, take your time to roll up through your spine to a light, buoyant neutral position.

Squat breath

- With your abdominal muscles relaxed and your feet apart, move into a low squat. Bend your knees as far as possible while keeping your heels on the ground. Slowly breathe in, directing your breath toward the floor. You should feel your breath extending deeply into your pelvic region. Hold this position while you inhale and exhale – six to eight breaths. Are you squatting around a tribal fire or at the backstop of a baseball game? How do you feel?

Feeling full

- Diaphragm activation and release. Drop the air down into your belly and fill your lungs completely. Once they feel comfortably full, try to take in a little more – the sensation for me resembles having eaten too much and feeling full. Hold that air for a few seconds, then relax and release it. Don't force the air out; just let it escape naturally, as if it were from a balloon. Check in with your body and breathe gently, noticing the release of any tension in your stomach area. These breaths can help you manage nerves and alleviate performance butterflies. Visualize a time and place where you might feel relaxed yet full. Where are you now? At a restaurant or perhaps enjoying a gourmet picnic?

Rhythmic breathing

- Count silently as you breathe. When you feel ready, add your imagination and make the counts count! Breathe to a rhythm or music. Perhaps you can choose world or culturally inspired music. Close your eyes and transport yourself to that place as you breathe. Visualize the environment and engage your senses – what are the smells and sounds, the tastes and textures of the location you've imagined? Are you on a beach in South America or in a high-altitude village in Nepal? Or are you in a pub in Ireland or a taverna in Greece? Can you taste the salt in the air, feel the chill on your skin or hear the sounds of joy and celebration?

Yoga – Breathe in a square

In Sanskrit, 'prana' refers to life energy, while 'yama' denotes control. Pranayama, or yogic breathing exercises, encompasses breathing patterns that can both energize and calm the mind while awakening and controlling the diaphragm and airflow. Yogic breathing employs nasal breaths to stimulate and stabilize the brain. One technique I often use with beginner students is my version of Sama Vritti (equal breath), which I call 'Breathing in a Square'. This method helps cultivate awareness of the beginning and end of the breath cycle, pausing on 'empty' and 'full' while recognizing the body's natural breathing response. Follow this four-part cycle: exhale, pause, inhale, pause – maintaining a moderate pace or slowing down for a more tranquil breath.

- While breathing through your mouth, use one hand to trace a body-width square in front of you. Count four clicks for each side. Exhale fully as you draw up one side of the square, rest briefly on empty while drawing across the top, then inhale through your nose and mouth as your hand descends down the other side, resting on full as you sketch the bottom side of the square. Repeat this pattern several times. What could that square and the clicks represent? What can you imagine? Are you the characters Riff or Anybodys from *West Side Story*? Or perhaps a magician?

The singer's and actor's breath

Traditionally, a singer's breath involves inhaling through the mouth, which opens the larynx and is efficient. However, breathing through both the nose and mouth is gaining popularity, and nasal breathing in specific contexts can open and awaken resonant spaces in unique ways. Practise inhaling air using these three ways.

In the complex world of musical theatre, our breathing fuels our singing, acting, and dancing. It is a vital part of storytelling. A 'story breath' conveys and integrates our physical needs with our emotional expression, signalling authenticity. Both a technical singer/actor breath and a 'story breath' can occur simultaneously; it's a case of 'and' not 'either/or'. However, let us begin with the technical aspect – the singer's and actor's breath.

There are several ways to teach breathing techniques to novice singers. The most common method is intercostal diaphragmatic breathing, which involves expanding the ribcage, engaging the intercostal muscles, and activating the diaphragm by relaxing specific torso muscles during inhalation and engaging them during exhalation. If you have been instructed to breathe with a soft abdomen, a feeling

WHOLE-SELF ACTIVATION AND BREATHING

of descent, and a gentle swing of the ribcage as you inhale, then that's the method you are using. This style of breathing can also be called belly breathing or floor breathing (diaphragmatic).

Wall breath, or back breath (intercostal), is another breathing technique that focuses more on the work of the intercostal muscles. It places energy slightly higher and is often used in more contemporary singing styles. Contemporary vocalists employ this higher breath placement in the upper body to achieve a louder, belting sound. Although this breathwork style is specific to high-intensity pop, rock, and musical theatre, learning to breathe deeply and access energy in the lower abdomen is essential for creating resonance and depth in vocal tone across all genres.

- Standing in a comfortable neutral position, gently blow out air, feeling and hearing it across your relaxed lips. Take a brief note of your sensation of emptiness. With your mouth closed, mentally count to three, then open your mouth and allow the air to drop into your lungs. Your diaphragm will descend naturally. The feeling is one of expansion into your pelvis and around to your lower back. Notice your floating ribs expanding at the sides. Visualize your torso as a piano accordion or a pair of bellows.
- Both the intercostal and abdominal muscles work to optimize subglottal pressure and airflow. During any diaphragmatic breathing exercise, use your hands to feel the abdomen at work. I often place my thumb against my navel and let my hand spread over my lower abdomen to sense the muscles contracting during an exhale. You can also move your fingers to locate the four muscle support points of a diamond, as described by Janice Chapman in her book *Teaching and Teaching Singing:*[2] the low abdominal/pubic symphysis, just above your pubic bone; the xiphoid region just below the sternum; and the muscles at the sides and back of your waistband, just inside your hip bones. Try saying *'Ha, ha, ha'*. As you exhale to feel these muscles engage.
- Practise a SPLAT breath (Singers Please Loosen Abdominal Tension): activate your diaphragm by relaxing your abdominal muscles as you take a quick, low breath. Then, exhale the air steadily and evenly. Repeat several times. You can use a straw in water to create bubbles or perform lip trills to engage those lower muscles. Often, in songs, the moments to breathe are brief. Learning to release the abdomen quickly in order to attain a deep supportive breath is essential. A thought can trigger that spontaneously.

Primal breath

A musical director once told me there are a hundred different breaths for a hundred different moments, and theatre practitioner Antonin Artaud agrees, stating, *'It is certain that for every feeling, every movement of the mind, every leap of human emotion, there is a breath that belongs to it.'*[3]

Inspiration – the intake of air into our lungs – is one of the most potent nonverbal forms of communication that humans use. Inspiration is, indeed, inspirational! Subconscious thought often triggers our breath intake before we realize we've taken it. Before we can fully recognize or articulate our thoughts, the breath needed to convey them is already present. And even before we utter a sound, the way we inhale sets the scene and begins the story we are either trying to tell or conceal. I can instantly tell when a singer isn't engaged or genuinely connected to their thoughts if their breath seems out of sync with the moment they are singing about. The efficient, supported airflow required for singing can also convey the truth of the moment; both can be achieved with a 'story' or primal breath.

Instinct-driven breathing is a subject I began exploring while teaching primal sound (see Chapter 11). A broad approach to breathing usually employs intercostal and diaphragmatic techniques; primal breath urges actors to intuitively link their thoughts with their breath, aligning it with the size, energy or strength of the emotion being expressed. Primal breath liberates the performer, allowing the intake of air to enhance storytelling, creating an impression of spontaneity or authenticity for the audience.

Utilizing primal breath does not require the abandonment of traditional breathing techniques; instead, actors can instinctively access the method, speed, and placement of their breath to convey the story. Furthermore, actors can cultivate this breath to make intentional choices, contemplating questions such as: Where do you find the thought? Can you extract it from the external environment and draw it inward, or does it emerge from within your body? These enquiries enable actors to intertwine thought and breath. When paired with established breathing techniques, primal breath can immediately connect the actor with the audience. Stimuli elicit instinctual or subconscious responses, and the breath used to express these will naturally reflect the energy and urgency of those thoughts. Your breath and sound can equally narrate the story of the song or scene.

> Hark back to Chapter 2 and our silent movie experiment with Clara Bow. We can also see the power of a telling 'story breath' by watching others with the sound off. Use a pair of earphones, and in a place where people are conversing, 'listen' without hearing, perhaps in a shopping centre, sporting event, or theatre foyer. Watch how their breath pre-empts the conversation and flags the mood, thought, or emotion before it is expressed.

Primal breath enables you to convey your story with the same energy as the emotions you express, all in a safe and supportive manner. Provided that the singing is not excessively high or vocally complex, primal breath will suffice for most sung phrases, especially for speech-quality singing in Golden-age or contemporary musicals. Primal breath can be layered over a lower singer's breath if increased air support is needed. Of course, there is less flexibility with the breath intake required in opera, which is not amplified and requires specific breath management to produce a complex and powerful vocal tone. Nevertheless, in musical theatre, integrating primal breath into a supportive inhalation can enhance good subglottal pressure, flow, and believable physicality. Veteran Musical Director Michael Tyack agrees, *'connecting breath to thought is another concept that will help synergise a performance'*.

Although primal breath is inherently instinctual, here are some tactics to stimulate it and to become more familiar with its value.

- When warming up, incorporate a reason or intention into your air intake. Give your breath a meaningful 'Why?'. Ask yourself, 'What am I thinking or feeling?' Then, using a specific 'stimulus' thought or subtext, inhale to convey that thought. You can also add this intake to the conclusion of your intercostal diaphragmatic breath. Short phrases like *'Oh no!', 'Yippee!', 'Stay!', 'Wow!', 'Wait!', 'Don't go!', 'I want!'* can guide your breathing. Consider these phrases as you inhale, without controlling your breath. Notice what your body instinctively and intuitively wants to do.
- As you contemplate a line's subtext, take an instinctive breath. Mentally narrate the story as you exhale instead of articulating the lyrics. On your second breath, express the lines during your exhalation, intertwining your thoughts with the text. Consciously consider your thoughts and what you wish to convey before speaking. Then, align that thought and breath with the actual text.

Primal breath serves as a shortcut to attaining the ideal setup for authentic communication. If you're uncertain about primal breath and how to integrate it into your performance, consider delving into the realm of primal sound, which will be discussed in Chapter 11. Above all, enjoy the journey of uncovering what your breath, imagination, and body can accomplish.

Grounding and connecting

Body awareness and groundedness are essential. Being grounded entails finding a good postural balance in a physically neutral position while accessing the physical, mental, and emotional readiness to engage. We began our activation by finding an engaged neutral stance. Now, let's extend that sense of balance and physical ease. With each exercise, allow your mind, heart, and senses to evoke a story, a memory, or an imagined scenario. Below are some simple suggestions to keep the imagination flowing. The best ideas are those that you come up with yourself.

Finding engaged neutral

Find your engaged neutral with small incremental check-ins.

- Feel the ground beneath your feet. With slight movements from back to front, rock forward onto the balls of your feet while keeping your heels on the floor and your knees soft – not locked. Circle your pelvis, then relax back to the centre. Slump forward, bending your spine from the waist, and hang for a moment. Then, vertebra by vertebra, slowly re-stack your spinal column and balance your head above it. The feeling should be one of release and ease.
- Roll your shoulders several times, lifting them before letting them drop. Then, gently swing one arm forward and back, followed by the other, allowing them to unwind and find their resting position. Swinging your arms while you breathe opens up the ribcage. Continue swinging one arm at a time – back, forward, then let it settle naturally. Inhale as your arm goes back, and exhale as it moves forward. Feel the power of an aligned body energized by breath. Repeat this six times, then let your arms find their still point.
- Recheck your head position – close your eyes, let your head drop to your chest, and relax there as you gently ease your neck and shoulder muscles. Stay in this position for ten seconds, breathing deeply, then slowly straighten up, breathing as you go, and imagine balancing your head atop a flowing stream of water – like a ping pong ball on a water bubbler. Open your eyes and gaze toward your imaginary horizon. Relax your facial muscles and slightly release your jaw. Breathe gently and deeply through your nose and mouth in this position, filling your body with buoyancy.
- In your grounded, neutral position exercise, incorporate some imaginary environments. For instance, visualize floating in the ocean: extend your arms out from your sides as if you are in the ocean up to your shoulders. Imagine the water on your skin and the gentle tidal movement lifting you onto your toes and then settling you back so your feet touch the sand; feel the support of water all around you. Dive down into the water, surface again, and float. The tide recedes, and now you are standing on solid ground. Your arms have come down to your sides. Walk back up the beach, feeling connected to the stable ground beneath you.

- Imagine you're flying. You're a bird – what kind? You decide. Move around the room. You're up in the sky, swooping and soaring over rooftops, looking down at the world. Or you're a sea eagle gliding over the water, catching a fish before rising into the sky. Breathe the rarified air. Return to earth, settle down, and bring your wings (arms) to rest by your side.
- Or imagine yourself as a butterfly in a chrysalis, ready to emerge. Standing in neutral, release your head and back, and roll down to hang. Breathe into your back and feel the shell beginning to split open. Sense that space expand, and from your rolled position, slowly straighten your body and unfurl your wings from your shoulder blades. Breathe deeply, inhale the air, and observe your new surroundings. Feel the breeze fluttering your wings (arms) and strength flowing into your legs. Prepare to push off the earth and fly.

Puppet play

- Practise muscle release through puppet play. Begin in a comfortable neutral stance, with your feet a hip-width apart. Raise your arms as if they are being held at the wrists by marionette strings. As the imaginary strings that hold you in place are cut, flop down in stages: one arm at a time, cutting the strings at your wrists, elbows, and shoulders, followed by your head to your chest, and lastly, from your chest to your waist. Hang from your waist and enjoy the complete release.
- Keep your knees soft, with weight balanced over them and your feet. Check your back, shoulder, and neck muscles. Lift each arm slightly and then let them drop. Now, release your hips and allow your pelvis to wiggle and stay loose. Jiggle a little in that position before slowly uncurling to stand upright. Puppet play can also be a fun game if you work in pairs – one person can act as the puppeteer, using verbal instructions or a gentle touch to direct various parts of the other person's body, the puppet, to move and respond.

Front foot rocks

You can add energy to your stance by gently rocking forward from a neutral position into a state of engaged readiness. I refer to this as 'front footing', which can help convey heightened emotions in spoken or sung text.

- Begin in a neutral stance or with one foot slightly in front of the other. Shift your weight forward a little, then rock back to a neutral position. Notice the difference. Rock back on your heels, being aware of how your body feels. Observe how it affects your breathing. Return to a neutral stance. As you transition from a forward, energized position to neutral, create a narrative. Are you waiting for your name to be called to join a team? Or are you waiting for a bus? Where, when or why? Connect your thoughts and emotions to your physical presence.
- Add shadowboxing to the front footing exercise. Come onto the balls of your feet and assume a boxer's stance, with your fists raised near your face and one foot positioned in front of the other. Visualize an opponent in front of you. Begin shifting your weight in the rhythmic boxer's dance, breathing freely and deeply as you move and weave. Return to a neutral stance and perform the

WHOLE-SELF ACTIVATION AND BREATHING

jelly wobble. As you breathe, picture yourself as jelly on a plate or a jellyfish swaying. Wiggle freely for twenty seconds.

Walk, run, stop

- Get the blood flowing and slightly elevate your heart rate. Keeping your body loose, begin an energized, focused walk, then run, and then back to walking, before standing still. Perform this in ten to twenty second intervals. If desired, you may play upbeat music in eight to sixteen bar segments.

- Begin your energized walk with a specific intention set in a distinct environment, such as hurrying along a bustling city street to meet an old friend. Alternatively, you might weave through the chaos of department store sales in search of a gift. Imagine yourself walking along a beach on the first day of a long-awaited holiday, or perhaps you find yourself lost in a forest, hearing wild animals behind you. In each scenario, spend at least thirty to sixty seconds visualizing the situation and fully immersing yourself in the thought and the walk/run/stop.

Allow yourself to be fully present in the moment, both physically and mentally. Don't force an emotional response; instead, pay attention to any feelings that may arise as you visualize. Always finish the exercise with a relaxed walk around the area, keeping your mind and body in a neutral state and breathing freely.

Ball work

Connecting with other actors on stage, with the story, and the audience creates transactional interactions that are essential for the 'It' Factor. Practise establishing connections with others as part of your activation. Giving, receiving, listening, and responding can be practised using Chekhov's ball-throwing exercise.[4] While best performed in pairs, if need be, you can also work alone: choose a bouncy ball and a wall space to throw against.

- Start with an imaginary ball of any size and later use a real one – a tennis ball size is the easiest to manage. This exercise links the mind with the physical body as you concentrate on the fluid motion of giving and receiving from your partner through the action of the ball.

- Exhale as you shift your weight forward and throw with a smooth, full swing. Inhale while catching the ball most easily with both hands, following through at each moment of catch and release. Acknowledge the brief pause at each change of direction, aligning with the transition from inspiration to expiration. Feel the air rush across your lips as you exhale and touch the back of your throat as you inhale. This exercise embodies Meisner's technique of listening and responding. You are connected to the ball – your energy flows to your partner, who receives it. As the exercise progresses, you can incorporate vocalization with your breathing. This practice sharpens attention and enhances the actor's specificity, linking mind and sight to body.

- Unleash your imagination while throwing the ball. You can try this in slow motion, especially in limited space. Picture yourself in a stadium, tossing the ball for a winning rugby team. Now, catch the ball and either run or kick it to score a goal. Alternatively, envision your hand as a tennis racquet, playing in the Wimbledon finals. After you hit the ball, let your feet dance until you see it return.

Imagine being at a wedding, catching or throwing a bouquet. Or visualize yourself in the shot-put finals at the Olympics. Will you make the winning throw?

Partnering work

Collaborating with others strengthens your connection with fellow actors on stage. If you have the opportunity to work in pairs, embrace the power of opposites that Chekhov explores in his psychophysical work.[5] He encourages participants to walk and move while improvising gestures such as pushing, pulling, lifting, throwing, gathering, and tearing. Think about some scenarios that could incorporate these actions. Below are two examples from my experience.

Sawing and see-sawing

- Imagine using a long-bladed two-man saw to cut through a massive fallen tree. This push-pull action requires synchronizing with each other, feeling and adapting to each other's energy and physicality, while vocalizing as you visualize the weight and difficulty of the task.

- Imagine you are six years old. With your partner, get on a see-saw in a park and start to see-saw together. Begin slowly and move from a squat at the bottom to a little leap on your tiptoes at the top. Find your rhythm together as you work in opposition. Add vocalizations as you enjoy the moment.

Improvising and atmosphere

'Creative Twisting' with physical imagination

This next warm-up exercise draws on clowning physicality and adapts Seidenstein's Creative Twist exercise alongside another of his exercises, Twist Choreography.[6] This excellent exercise stimulates the imagination and encourages actors' instinctual responses through physical improvisation. Creative twisting uses physical techniques to simultaneously loosen both the body and mind.

- Begin by standing tall with your feet slightly wider than your hips and turned slightly outward. Keep your mind neutral. With your arms relaxed by your sides, use your pelvis to twist to the left, then to the right, repeating this motion four times. As you twist, your arms, though relaxed, will naturally splay to about forty-five degrees. Ensure you release your opposite heel during the body twist to allow for free movement. Keep your eyes following your twists; look to the back of you, then forward as you move back through the front position to the opposite side. After the four twists, perform four smaller rotations to gently unwind, with your arms down by your hips. Then return to two larger twists. On the third rotation, pivot into a natural turn, finishing with a spin that allows your arms to move freely. Without cognitive planning, go where your body leads, and let your intuition guide your movements. Allow your physical movement to continue for several moments, nurturing your imagination by adjusting your legs, arms, and/or voice. Trust that your body and subconscious mind will convey a story without interference from your thoughts. Don't try to force anything. You might trigger a character, a scenario or a feeling. Explore. Play.

This outside-in exercise allows the body to influence the mind rather than the other way around. Your improvisations, following the physical twist, should last thirty to forty seconds and can morph and change as your whim takes you. If you wish, you can add vocalization to this exercise as it progresses. It often feels strange to start; the mind wants to know what to do before we do it, but we must trust the moments that happen after the twist. You will discover that something will emerge!

'Nothing' Exercise

Another improvisational exercise is Ira Seidenstein's Nothing Exercise[7], which is designed to ignite our creativity and emotions. Ira explains that as we create, we engage our bodies, emotions, imaginations, and intellects. Instead of restricting our abilities, we can learn to navigate through them together and improvise.

- Breathing freely, naturally walk forward about six or seven steps, while moving your arms into three random positions. Keep your arms in the third position as you come to a stop. Pause for a few seconds in a relaxed neutral before moving your entire body at once. This will evoke a feeling within you. Embrace that feeling and explore wherever your body guides you for about thirty to forty seconds. You may feel inclined to vocalize. Follow your body's lead.

  This exercise is about having fun and exploring. Don't let yourself settle or feel stuck. Add a detail to refresh the moment and play.

- The Nothing Exercise can be expanded by working with opposites. After ten to fifteen seconds of your initial improvisation, switch to an opposite – whether it's an idea, feeling, direction or physicality. One of your processes will trigger this intuitively. It could be your body, emotions or imagination. For instance, if your first improvisation is loud and boisterous, brimming with energy, you might contract into someone timid, small, and cringing. Explore that state for a while before returning to the original idea. You can experiment with several opposites.

> When you exercise, create the bigness of the world you imagine you are in. Give yourself room to move in the story and world you are creating. The bigger your story, the more play space you can subconsciously create for us.

Maintain a clear mind while standing in a neutral position; allow your body the freedom to decide what to do. The goal of this exercise is to remove premeditated thinking and encourage a sense of spontaneity and play that links instinctual responses with physical freedom and expression.

The Twist Choreography and the Nothing Exercise can serve as a starting point for an improvised Atmospheric Walk. Allow your body to lead the way; access your sense memory, and your imagination will follow. This 'outside-in' approach balances the 'inside-out' method that many actors are more familiar with.

Atmospheric walks

Atmospheres are carriers of emotion. Creating an atmosphere, or recognizing and engaging with an existing one, is a powerful way for actors to express themselves and forge palpable connections with the audience. We experience atmospheric energy when our cognitive and instinctual thoughts, feelings, and imagination interact with others or the environment. Additionally, we can join and respond to atmospheres created by others.

The Atmospheric Walks exercise is another psychophysical practice I've adapted from Chekhov.[8] Here, we explore atmospheres and our movements in and through them. In the past, I have provided side coaching for this scenario while an accompanist improvised atmospheric music. You may wish to find an instrumental soundtrack to support your imagined story or opt for the power of silence. If space allows, feel free to move around the room or, if necessary, select a more confined setting. Below is an example; create and improvise your own sensory stimulation. Two scenarios are narrated for you on the companion website.

- Imagine taking an atmospheric walk at night. Step out of the darkened building onto a cold, wintry path. You are alone and heading home. Move through your space, envisioning the biting cold air and the snowy ground. Imagine physical sensations: feeling like a block of ice inside, with stiff fingers and joints, trudging through the difficult terrain. Stop momentarily to remember something you have forgotten and left behind. Will you go back? Breathe in the icy air and look at where you have come from and where you are headed. Make a decision. Your choice! Finally, you arrive at the door of a home. Is it yours? Or a friend's? How do you get in? Do you have a key, or do you knock? The door opens to a warmly lit interior, filled with the warmth of a roaring fire, a waiting family, and a sense of welcome.

Imaginative vocalizing

Exploring resonance

We are now ready to begin vocalizing. Instead of using the traditional 'singer's breath', relax, breathe freely, and allow your body to access what it needs. Connect with your body and imagination!

- Hum into your body to awaken resonance. Direct your sound into various parts of your body and gently pat those areas with your fists or open palms. As you hum, begin with your chest and move to your stomach, back, buttocks, legs, and arms, spending about eight seconds on each area.
- Add rhythm and accent to your sound to connect your breath with your voice. The Accent Method[9] breathing utilizes voiceless and voiced fricative consonants to create a semi-occluded or half-closed vocal tract shape. Incorporating rhythmic patterns to enhance breath and body awareness is the cornerstone of this method.[10] Use voiceless fricative consonants such as *s, f, th* (as in <u>th</u>in), *and sh*, along with their voiced counterparts – *z, v, th* (as in <u>th</u>e), *and dj* (similar to <u>judge</u>). Begin by taking a low, easy breath and vocalizing during exhalation. When you feel ready, introduce a rhythmic pattern during exhalation, repeating it as you work through the voiceless and voiced consonants.

'Swiss Army Knife' exercise

This next warm-up, which I affectionately call my Swiss Army Knife exercise, serves as my go-to, multi-use tool for a quick vocal check-in. This exercise:

- reminds the body to engage breath support low in the torso through rhythmic, emphasized sounds,
- covers the five pure vowel sounds,
- positions the sound in five resonant spaces within our vocal tract,
- utilizes a complete vocal range from low to high,
- imaginatively connects sound to a character or story.

Keep in mind that this exercise focuses on making sound rather than singing, so don't strive for a beautiful tone. Just vocalize and think about how to place the sound in the different spaces we can open up. Have fun and experiment with it; don't overthink! Here it is:

- Running at a tempo of around mm=108, the exercise consists of 4/4 bars, each featuring three rhythmic vowel sounds followed by a low belly breath intake on the fourth beat. This pattern repeats seven times for each vowel sound, and on the eighth bar, say the phrase or word that captures the essence of the sound. Then, continue the pattern with the next vowel. The order of the vowels is intentional.

1. Ho, Ho, Ho, breathe, seven times. Then say, '*Merry Christmas!*' Breathe low and think the Ho sound down in your belly, tapping into lower resonances as we imagine being Santa Claus.
2. Ha, Ha, Ha, breathe, seven times. Then say, '*La–di–da!*' This vowel is voiced on a descending pattern of high, medium and low, with each sound accessing the space created by a raised soft palate. Think opera diva!
3. Heh, Heh, Heh, breathe, seven times. Then say, '*Have I got a deal for you!*' Reverse the direction of pitch and use your speech-quality sound (M1) to go from low to medium to high. Imagine this sound coming from wide in your neck and back of your mouth, creating retraction or a laugh space in the larynx, where the false vocal folds can retract to create greater width in your timbre. This vowel will also extend your speech-quality range. Try and locate the chuckle space we can feel in our neck. Think dodgy car salesman!
4. Hee, Hee, Hee, breathe, seven times. Then say, '*Cheeky monkey*'. Feel like a cheeky monkey and place this sound in your lifted cheeks, vocalizing around Bb 4 to Eb 5. It encourages forward resonance and brightness in the tone.
5. Hoo, Hoo, Hoo, breathe seven times. Then say, '*Sad owl*'. The vocal pitch for this sound is higher, in M2 or head register, possibly around F5 to Ab5, and it comes with a laryngeal tilt or a sense of leaning or crying into the sound, expressing sadness, almost like a Boo, Hoo, Hoo.

Loaded SOVT sounds

Semi-occluded vocal tract (SOVT) sounds are excellent for warm-ups and rehabilitation.

- Using the power of your thoughts, direct them to various parts of your body. Visualize a sound in a specific area within you, and then feel it resonate there as you vocalize. Experiment with positioning it in your gut, chest, face or at the top of your skull. Envision the sound emanating from your belly or your hand.
- Next, visualize the sounds existing outside of you. Examples include 'zzz' – the buzz of a bee; a low lip trill – the deep sound of a large horse; 'mmm' – a deep moan from your pelvis; 'vv' – the whine of an electric drill; or the sound of playing a toy trumpet in a jazz band using puffy cheeks. Infuse your sounds with imagination and narrative as you move around the room. Pay attention to how your abdominal muscles engage with SOVT sounds.

Vowels with attitude

Open your sound now into vowels with attitude! Use a pure vowel as your text and discover the meaning that can reside in each vowel. This will come easily if you respond instinctively – don't overthink it!

- Choose one vowel sound as a trigger, for instance, 'Ah'. Say it and go where your sound leads you. You may use long sustained sounds or shorter utterances at any pitch or melisma. Let the meaning of this vocalization arise without preconception.
- Stay in that moment and allow it to develop as you vocalize. Take ten to fifteen seconds to focus on that thought and notice what your voice does without any cognitive planning. You may uncover something playful or cathartic.

This exercise utilizes the concept of primal sound and prepares us for spontaneous play, something we will explore in the next chapter.

If you find that challenging at first, you can start with a subtext or key phrase like 'I want to!' Visualize the phrase and then vocalize the thought using the vowel. Here are a few simple examples:

- Ah – can be a sigh; it can mean boredom, relief, tiredness or waking up. Or 'Ah, I get it!' Find your own thoughts. Notice how pitch, airflow, and vocal tone will change instinctually to match your thoughts.
- Oh – can be disappointment, dismay, embarrassment or surprise.
- Eh – can be a question, a realization, resignation or boredom.
- Ee – can be a squeal of excitement, or terror, a cheeky laugh or pain.
- Oo – can be awe or wonder, the unexpected or pain too!

Notice how your breath intuitively adapts to align with the underlying narrative. The speed of your intake, whether your breath pauses briefly before being released, and the intensity and duration of your exhalation are all subconsciously shaped by the power of your thoughts.

Finding energetic focus and readiness

Finish your activation with a focus exercise. Depending upon when and where you are warming up and the energy level you require for the moment before you, you may choose something energetic or calming. I have seen actors stretch or jog on the spot and shake out their limbs on the side of the stage. Some speak a personal affirmation and find a point of stillness. Below are two focus exercises I have used in masterclasses.

Energizing meditation

The first is an eight-minute guided meditation. The purpose of this one is to ignite inner radiance by awakening the senses and internal energetic centres – mind, heart, will, and body, including arms, legs, and loins. It can lead you to a place of calm readiness. I have narrated this for you on the companion website.

Meditation is an effective way to focus the mind and create space for your imagination. While the energy valence for this exercise may appear low, the radiance gained can be powerful. Remember to breathe deeply, keeping your body relaxed. You will feel energy warming your body as you imagine the space inside your skin filling with light or with a liquid river that can flow through you. Take time to cultivate an awareness of the natural energies that reside within you and practise harnessing those energies at will.

'Crossing the Threshold' exercise

The second focus exercise is shorter and employs the Chekhovian concept of crossing a threshold. I first encountered this idea at a Music Theatre Educators Alliance Conference in New York several years ago. In acting terms, the concept of the threshold represents the liminal space or boundary that separates the everyday, non-performance world from the artistic realm of performing, imagination, and narrative. 'Crossing the Threshold' serves as both a physical and a psychological tactic for centring personal energy and fostering a sense of readiness. There are several ways to achieve this – this is one I use:

- Stand tall in a relaxed, neutral position and breathe deeply. Using your imagination, visualize the performance world you will step into; it may be the stage or platform that actually awaits you. But first, you must cross a threshold to get there. This threshold can be internal or external – a closed door, a curtained doorway, a small brook or a low hedge – anything that separates two spaces.

- Look around and using your senses, take a moment to mindfully acknowledge the space you are currently in as you prepare to cross over into the performance space that awaits. Look up into the sky, through the roof, the clouds, and toward the stars and planets beyond. Imagine a bright golden ball filled with energy from a distant galaxy speeding toward you. This faraway ball of energy grows larger, stronger, and brighter like the sun. As it reaches you, extend your hands to grab that ball of energy; it is as wide as your shoulders. Hold it out in front of you and using your hands, squeeze and meld it, compressing it in size so that it can fit into your hands.

- Focus on that energy ball and feel its dense power. Then, imagine opening your chest cavity and place that ball of energy firmly within you. Close your eyes and sense the ball inside you illuminating your being, sending radiant energy flowing through your veins into your head, flooding your torso, coursing down into your legs, and extending to your fingertips. You are a ball of energy. Open your eyes and feel the light inside you radiating outward. You are radiant.

- Look at your threshold, and confidently and purposefully, take the step or steps and cross it. Pause, stand there and breathe, taking in the view. Claim that new space; make it your own. Breathe in the new air or atmosphere, absorbing it as you radiate warmth into it. If you are in a theatre, take a few steps into the world of the story you're about to tell. It's more than just a stage now. Leave behind the old space, you have reenvisioned your environment; it is ready for your exploration. The ground you walk on now is different.

- Look around you. Are there real or imagined people present? Recognize them and radiate love and joy toward them. If you are in a theatre, gaze out into the auditorium, beyond the world on stage, and see your loved ones sitting there and send your love to them.

Ultimately, that's what all of this is about: love. You are ready.

11
TOOLKIT TECHNIQUES: ACTING AND SINGING

A productive teaching studio is a safe, experimental space where technique and confidence can grow. Arriving with an open mind, a full heart, and a desire to try new things can yield wonderful results for the actor as they explore. Creativity flows, ideas flourish, and metaphors and analogies emerge like thoughts plucked from a river of intuitive energy. In my studio, sometimes new ideas stick and become favourites. Other times, they create pathways for a single performer in a specific moment; they fulfil their purpose and may not return. I often tell students, 'Write that thought down before it's gone!'

Michael Chekhov stated, *'What we usually call "developing one's talent" is often nothing more than freeing it from the influences that hamper, occlude, and frequently destroy it entirely.'*[1]

In this chapter, I will share some of my favourite acting and singing tools and suggest ways to apply them in scene work and song study. Each tool can be used to encourage and combine your intrinsic performative processes (as discussed in Chapter 3). Acting exercises and imaginative play can be incorporated into most singing exercises, and vice versa; combining skills by cross-training energizes the synergized performer.

Exercises are loosely organized around the intrinsic performative process they influence. Some tools engage multiple processes. For instance, creating and inhabiting an 'atmosphere' involves strong visualization (*sensate*) merged with imagination *(psycho)*; the accompanying release of emotion (*emotio*) brings it all to life. If necessary, refer back to Table 3.2 to remind yourself of the characteristics of the seven performative processes and understand what qualities the toolkit can unlock.

Acting tools

The acting tools included in the kit come from various sources: traditional techniques, physical theatre, clowning, and some of my own ideas and hybrid combinations.

My approach is built upon the sure foundation of acting masters Michael Chekhov and Konstantin Stanislavski. Their practices and exercises engage both the body and mind to create believable characters, evoke emotions, and generate energetic flow. I have also drawn inspiration from various other acting methods, including those of Sanford Meisner (1987), Uta Hagen (1991), Ira Seidenstein (2018), Ivana Chubbuck (2004), and Rudolf Laban (Newlove and Dalby, 2004); I have explored their methods in classes and some of their concepts have been adapted and incorporated here. I selected tools from these sources that stimulate specific performative processes, including the senses, cognitive thought, text-based work, instinctual and imaginative play, psychophysicality, and the activation of energetic centres. As noted in the previous chapter, breathwork plays a vital role in accessing these processes.

Sensate tools

Our senses help us learn and recall information in various ways, often blending visual, aural, and kinaesthetic elements. When actors freely access a sensory experience – whether real or imagined – and immerse themselves in that moment, the audience embarks on that journey with them and responds with empathy. Recently, I watched a video of my son walking to the edge of a mountain precipice on the Eiger in Switzerland; he gazed over the edge, thousands of feet below. My sensory response transported me there; my heart raced, and my skin tingled. I felt fear, even though he was safe on the ground while I watched the video. We can evoke similar responses from audiences through the power of effective sensory stimulation, creating truthful storytelling. Try experimenting with:

- Five-sense stimulation. Using real or imagined stimuli allows the body's sensory connections to generate an authentic response. Awaken each sense in turn and explore it fully. Begin by listening to and engaging with your imagined environment. Active listening, a cornerstone of Sanford Meisner's work (1987), sparks an actor's authentic response.
- Practise using your visual memory to awaken your imagination. A simple way to start is by slowly turning in a circle and observing your surroundings. When you face forward again, try to recall what you saw behind you – the space, the furniture, and the energy – and visualize it without turning around.
- Sensory recall: The faster you can dimensionally access your environment, the easier it becomes to immerse yourself in your imaginary world. Practise engaging all your senses by recalling familiar objects:
  - Sit or lie down in a comfortable position. Close your eyes. Breathe easily and find your resting state.
  - Imagine an everyday object – something you use regularly, like a set of keys, a phone or laptop, or cutlery.
  - Look at it with your mind's eye. Visualize it in detail, including colour, shape, design, weight, and texture.
  - Imagine holding it. What does it feel like? Its texture and weight?
  - If you put your tongue on it, what would it taste like?
  - Does it have a smell?
  - What sounds are associated with it? Can you tap or shake it? What sound does it produce when you place it down? Expand your sensory recall.
- Visualize a scene. Drawing from memory and imagination, construct a virtual visual world. Focus on creating a 'real space' where you can position yourself and share your story. Determine the location of all elements in your field of vision. Use your imagination to establish the atmosphere. Identify the stimuli within your world that can drive the dramatic action of the scene. Make discoveries. Incorporate targeting and referencing to enhance clarity.

Ideational cognition: thought, text, and music-based work

Traditional acting and directing methods often include a 'table read' to establish the characters' backgrounds and the context of the story or scene. Cognitive dissection and the work conducted in this area create the fertile soil in which an actor's craft can grow and flourish. Engage in this work but recognize that it serves merely as the foundation for layering performative processes, not the final product. Here are ways to enhance depth.

- Create a subtext. Identify the specific thought that drives the idea in the text and give voice to that thought that is underlying the actual words. This might be a phrase, a question, a statement, or even an expletive. Sometimes, it might be just a grunt or groan, as no words can fully capture the thought – that's okay! Any vocal or physical expression of the thought adds dimension to the lyrics you will sing.
- Mine the text. Deconstruct the lyrics to construct meaning by exploring grammar, consonants, vowels, transitive (actionable) verbs, imperatives, negatives, adjectives, and adverbs (descriptors, colours). Investigate the sound, including alliteration, assonance, consonants, and vowels. Roll these sounds around in your mouth and body. Relish the richness of language and etymology. Don't overlook seemingly small words like 'if', 'and' and 'but'.
- Monologue the text. Songs transform into scenes, and scenes become songs when you find the rhythm, ebb, and flow in the words. Musicality can become a part of the communication norm. Play with your delivery: breathe a spoken line, then articulate it or spontaneously improvise a melody to express the thought that forms the subtext. Try speaking the text while the accompaniment plays to discover the natural ebb and flow of the lyrics.
- Find intention. Ask questions to establish focus and direction, such as: 'What do you want?' 'From whom?' and 'How will you get it?' This fundamental technique promotes specificity and energy and explores action words that open options for actors to explore (Hagen, 1991; Moss, 2005; Stanislavski, 1980).
- Look at 'the moment before'. Thinking and breathing in that moment will add impetus and dimension to the following scene. Your psychological connection and awareness of the moment before will invoke thought and breath, empowering the voice.
- Utilize both 'inside-out' and 'outside-in' approaches to cultivate easy access to thought. Identify your natural tendencies and the intrinsic personal traits you bring to the character to bring it to life (inside-out). Next, envision the character as fully formed and embody that: the look, the gait, the posture, and other aspects of the physicality that you can make your own (outside-in).
- Look for the universal truth within the text, character, or story. Energy levels increase when you actively connect with the fundamental truths reflected in a character's plight; embrace these truths as they resonate with the journey of life. A good starting point can be the composer's subtext (underlying thoughts) or the song's overarching *raison d'être*; these ignite passion and energy. It could involve justice, hope, dreams, desire or purpose. These universal concepts act as powerful bridge builders.
- Examine the transactional thoughts present in the text and note the possible choices before responding. Practise discovering the space between thought, emotion, and decision-making, and

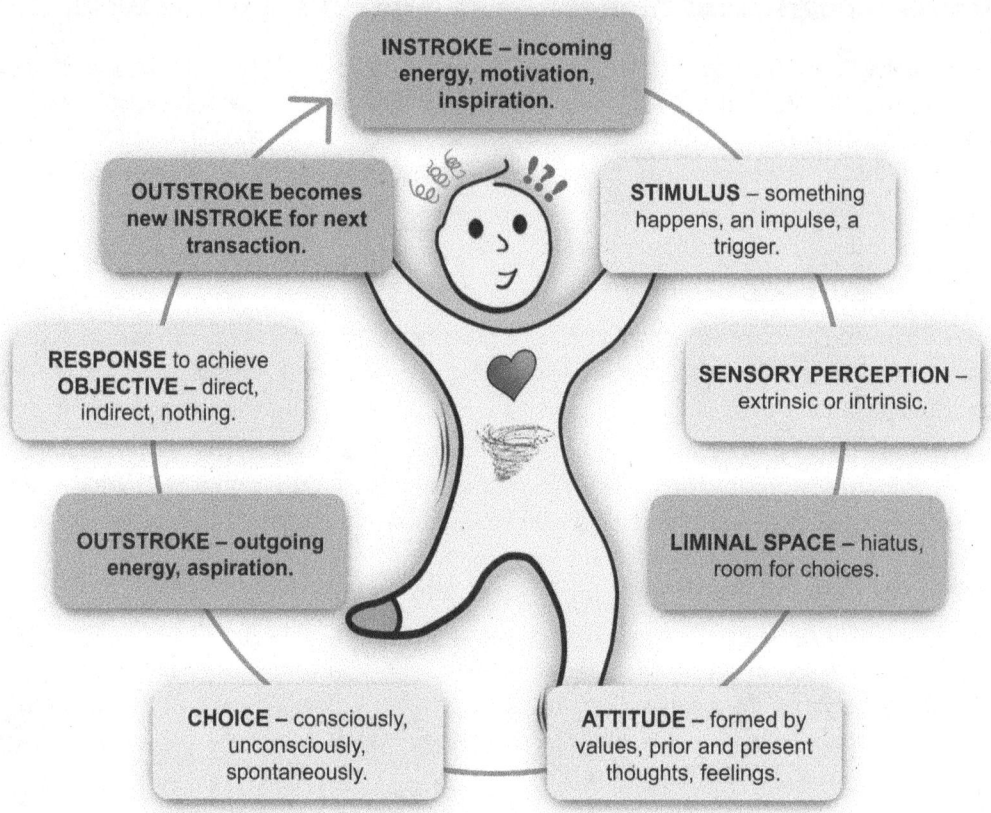

Figure 11.1 What happens between stimulus and response.

actively make a choice. Holocaust survivor and psychologist Viktor Frankl observed the power in the choices we make in the liminal space between stimulus and response. A saying often attributed to him states, '*Between stimulus and response, there is a space. In that space is our power to choose our response. In our response lies our growth and our freedom*'.[2] This space may only last microseconds, but the audience engages with the actor as they make choices in these brief moments. This aligns with a cyclical action-response transaction graph I encountered as a young theatre student, the elements of which are explained in Figure 11.1.

Your response to the stimulus becomes the new stimulus for the next response, and so it continues. Apply this concept to a section of text. Take your time to explore the space between each stimulus and your response.

Intuitive cognition: imagination and instinct

Your imagination is an extraordinary tool for creating habitable new worlds out of thin air. As Dr Seuss writes, '*Oh, the thinks you can think!*'[3] By tapping into the mind's spontaneous, playful, and often hidden workings, a wealth of possibilities emerges for developing and layering a character. I firmly believe that engaging in the imaginative or 'psycho' performative process can have the most immediate and

ACTING AND SINGING

influential effect on the 'It' Factor. Much of my inspiration for unlocking imaginative play comes from Michael Chekhov's psychophysical exercises – some of which I will reference in the next chapter, as they are both psycho and physical. Below are some additional ideas in my toolkit.

- Perform the Nothing exercise or the Creative Twisting exercise (Chapter 10) and, as you finish the pause or spin, speak the lyric.
- Alternatively, combine the lyrics of your song with its subtext. Weave them together, and, just as a jazz singer improvises new melodic ideas from the original, riff on the thoughts behind the lyrics or text – your subtext. Express these new lyrics as you explore your feelings.
- Incorporate the ball throwing exercise from your activation warm-up to remain loose and spontaneous. If your lyrics are directed toward someone, vocalize the lyrics during your throw and respond to the stimulus for the next line as the ball is returned. As mentioned in the previous chapter, you can practise this with a tennis ball against a wall.
- If you work in pairs, start a conversational improvisation using a line or two from the text or song. Your partner then makes an offer, either a verbal or physical response to that line, without any preconceived notion of where the story or conversation might lead. Incorporate a physical element, such as throwing a ball, playing an imaginary sport, or dancing together. Engage with the exchange of receiving and responding to another's offer as you explore your intuitive, spontaneous responses.

Make friends with the concept of improvisational play. Many novice performers have expressed discomfort with improv, as they envision it being about performing or presenting a scene rather than inhabiting the moment. Pioneer improvisation educator Viola Spolin[4] provides a wealth of exercises that encourage actors to accept and make offers. Improvisation helps them tap into their instinctual responses to stimuli and connect with their creative selves.

This exercise combines cognitive thinking (*neuro*) with intuitive, spontaneous play (*psycho*).

- Select two fixed points in the story, text, or song. Using these as your starting and ending points, explore and improvise the journey in between. For example, in the song 'Somewhere Over the Rainbow' from *The Wizard of Oz,* two points could be the beginning of the bridge: '*Someday, I'll wish upon a star and wake up where the clouds are far behind me*' and the last line, '*Why, oh, why can't I?*' The first line is hopeful and optimistic, while the last feels wistful and unresolved. What journey can you envision to transition your thoughts from one point to the other?

Using our imagination and visualization can deepen our understanding of the character and reveal a deeper level of emotion that we can then use to bring the character to life.

- Begin a conversation with the character you are portraying. Instead of objectively questioning the character's scene (*neuro*), engage in a dialogue with your imagined character about how they relate to others, participate in specific activities, or express their feelings. As you ask questions, explore the imagined external (*persona and physical*) and internal (*neuro, psycho, emotio*) aspects of your character's life. Create an open space and allow your imagination to receive their responses. Spending time exploring the character's intrinsic processes encourages a deeper level of character development. The character can become fully realized before the actor embodies it, leading to more fulfilling and inspired outcomes, as our life experiences and understanding are not limiting them.

Emotive processes

To introduce the emotive tools, let's explore how emotions manifest and how they can empower an actor's 'It' Factor.

Developing emotional intelligence and maintaining easy, clear access to our feelings are essential life skills. Some Western societal and cultural norms inadvertently teach us to compartmentalize, subjugate or regulate emotional responses under the guise of 'appropriate behaviour'. However, unrestrained access to emotions is crucial when engaging our seven performative processes. These processes inform and empower each other and:

- our senses become our antennae, situating us in time, space, and circumstance,
- our cognitive thoughts provide structure and direction to our intentions,
- our intuitive thoughts open us up to potential and new possibilities,
- our emotions – our inner embodied state of physical and psychological arousal – can fuel both conscious and subconscious thoughts, acting as a springboard for physical action, shaped by individual personality and expressed through technical skill.

Conversely, physical activity – rather than thoughts – can also trigger emotions. The body holds memories buried deep within the muscles and tissues, which can elicit an emotional response. Understanding how these performative processes support and enhance each other is key.

Trying to find or manipulate a feeling is deceptive – the antithesis of our 'It' Factor. In his book *The Intent to Live* (2005), Larry Moss warns actors against playing a mood, as the word spelled backward is 'doom' – a fate that might befall those who make emotion or mood their ultimate goal.[5] Instead, emotion should emerge as a byproduct of conscious or instinctual thought. Unlocking this process requires trusting a strong thought and its inherent power to evoke feelings. In the 1980s, Australian master director and educator Dean Carey taught me this through a simple side coaching exercise he employed in a directing course I took in Sydney. He would say, '*And again*', meaning '*I don't believe you*', repeating it each time I delivered a line or expressed a thought without fully engaging with it.

When thoughts are inhabited rather than merely expressed, emotions flow. They arrive alongside and foster clarity and perceived truthfulness, traversing the subliminal bridge that connects the audience and the performer. This nonverbal, subconscious trafficking of story and emotion creates a platform for participatory inclusion.

So, how can we practise expressing emotions truthfully in imaginary circumstances? There are various approaches to acting with emotion, and depending on your prior experience, some tools may be more effective for you than others. At first glance, some exercises might appear contradictory. Explore which ideas resonate with you or stick with what already works for you.

Sense and emotion memory

Stanislavski promotes the notion that emotions serve as the invisible link between an actor and their audience. His early techniques advocated using actions, personal memories, and empathy; when combined with artistic skill, these practices can evoke emotions during a performance. Stanislavski particularly valued engaging the five senses to stimulate creative imagination and evoke emotion or

ACTING AND SINGING

affective memory, which is a valuable tool for the actor.[6] Stanislavski's early work promoted the inside-out approach for character building, drawing on an actor's cognitive understanding and personal reservoir of experiences. Later, he examined the power of the mind and body in activating emotions.

Here are a few of my 'Stan' based ideas.

- Select a song lyric and explore the thoughts it evokes – considering both the super-text and subtext. Express these thoughts aloud, repeating them to discover fresh perspectives as they evolve. Engage your sense memory to create a personal connection with the essence of the lyric. It may relate to a similar or parallel experience, whether real or imagined, drawn from your memories, dreams, or imaginings. Observe your emotional responses to these thoughts as they emerge.

- Try saying the lyric and your expanded thoughts from a different place in your body to engage other performative processes or energetic centres. This is helpful if you feel trapped in your head or in cognitive understanding and need to move the thought down into your chest or belly or elsewhere in your torso to access your personality or emotions.

- Add physicality to your story; if your body feels stuck, consider moving and pacing or doing something mundane and repetitive, like pretending to vacuum or clean – anything that gets your body moving.

- Alternatively, try the opposite: shut your body's energy away or shake it off. Take your thoughts deep into yourself and quietly look inward to what may not be visible. Tap into that inner well and then express the lyric line. Employ physical forms of expansion and contraction (more on that in the next chapter). Just let any emotions that arise in your body come to the surface and guide you.

- Improvise with tempo and rhythm, which can be created two ways: from the outside in – for example, a leisurely stroll or running late for a train, or from the inside out – an internal response to a given circumstance that reveals itself physically. Contrasting inner and outer tempi creates exciting theatre. Imagine finding quiet stillness amid external chaos or experiencing intense inner turmoil during a funeral.

As you observe different emotions, find a helpful vocabulary for them. Research from the University of California, Berkeley, has identified a rich palette of human expression – at least twenty-seven distinct varieties of emotions, which are often experienced in combination and varying ways.[7] Brené Brown's book *Atlas of the Heart* (2021), also aids our understanding and provides nuances for various emotions and states. She notes: '*Human emotions and experiences are layers of biology, biography, behavior, and back story*'.[8] How many emotional states are on your list?

- Your memory is a powerful resource. 'Reverse engineer' your pathways by connecting your cognitive mind with your emotions: Choose one of the emotions listed and reflect on a time when you felt that emotion or could empathize with someone experiencing it. Quietly and internally, explore that real or imagined memory or response. Sit with the thought and the emotion together. Notice where you might feel it in your body. You might consider journalling your findings if it helps.

As you contemplate these words, explore primal breath and your natural physicality that can convey them.

Accessing objective atmospheres, the 'Higher Self' and love

As discussed in Chapter 4, atmospheres are a powerful link connecting actors to their audience, creating an environment where authentic feelings can emerge. Chekhov's objective atmospheres operate differently from the personal emotions performers can bring to a scene or narrative. They are established around a depicted event or circumstance, which fuels and enhances the actors' emotional journey while also impacting the audience. Objective atmospheres and the feelings they evoke transform intellectual concepts into visceral experiences. The actor and audience begin to share and breathe the same energetically charged air.[9]

- Atmospheric walking. We explored this during our warm-up; it is a wonderful way to claim the physical space you are working in. This psychophysical exercise adds physicality to the imagined atmosphere, allowing the entire body to experience changes in that atmosphere. The more we connect with our imagined surroundings, the greater our access to energy outside ourselves that can be harnessed and integrated.

Chekhov taught his students the power of accessing a palette of higher, purified emotions that are artistically true, which he called the higher ego. By leaving behind the earth-anchored mundanity of everyday life, the performer can reach an inspirational state that transcends yet is felt and perceived by the audience as real. Chekhov also teaches that love must infuse and empower us. Indeed, all I interviewed spoke of how their love of theatre, acting, and sharing stories motivated them. They tapped into something 'other' – their higher creative selves: *'for it is from no other source but the higher self within us that our artistic, creative love derives.'*[10]

- Find a comfortable position and take a moment to clear your mind of the activities that brought you to this moment. Close your eyes and breathe deeply and gently. With each inhalation, imagine pure energy and love flowing into your heart and body. As you exhale, release thoughts that limit your potential, as well as your worries and concerns. Gently expel the last remnants of your everyday self. If it helps, visualize gathering those parts of 'yourself' released into the air and placing them into an imaginary box or container, waiting for you to reconnect with them when needed. (I sometimes envision blowing them into a balloon, which I tie off and set aside.) With every breath, feel yourself filled with light and love. You are now ready to meet your character, step into their story, and inhabit their world, free from personal restrictions or limitations.

Persona processes

Your personality is a wonderful resource to draw upon. While Chekhov promotes the emptying of ego and self, allowing actors to step into their imagined selves, Stanislavski encourages actors to tap into their inner lives and draw from their personal experiences to develop their characters. Whether you embrace one method or both, igniting your 'persona' process involves acknowledging your uniqueness and how it can colour and energize your character. Take time to recognize and appreciate who you are and what fundamentally represents 'you' that you can bring to the stage and to the character. Cultivate and harness your personal, energized power through focused deep stillness, building inner presence and radiance.

Energetic centres

- Explore and access your energetic centres. Your centres are uniquely you and carry overtones of your personality and character. Place or discover your thoughts in various locations: the head, heart, soul, will, and loins. Consider which space to focus on based on whether you are working through something, uncovering a new idea or emotion, feeling something profoundly, or committing to something significant. Remember Simon Phillips instructed his actors to '*Put your brain in the bottom of your stomach; put it there and take a breath to access it.*' Chekhov proposes that action arises from your will, which is centred in and around the solar plexus or gut. If we 'think lower' – down in our gut – we will breathe there. Thoughts generated from a lower place in our body add physical commitment and our personal engagement to the sounds produced. Place your thoughts there, and breath will follow. Following the breath comes physical movement.

- Explore the distinction between thinking and singing or speaking from your head, heart centre, and gut centre. Depending on the material, you can drop the centre even further and place it in your pelvic centre. Take a moment to sing a line from a love song and notice how the placement of your thoughts and the energy you harness affects your experience. One enjoyable song to experiment with is 'Sooner or Later' from the musical *Dick Tracy*. '*Sooner or later, you're gonna be mine. Sooner or later, you're gonna be fine.*'[11] This line serves well as a choice and decision, a heartfelt emotion, a 'boots and all' commitment to the future, or an invitation to bed. Or perhaps it suggests all four possibilities in varying amounts!

- Practise moving different parts of your body from various energetic centres. Imagine your core directing your arms up and down or visualize your energetic pelvis guiding your legs as you walk. Place your sense of self outside your body. Picture yourself as a person of great power, perhaps a pharaoh or Cleopatra from ancient times, with your entourage leading the way as you walk or glide. Feel the expansiveness of your energy extending in front of and behind you as you move forward. The strength of your imagination will activate a personal energy that makes you larger than life in every direction. I once practised this exercise on a busy street in New York, and although I might have imagined it, I felt the oncoming foot traffic parting to make way for me as I walked up West 40th Street. Regardless, the personal power and energy I felt in those moments were genuine.

Psychophysical embodiment

Theatre audiences connect visually to the drama on stage through an actor's embodiment of their character. While much of an actor's work is internal, it must translate into larger performance spaces. The next chapter will provide more ideas on using movement-based exercises to create that heightened embodiment; however, below are a few ways to embody thought.

- Identify the targets and references in the scene. Who are you talking to? About what? Where are they located in your immediate environment? Declan Donnellan's techniques help integrate specificity and direction into the active thought process, bringing imagined environments to life.[12] The audience can perceive even something as simple as the focal point of your eyes. While your physical energy must fill the performance space in which you work, the gaze and focus of your eyes must remain true to the story. Truly 'look' at those imaginary people and things around you.

- Imagine an idea as an entity that arrives or comes to you. Play with how it manifests. The speed and origin of thoughts influence us subliminally and are subconsciously indicated through various means. Ideally, we want that physicality to appear spontaneously, guided by the thought. However, we can practise discovering them.

- Physicalize the location of a thought or idea and how it arrives. Sometimes it hits you; sometimes you must really search for an idea; sometimes you can pluck it out of the air. Thoughts can also feel like a connected stream. What speed is the stream flowing? Where are you in relation to the stream? Are you in the middle of it or on the bank, wanting to dive in?

- Practise finding it in different places: in front – instant realization, which may come with varying intakes of breath that occur simultaneously or afterward; or does it suddenly hit you from behind? Or to one side – up, middle or down – accessing memory or embedded knowledge with different sensory stimuli reminders. What word in the script describes that? Are there indicators? Practise finding the thought in your periphery – a thought arriving from behind or right at the edge of your vision.

Once you have played with physically finding a thought, take those same feelings and energy and internalize them while you deliver the thought or line.

- Physically chart the trajectory of the song or scene. Connect your body to your mind; visualize the beginning, middle, and end. Move around the room and map it out with your body as you sing or speak it. Physically feel the dynamic intensity and changes – the highs and lows, the expansions and contractions, the reflective and the offensive. Pay attention to where your thoughts take you.

Another Chekhov-based exercise I learned at a theatre educator's conference is to mould your character out of a block of clay.

- Like Michelangelo carving the statue of David, walk around an imagined life-size block of clay and, bit by bit, remove the excess as you carve and shape the outer form of the character you will inhabit with your hands. Consider their physical features, traits, posture, and facial features. When you are satisfied that your character is before you, undo an invisible zip at the back of the statue and step inside the hollow space. Touch your nose to zip it up at the back and feel the clay exterior as the character conforms to you, moulding to your body as you embrace new characteristics. You are now free and ready to work without inhibition. When you are finished, unzip and exit your character's skin. You can crumple it up, discard it, and start anew next time, or fold up that skin and place it 'somewhere safe' – in an imaginary drawer, back pocket, or shelf, ready for use the next time you embody that character.

There are many more resources available beyond those I've listed. Add any you know and like to your toolkit and look for others that inspire and challenge you. Above all, have fun exploring.[13]

Singing and musical tools

There is no doubt that technical competency across the triple-threat skills forms the foundation of an exciting performance. However, technique training, especially in singing, can be both a blessing and a

ACTING AND SINGING

curse. While providing essential scaffolding for safe vocalization in a discipline that demands extreme skill and stamina, the rigour of some methods can create overt singing skills that can overshadow and hinder truthful, emotionally connected storytelling. It's important that the audience doesn't notice more technique than character. The following tools aim to build and support competency while freeing actors who may have become technique-bound – who focus too much on the singing process rather than allowing its embodiment to feel natural and effortless.

In Chapter 4, we explored external elements – the story, space, time, and environment – that create context, and the atmosphere that shapes the audience's perception of the 'It' Factor. When it comes to songs performed in musical theatre, carefully crafted melodies, harmonies, rhythms, and accompaniments are just a few powerful tools available as you delve into a character's identity, current intention, and depth.

During my years of teaching, performing, and directing, I've discovered that cross-training is essential. Acting techniques serve as invaluable tools when singing musical theatre songs. Vocalization with intention produces immediate and rewarding results. Here are a collection of helpful tools – some I have developed, and others I've gathered from directors or coaches I've worked with. Some of these techniques involve using the body to stimulate the mind, merging multiple performance processes rather than isolating them. For example, in a specific moment, a breath (*psycho/physical*) triggers the imagination (*psycho*), activates the body (*physical*) and thought (*neuro*) and influences a sung note (*technico*) to convey emotion (*emotio*). Often these processes seem to occur simultaneously.

Sensate – the senses

Your senses can stimulate your imagination, and vice versa. For instance, envisioning a gooey dessert can trigger saliva production, just like the aroma of freshly baked bread. Engage both your senses and imagination and work them in tandem.

- Use the accompaniment to help you visualize your surroundings and create an atmosphere. Vividly picture the world you imagine. As your sense memory awakens, immerse yourself in the sensations of the elements – the texture on your skin, the scent in the air, the taste on your lips, and the sounds enveloping you. This technique enables you to discover and respond to the stimuli in the atmosphere ignited by your imagination. Live authentically in the moment, describing the scene and expressing what you perceive through song. Do not sing until you can visualize and fully experience it in detail.

Here is an example how to engage your senses and imagination using the song 'How Far I'll Go'[14] from the movie musical, *Moana*. In the first line Moana establishes the environmental context: *'I've been staring at the edge of the water for as long as I can remember, never really knowing why.'* Immerse yourself. Remove your shoes. Wriggle your toes into the warm, wet sand. Close your eyes and feel the sun on your face, hear the distant thunder of breakers crashing on the reef, and taste the salty air. Breathe it all in. Now open your eyes and look at the horizon, and *'See the line where the sky meets the sea.'* What does that line look like? Is it midnight blue merging into deep turquoise? Are there flecks of white surf out there, ruffled by the breeze you feel on your face? What colours fill the sky? Is it dawn, noon or dusk? Stretch out your arm and, with your finger, trace that straight horizon line that gently curves at the edges. Focus your eyes on that faraway delineation. Imagine flying like a bird toward that horizon, your energy expanding and soaring, skimming across the water. Now, bring your body energy back into yourself, feel the contraction inward, and look down at your feet. The crystal-clear, sparkling edge of the water is just inches away. One step, and you are in the water. But you are not. Let your feelings arrive. The accompaniment plays a high tremolo as you fully absorb this scene. The sound is the vibration in the island air, the diamond sparkle of the water at your feet, and the sound of your body's electricity as you plug into that world. Open your nose and mouth and sing.

> *Anything one man can imagine, other men can make real.*
> –Jules Verne, *The Mysterious Island* (New York: Signet Classics, 2004), 225.

This song was performed during the PhD workshop I led. Once the actor connected with the song's environment through their senses, a palpable atmosphere emerged, creating a completely different foundation for singing about longing and breaking free.

- As you sing a phrase, visualize a colour or shape. One musical director would say to her ensemble, 'Sing that bit yellow,' or 'think that phrase red.' Another musical director would ask the ensemble to draw geometric shapes above words or notes and look at them as they rehearsed. Without explanation, the chorus, seeing those shapes as they sang, would adjust their sound to emulate the shape – specifically, a rectangle placed vertically would produce a different elongated north/south resonant space than those sounds sung while observing a horizontal rectangle, which creates a more spread, wide, and brighter sound. Instinctively, the vocal tract and the sound would change.

- Think about the temperature of your breath and how it feels against your skin or inside your body. Sing a phrase from a song, then repeat that line while creating a 'warming' effect with your breath. Perhaps your breath is like gentle summer breeze, or maybe you are blowing on your icy fingers chilled by the cold outside. Alternatively, imagine that you are exhaling fire or ice. Observe how the sound changes effortlessly, without conscious thought.

Ideational cognition – cognitive understanding

Many acting tools can be easily applied to song lyrics. These tactics help to focus attention to the melody and musical accompaniment, adding dimension to the storytelling.

- Vocalize the melody without words. Use fricative consonants and vowels, choosing their sounds to reflect the meaning of the phrase and the song's trajectory. Recognize the significance of the written musical material, letting the arc of the melody convey the story. Focus on the intervals and the quality of the scale degrees used to enhance or colour the emotional journey. Be attentive to rhythmic devices, the effects of long and short notes, and repetition.

- Explore the OOPS to UBU continuum. Your voice encompasses a variety of timbres and qualities that can vocally bring a character to life. Golden age musicals (pre-1960) specifically utilize tonal beauty to paint elements of character aurally. However, your 'One and Only Perfect Sound' – OOPS – is merely one hue in your toolkit. Experiment with your sound using a story-driven continuum of diverse timbres: all sounds ranging from 'OOPS' to 'Unusual (Ugly) But Useful' – UBU.[15] Try experimenting with touches of nasal tone or twang or placing resonance in specific areas of the vocal tract. The colours you can find are filled with rich story and nuance.

- Sing the subtext. Similar to the acting tool mentioned above, set the actual lyrics aside, improvise, and vocalize other thoughts while following the melodic contour, connecting these thoughts with breath and primal sound. This process enlivens and expands your thoughts, aids the external expression of your internal life, and fosters a focused, cohesive approach to storytelling.
- 'Mine' the music for meaning. Composers employ specific techniques to emphasize the dramatic intention of the song; for example, melodic rhythms can either complement or contrast with the accompaniment to create tension, suspense, and a sense of discovery or excitement. The chosen notes of a sung scale, together with the length, arc, and shape of the phrases, reveal the composer's thoughts. Even the melodic intervals surrounding significant lyrics contribute to the song's emotional power. Examine how the text is paired with music to convey meaning and inspire thoughts as you sing.

Intuitive cognition – imagination and instinct

Our natural, instinctual vocal responses to stimuli captures some of our individuality and the essence of our humanity.

Primal sound

Primal sound was first coined by classical singing pedagogue Janice Chapman and later developed into a method in the UK by Dane Chalfin.[16] A popular technique used in contemporary singing, primal sound is a safe and effective method for creating authentic sounds that resonate with human emotion. This approach is linked to Estill's method of compulsory figures (1996) and taps into the body's natural responses for instinctual expression – such as whimpering, whingeing, calling out, and sighing.[17] Primal sound enables singers to access a technically safe vocal setup tailored to the specific song genre, timbre, and emotion. This natural neuro-psycho-biological interface between sound production and authentic emotional expression creates a broad timbre vocabulary. Try tapping into naturally occurring sound qualities – like laughing, whooping, giggling, chuckling, wailing, moaning, cooing, keening, sobbing, sighing, and humming. Even an instantaneous, vocalized response to pain or shock produces a primal sound.

Primal sound scenarios

- Explore and practise primal sounds in various scenarios, with or without matching lyrics or phrases. Incorporate storytelling into your primal and instinctual understanding to uncover nuances in tone and resonance. For instance, embody a four-year-old whining 'I want' across different pitches; vary the settings, such as being in a grocery store desiring candy or at home wanting a parental hug. Investigate the differences in primal sound between 'I want' and 'I need'.
- Unpack the lyrics and assign a primal sound to each phrase. Mix, match, and overlay these: laughing, crying, moaning, sobbing, wailing, whining, giggling, chuckling, sighing, whimpering, crooning, keening, pleading, cajoling.
- Unlock your instinctive understanding of the depth and power of instrumental sounds: the warmth of the trombone, the piercing brilliance of the trumpet, and the legato richness and emotion of the

violin or cello. Tap into the feelings these instruments can evoke – their beauty, tonal quality, and your natural responses to them. Delve into any buried emotional reactions stemming from past experiences.

Emotive processes

Remember, your emotions are a byproduct of your thoughts or your physicality. Even how you breathe can prompt emotions to rise. Take time to note how a strong thought or an engaged physical stance can inform your vocal tone.

- Draw on your passion and energy and observe how your voice changes when you front foot or back foot a song.
- Sing silently. Breathe in the thought that lies beneath the lyrics and breathe out the lyrics and emotion as the accompaniment plays while you sing the lyrics in your mind. Connect that breath to the airflow and pressure required to sing the song and feel the power of breath to release the physical energy that matches the story and lyrics.

Intrinsic persona – individual personality

Elements of your individuality will inform the personification of the character you play. Don't fight that. Only your 'unique you' will bring something fresh to the character. As you embrace the role, let the music and your voice – your timbre and dynamics find and tell the story.

- From a place of connection and groundedness, let the melody and accompaniment narrate the story and shape your energy response. Consider the accompaniment as part of your sound. Become one with it as you immerse yourself in the music – an aural representation of your thoughts and heart energy. For instance, listen to 'The Life I Never Led' from *Sister Act* by Slater and Menken.[18] Absorb the spartan simplicity of the convent atmosphere in the open block chords during the first verse. As the story gains momentum, the quaver arpeggios in the second verse flow through suspended chords. Notice the rising turmoil and longing in the faster tempo and the accompaniment's escalating patterns. Often, a composer's tempo or rhythmic movement serves as a revealing indicator of a character's heart rate. Whisper the lyrics as you let the accompaniment pour and flow through you. The rising intervals at the beginning of each phrase in the bridge grow larger – '*And now ... And now ... But how ... ?*' These wider intervals reflect the escalating emotion and urgency that Sister Mary Roberts feels. The song naturally expands as her thoughts flow and spill out. Then we witness a contraction, as the accompaniment reverts to crystalline chords while she emerges from her imaginings and dreams back into her convent surroundings, just before the modulation and energized accompaniment expand and propel the story forward. The interplay between these two accompaniment styles deftly paints the conflict embedded in the lyrics. There is a river of story, filled with twists and turns in the accompaniment. Let your character's persona connect with it and inhabit it.

Physical embodiment

Your physical portrayal of the characters you embody will be unique, just like your voice and persona. Embrace it.

- Monologue the music with your body. Allow the accompaniment to ignite your imagination: dance or conduct the melody or accompaniment as you sing it. This technique encourages you to embody the musical elements of the story and helps integrate the physical aspects of singing with the inherent qualities of the music.

- Alternatively, dance and improvise to the music using contemporary dance or ballet; move in any way your body desires, exploring the sensations of flying, flowing, moulding, reaching or gathering. Seek out the orchestration in backing track form, listen closely, and conduct the instruments, responding to all the nuances of the composer's intention in the orchestration.

The acting and singing tools listed in this chapter are just some of the ways I try and open the singing actor's mind and body to the richness that lies in every song and scene. Experimenting with these exercises as well as your own is vital. Pioneer theatre performance practitioner, David Craig, in his seminal work, *On Singing Onstage,* gives some pithy advice about doing, '*The rule here is: Do it. Do it. Do it 'til you become it. Eventually, all performances get better, and better yet, get hired.*'[19]

The next chapter will introduce more tools to play with.

12
TOOLKIT TECHNIQUES: PHYSICALITY AND PSYCHOLOGY

Every time actors step onto the stage, their role is to effectively convey their inner psychological world through outer, physical expression, forging synergistic connections with their character, fellow performers, and the audience. Physicality serves as the visible manifestation of an unseen inner realm. When these elements are congruent, the 'It' Factor can emerge, making performances thrilling and dynamic.

In this chapter we will explore toolkit exercises specifically designed to engage the physical performative process, which in turn illuminates other intrinsic performative processes. We will then examine tools that foster a positive psychological mindset – a crucial trait that underpins all technical competencies and informs and empowers performance.

Physical tools

In musical theatre, dance is a vital component of the triple-threat portfolio. Traditionally, it has been viewed as an integral and heightened physical extension of the narrative, particularly in twentieth-century book musicals. An adage encapsulates their formulaic structure: you speak until that's not enough, then you sing until that's not enough, and then you dance. Dance training for actors is invaluable; mastering technique and developing an expressive body opens a portal for the audience to engage with the story more readily.

The role of a grounded yet adaptable physicality to facilitate synergistic flow became evident during the interviews. Choreographers spoke in depth about the effortless presence and latent power residing in dancers and actors who are comfortable in their bodies and fully connected to their physicality.

Many acting methods also regard acting and movement as two integral components of a unified whole. The physical tools in my SASS! toolkit are designed to enhance that mind/body connection through movement, physical acting, and psychophysical work, rather than through specific dance techniques. This approach reflects

> One of the most enthralling actors to watch is one of the least publicly recognized – Andy Serkis. His embodiment of iconic roles like King Kong, Gollum in *Lord of the Rings*, and Caesar in *Planet of the Apes* uses 'a complete marriage of skills'. Advances in motion capture have mapped the nuances of his physical portrayals to bring fantastical characters to life. This video essay is worth a look to inspire you to find and explore the edges of your physicality.
> https://www.youtube.com/watch?v=DFQ9JvtqTtA

not only my limited knowledge and expertise as a professional dancer but also the evolving role of physical movement in various contemporary musical theatre styles.

There is a truism: '*We listen with our eyes.*' When an actor's physicality does not convey the same story as the lyrics or emotions, their constructed, imaginary theatrical world can easily crumble. In *To the Actor*, Chekhov observes that some actors fail to communicate their feelings effectively to a broader audience when their inner life is not clearly expressed through their physical bodies. He notes that these '*wonderful thoughts and emotions are somehow trapped within their underdeveloped bodies*'.[1] Chekhov suggests that the actor's primary concern should be to train their body to become a '*sensitive membrane, a kind of receiver and conveyor of the subtlest images, feelings, emotions and will impulses*'.[2]

Wake up your body

Start by connecting your physical self to your other performative processes: your senses, mind, imagination, heart, and soul. This is the essence of the whole-body activation in Chapter 10. By now, you should have explored some of Chekhov's techniques or engaged in the clowning exercises presented in the warm-up. If you wish, take a moment to enjoy throwing balls, creatively twisting, and walking through various atmospheres.

You may also have your own exercises that connect your mind and emotions to your body. Your thoughts influence and shape your physicality, both positively and negatively, in performance and everyday life. You can create a positive exterior-interior-exterior loop that encourages the free flow of body–mind energies in a cyclical manner.

In *The Acrobat of the Heart,* Stephen Wangh describes his stream-of-consciousness warm-up process with actors. He encourages them to utilize their familiar warm-up and stretching routines and, while doing so, to gently notice and connect their thoughts to their bodies and their bodies to the mind's stream of consciousness, '*accepting all of our "irrelevant" thoughts and impulses as creative inspirations for our work*'.[3]

Wangh, who trained with acting and directing master Jerzy Grotowski (1934–1999), encourages actors to find their way back to the *via negativa* – their childhood origins. Proprioception is merely the tip of the proverbial iceberg regarding what our bodies remember. Our bodies contain a myriad of memories and learned childhood behaviours, some of which began as forms of protection or cultural socialization. If you feel safe and supported in your sandpit of imaginative play, explore your mind–body connection and allow any restrictions to loosen and disappear. In our earliest years, primal sound served as our primary form of communication, and uninhibited physical play was one of our modes of personal expression. Both still reside within us, awaiting rediscovery.

Regardless of your approach, a fundamental physical warm-up helps you discover your physical centre. Deep, effortless breaths, fluid thoughts, and an open, flexible body facilitate the expression of natural and spontaneous emotions.

> What does your body say to your audience? How you hold your arms, your head, how you stand, and where your weight is placed in your body dramatically changes your physicality and observer perception. Observe others around you. What does their posture tell you? Where is their centre of gravity? Where is the weight on their feet?

PHYSICALITY AND PSYCHOLOGY

- Take deep breaths to activate your brain and find cognitive focus.
- Feel the ground beneath your feet; it subtly connects you to the greater world and everyone who lives in it.
- Stretch out your muscles and limbs to embrace the space you are in.
- Align your unique centre – that single, straight line connecting the top of your head, through your neck, ribcage, and pelvis, down to the ground between your feet – links you from the earth to the sky.
- A simple sound, an instinctive, primal utterance, or a vocalized vowel or hum from deep within you will anchor your sound in your physical core. Project that sound into the space around you and connect with the real or imagined people in your immediate vicinity.
- Listen. Receive and give with your body, as well as your mind and heart. You will feel ready to begin work.

Body centring energy

In Chapter 11, we examined energetic centres and explored how to channel thought and sound into various parts of our bodies. Let's delve into your body's energy once more, identifying where you feel it and how you can focus, empower, and centre that energy in different areas – be it the head, the heart, the solar plexus, or a combination of these. Remember the director's instruction to direct your thoughts into your abdomen?

It is worth acknowledging that both Eastern mysticism and Western thought recognize seven energy centres, or chakras. In her 2020 book, *The Lucid Body: A Guide for the Physical Actor*, Fay Simpson explores the potential for growth that actors can achieve by understanding chakras and their specific energies.[4] She states, '*Acting needs flow – blood flow, emotional flow, breath flow and physical flow in order to recreate organic life on stage.*'[5]

Her method examines how these energy centres can connect to our inner lives. She quotes Dr Robyn Powell from NYU, who identifies chakras as '*a spinning sphere of bio-energy emanating from the major nerve ganglia branching from the spinal column*'.[6] These ganglia generally correspond to our endocrine glands, which regulate the nervous system.

Figure 12.1 illustrates the seven centres, along with their locations and energetic focus. Interestingly, they generally align with the seven performative processes I uncovered in my research, as well as Chekhovian thinking.

We began exploring energetic centres during our whole-body activation in Chapter 10. Let's continue to gather and radiate energy from these focal points physically. Here are some additional ways to explore the connection between the body, heart, mind, and will.

- Revisit the energetic centres exercises in our persona processes acting tools (Chapter 11)
  Try placing your thoughts in various areas of your body and connect your physicality to them, delivering movement from the same energetic centres as the thought and text. For instance, several Chekhov exercises encourage us to envision movements originating from an imaginary centre in our chest.[7]

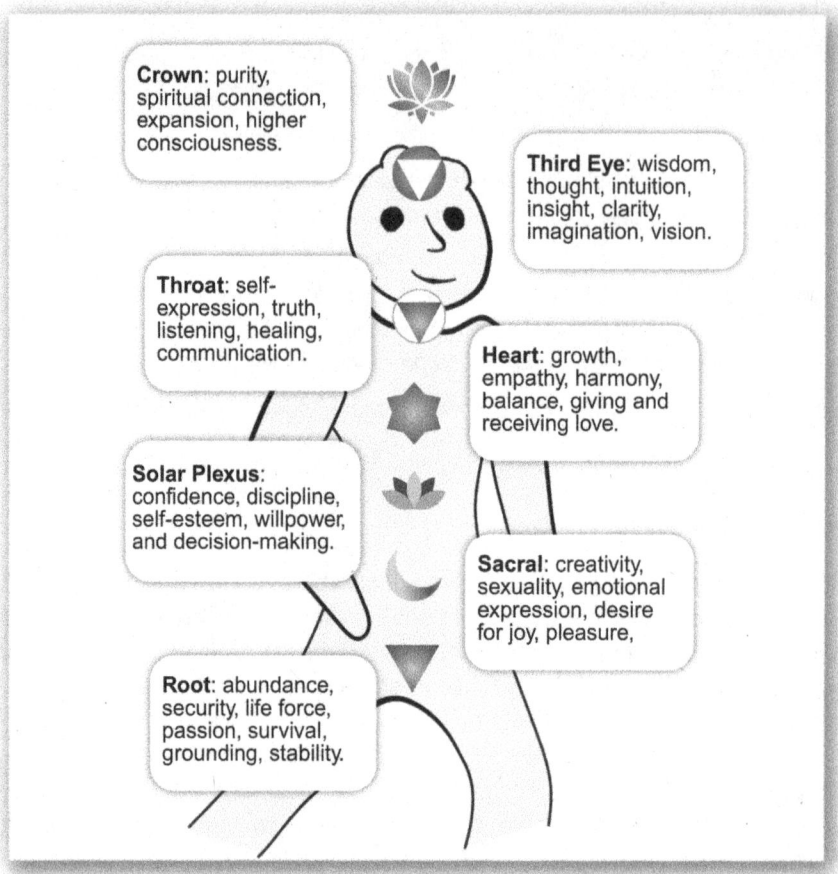

Figure 12.1 Seven energetic centres in yogic thinking.

- Project a sense of determination and strength by straightening up and planting your feet. Transfer your weight from one supporting leg to another. Find your balanced, neutral posture. Next, move in and out of your centre, taking small steps forward and backward and from side to side, feeling the floor through the balls of your feet. Take that further with lunges – forward, backward, and to both sides. Notice what your body weight and position might suggest to you imaginatively.
- Engage in imaginative sports games. Expand the ball-throwing warm-up by incorporating creative scenarios that merge memory, imagination, and physical activity. Visualize playing tennis, golf, pitching baseball, or casting fishing lines or nets, either alone or with a partner. Imagine you are an elite athlete at the Olympic Games; take your starting position for a sprint and react to the sound of the gun or the bell in boxing or fencing.
- Practise delivering the lyrics of your song or text as if your feet and legs are doing the talking. Notice how your body responds as you feel the stakes rising and adjust your stance by shifting your centre of gravity.

- Move around the room, allowing different centres guide you. Visualize an invisible horizontal line connected to the centre you focus on – head, chest, heart, persona, gut, hips, pelvis, legs, or arms. Feel that line drawing you around the room. Then, shift the impetus. Instead, sense the line is pushing you from behind, impelling you forward.

- Experiment with imaginative walks across various terrains to help you notice both centred and uncentred movements. Imagine hiking through a bush, climbing a mountain, wading through water, trudging in deep mud or sand, riding a bike, fencing in a competition, shovelling dirt or snow, chopping wood, doing a cartwheel, tumbling, or practising gymnastics. Then, engage in these different walks while narrating the story of your lyrics to someone.

- Work to music. Let the sound guide your body's response and dance: animal moves, era-inspired dances, or even imaginary hopscotch. Dance and freeze, becoming aware of your shape and energetic centre. Then, do it again to discover something new. Add a creative twist or simple turns to extend your imagination and improvise. Don't force it or try to 'present' or 'represent' what's in your mind. What naturally arises is the best starting point.

Laban's Eight Efforts

Choreographer Rudolf Laban (1879–1958) was a master teacher and choreographer who developed a method for exploring the quality of movement in human body mechanics. He established the 'Eight Efforts' or qualities he observed permeating our physicality: wring, press, flick, dab, glide, float, punch, and slash. Laban further expanded these movements by incorporating aspects of direction, weight, speed, and flow.[8] While experimenting with these qualities in your body, consider applying them to your sound and breath delivery.

- Practise these efforts individually. Start by expressing them physically while varying the direction, speed, intensity (weight), and flow. One simple way to do this is to add an Effort as you imagine completing everyday tasks, such as weeding the garden, doing laundry, or cleaning the house. Try washing by hand, hanging out clean clothes, ironing, vacuuming, punching, and fluffing cushions using various approaches. Experiment with these movements first arrhythmically, then to a beat or soundtrack.

- Return to your text. Let the intention of the lyric or the quality of the accompaniment suggest an Effort. Play with the body's expression of that Effort while speaking the text or singing with or without words. Imagine your breath and sound as part of that same expression.

- Alter the Effort but maintain the same text and feel and observe the difference. Consider layering two Efforts to create a more subtle, complex approach. For example, the bridge section of 'Somewhere Over the Rainbow' might be an ideal spot to incorporate glide, float, dab or even flick ('*Someday I'll wish upon a star and wake up where the clouds are far behind me*'). Alternatively, take the song 'Somewhere' from *West Side Story* and experiment with press and wring if focusing on the longing or striving to break free, or use float and glide if exploring the hopeful, dreamlike aspect of the song ('*We'll find a new way of living, we'll find a way of forgiving, somewhere*').

Integrating Chekhov's psychophysical exercises

Much of Chekhov's work emphasizes an actor's psychophysical approach to character development and the evocation of emotion.[9] His impactful exercises and principles form part of the toolkit's loosening exercises in Chapter 10. Through these body–mind practices, actors connect their internal and external worlds. Here are some ways I integrate them into songs and musical theatre scenes.

- Expanding and contracting – opening and closing, growing and shrinking – are fundamental of life. Chekhov explores the body, the organs, the senses, and the spaces that expand or contract.[10] A character's emotional state in the text and story affects the extent to which an actor may engage in expansion or contraction. As you analyse lyrics, melody, and narrative, identify the moments when the mind and body feel larger or smaller.

- Utilize Chekhov's staccato/legato exercise to explore six directions for creating energetic flow throughout your body. From a neutral position facing forward, turn and lunge sharply in staccato to the right, keeping your arms extended at chest height away from your body. Return to a neutral stance, then repeat to the left, upward, downward, forward, and backwards. Between each movement, return to neutral. Next, repeat the six positions at a slow-flowing legato tempo. This exercise warms up the body and stimulates the mind, allowing for the addition of new layers, intentions, atmospheres, and gestures. Consider which part of the song could correspond to each direction, whether delivered swiftly and sharply or with a slower, gliding approach.

- Chekhov's 'Qualities of Movement' relates to four universal elements: earth (moulding/sculpting), water (floating/flowing), air (flying), and light (radiating). An actor's physicality responds to these distinct qualities inherent in energetic forces. Similar to Laban's approach, harness the power of your imagination to bring these qualities to life in the lyrics and melody. Experiment with different choices and observe how that releases thoughts and energy.

Chekhov specifically employed his qualities of movement exercise to awaken sensations and evoke new feelings. He instructs:

Lift your arm. Lower it. What have you done? You have fulfilled a simple physical action. You have made a gesture. And you have made it without any difficulty. Why? Because, like every action, it is completely within your will. Now make the same gesture, but this time colour it with a certain quality. Let this quality be caution. You will make your gesture, your movement cautiously. Have you not done it with the same ease? Do it again and again and see what happens. Your movement, made cautiously, is no longer a mere physical action; now it has acquired a certain psychological nuance.[11]

- Outside-in. Like other body–mind exercises, this practice unlocks the story by encouraging the actor to respond physically to external stimuli, such as music and imaginary environments. Physicality connects the body to thoughts and feelings. The premise of the exercise is that as you move in response to stimuli, your body will reveal a feeling. For instance, listen to the song's accompaniment and allow the music to guide you. Don't attempt to interpret it; simply respond to it. Follow the impulse it generates in you and discover a physical expression, whether grand or subtle. Feel free to dance to it.

PHYSICALITY AND PSYCHOLOGY

Another example of outside-in work is incorporating one of Chekhov's qualities of movement or Laban's eight efforts into a specific scenario.

- With or without the song's accompaniment, create an environment that suggests a metaphorical element – trudge through heavy, restrictive substances like mud, walk across hot, burning desert sand, tread water or slip and slide on an icy street. Walk on a rope bridge high in the treetops or on a tightrope under the big top. Use slow motion to enhance these scenarios; it brings focus and intensity to your physicality.

- Practise physicalizing the moment a thought is discovered or arrives. The speed and source of thought affect us subliminally and are expressed through our physicality in various ways. Ideally, this physical expression should arise spontaneously, driven by thought; however, we can practise finding it. Where do you locate it? Try plucking the thought from outside yourself, as if it is flowing past you in a river of thoughts, and you discover and choose it. Alternatively, envision the thought on the horizon, moving steadily toward you as it seeks you out and focuses on you. Or perhaps, like dawn, you see the thought resembling the sun rising slowly in the east. It could also feel like an electric shock somewhere in your body or a light bulb illuminating inside your head. As they arrive, allow these thoughts to reveal different ways to sing the words – the subtext or ideas – into the accompaniment to tell the story.

- Visualize the thought in front of you as an instant realization; it may come with varying breath intakes. Alternatively, place your thought on one side – top, middle or bottom – to access memory or embedded knowledge alongside diverse sensory reminders. Is it auditory, kinetic or visual? Position it in your periphery – a thought emerging from behind or just at the edge of your sight, a dawning realization or something out of reach that you are seeking.

Psychological Gesture – one of Chekhov's key psychophysical contributions – involves discovering a physical shape or position that embodies a character's essential qualities, including their wants and desires. Once identified, the gesture influences the actor's thoughts and emotions, awakening their intrinsic processes.

- Select a gesture that embodies a single quality found in a simple text or lyric. Combine the gesture with the lyric; repeat the words until you feel them settle within you, then subtly adapt the gesture. Observe how your body influences the line and vice versa. For example, you might sing or say a simple phrase like '*I don't want to.*' Repeat it until it resonates within your body, then create a gesture. This might involve a wide stance, with hands thrust forward, palms up in a pushing position, weight leaning forward, energy centred in your torso, chin slightly raised, and a direct gaze. As you repeat the phrase, gradually adjust your body position and notice what unfolds.

- Unlock your physicality. Imagine your body as a puppet and you the master puppeteer. The audience doesn't see you, telling the story as you pull your own strings. This concept is an excellent way to cope with anxiety. Lose yourself to discover the character – almost diametrically opposed to using yourself to find the character.

Psychological tools

We often 'get in the way' of ourselves and our abilities. We overthink or worry about our capability to accomplish the tasks ahead. An integral part of an actor's PQ includes self-belief, confidence, boldness, trust, and freedom. Actors must be vulnerable to create synergistic performances, turning that energy on in a heartbeat.

These tools differ slightly from others in the toolkit. While the previous singing, acting, and physical tools provide exercises that can be explicitly applied to character and role formation, the psychological prompts listed below focus on the inner personal work we all undertake in different ways. In her book, *The Lucid Body: A Guide for the Physical Actor,* Fay Simpson encourages us:

> *Our bodies house a spirit full of poetry, imagination, and expressiveness. Every step we take can produce an impulse, a memory, a feeling of some sort that know ourselves a little bit better. Knowing ourselves means knowing our potential and being that much more effective as an actor on the stage.*[12]

The following resources encourage actors to adopt an engaged, positive psychological stance that opens pathways for creative thought and synergy.

As mentioned in Chapter 8, building positive psychological capital is essential for encouraging and unlocking the 'It' Factor in ourselves and others. To cultivate a mindset that is open, free, curious, empathetic, generous, and receptive, The toolkit includes four specific tools: personal exploration, affirmations, meditation, and journalling.

Personal exploration

An ancient Greek Delphic maxim exhorts us to '*Know thyself*.' Over the millennia, this has been interpreted in various ways, such as understanding your abilities, your limits, social position or your soul. Self-awareness serves as the foundation for personal growth. Two cognitive-based tools I have found helpful in this endeavour are:

1. VIA Character Strengths Survey (VIA Institute, 2022). This free online tool uses a series of questions to help identify aspects of an individual's personality without imposing constraints or limitations. It encourages individuals to explore their character traits, fostering a deeper personal understanding for them to draw upon. Twenty-four character traits are assessed, including appreciation of beauty, bravery, curiosity, fairness, forgiveness, gratitude, honesty, humility, humour, kindness, love, perseverance, prudence, spirituality, teamwork, and zest. Taking the test helped me understand why certain aspects of performance came easily and where my challenges lay. The opportunity to work on the 'tricky bits' of ourselves arises when we comprehend our strengths and weaknesses.
2. Pip McKay's eight archetypes[13]. McKay's work is grounded in Jungian concepts of archetypes. Recognizing the traits of these archetypes – templates of collectively developed thought patterns – within ourselves can enlighten the user and provide greater self-awareness, as well as insight into the structures that stimulate our creative activity. I have participated in several workshops using archetypes, and each time, I felt validated and uplifted as I recognized the inherent *modus operandi* I employ in my daily life. While there are various approaches to

archetypes, I found McKay's eight basic archetypes to be particularly helpful: the ruler, the knight, the oracle, the creative nurturer, the innocent wanderer, the magician, the lover, and the sage. These aspects reside within us at varying times, although four will be more prevalent and relevant, illuminating how we instinctively live, work, and relate to others. My four are the knight, the creative nurturer, the innocent wanderer, and the magician. What archetypes help you understand your natural tendencies and *modus operandi*?

Affirmations

We are multifaceted individuals living in a busy, sometimes chaotic, seemingly fractured world. Affirmations can centre and focus our thoughts, calm anxiety, connect us to our inner essence, and release energy for the tasks ahead. Many options are available.

- Verbal Affirmations. Choose or create affirming phrases and incorporate them into your daily routine by saying them out loud. Speak, sing, shout, and act them out, and enjoy the process. These can be as simple as looking in the mirror at the start of each day and saying, '*Good morning, let's have a great day.*' If you have time, select one or two parts of your body and use the 'Hello to You' isolation exercise to give yourself a little TLC. Actors give deeply of themselves when they perform, which requires immense self-motivated energy. It is essential to fuel the internal tanks we draw from daily.

- Visual affirmations. Find a quiet space and breathe gently but deeply. Visualize yourself engaging in something you love. Absorb every detail; focus on your energy and notice the joy on your face and the connections you are forming with the person, place or thing that is part of that vision. Celebrate and affirm this part of yourself. Mentally gather that aspect of you and bring that feeling of well-being back to your present moment.

Actors often use affirmations as part of their 'moments', waiting in the wings before entering a scene. One actor spoke of gathering energy by focusing on a spot on the wall, side of the stage; another visualized herself performing on stage, affirming her role and character.

Group affirmations can build both individuals and teams. I have worked with some fantastic community theatre actors, and one circle affirmation used before a performance boldly declared, '*You are a star! People pay to see you on stage! So, shine, dammit, shine!*'

The power of articulating what you desire cannot be underestimated. I learned this lesson years ago while teaching piano to young beginners. 'Say it as you play it' is a maxim I used to engage multiple senses to coordinate reading, listening, and playing skills. My adaptation for singers is to encourage them to vocalize what they want their bodies to do. Singing '*More flow*', '*Round sound*', or '*I want*' naturally engages the subconscious, enabling the body and voice to follow your verbal guidance while employing a simple arpeggio or five-note scale. Something transformative occurs in the brain when the three senses of hearing, seeing, and feeling align into a single thought: your ear perceives what the mind has directed your voice to express while you read the words and physicalize concurrently.

Affirmations are also powerful tools for overcoming internal roadblocks and self-doubt. One notable resource is Niki Flacks' 2015 book, *Acting with Passion*. She highlights how the criticisms, pressures, and commands from our 'inner critic' can hinder performers from being fully present in the moment. Flacks offers strategies to free actors from restrictive or debilitating critiques that obstruct a genuine connection to the story. Her method includes scripts and affirmations aimed at relieving chronic muscular tension, confronting the inner critic, and accessing a subconscious stream of thought to evoke emotion.

Meditation

Many actors I interviewed emphasized the power of meditation in focusing and empowering their creative energy before stage performances. Research has demonstrated that meditation positively impacts the brain by altering hemispheric activity and slowing processes, thus fostering focus and calm. Online and app resources are available, or try using the energizing meditation I created for you, available on the companion website. Alternatively, consider recording your voice to guide yourself through a preferred meditation. Meditation can help you to let go of fear, and synergy blockers, and create opportunities to awaken your inner energy and explore it. Practise channelling your energy to connect with someone or something and then reel it back in.

Journalling

Journalling is not a new practice. We all know there is power in writing things down – by hand! It is through thinking, doing, and reflecting on what you've accomplished that the mind and body connect. These could be stream-of-consciousness pages that may never be re-read, carefully considered kernels of thought derived from philosophy, commentary on your daily readings, lists of goals, dreams, random ideas, or aspirations for the day. Whatever they are, just write. In her book, *The Artist's Way* (1992), Julia Cameron champions journalling and encourages us to write three pages of longhand first thing in the morning, capturing whatever flows out in a stream of consciousness.

Mindful practice is another approach to journalling. Start a gratitude diary and, each day, note three different things for which you are thankful. Be curious, look beyond yourself, acknowledge even the smallest things or moments, see the positive, and celebrate yourself, others, and this planet.

The 5 'W's: The who, what, when, where, and why of you and your story

The toolbox introduced in the last three chapters offers numerous approaches to finding characters and telling stories. One approach that has not yet been explored is that of Uta Hagen (1919–2004), a highly influential actress and esteemed acting teacher. Her work on and off the stage and screen championed realism and promoted Stanislavski's methods worldwide. Hagen's acting approach fostered synergistic connections; she advocated for what she termed 'transference', enabling actors to draw on their personal recollections and experiences to create believable characters while inhabiting the given circumstances of a scene or song. Her teaching method focused on asking questions to establish the scene, the character's persona, and their dramatic relationship within that scene – their wants, needs, and intentions. One of her object exercises employs these questions to keep actors self-aware and audition-ready. She encourages actors to observe and record the components of two minutes from their lives, using questions to explore their inner and outer worlds.[14] Try her exercise and document two minutes of your life; it is beneficial for personal housekeeping and internal auditing.

PHYSICALITY AND PSYCHOLOGY

Asking 'W' questions of yourself and your life journey can yield valuable insights. I encourage you to examine them from your 'inner visionary' as well as your outer experiential self. Who, what, when, and where are you? Why are you here? And where do you want to go? Table 12.1 could be your starting point. It outlines Hagen's who, what, when, where, and why questions in the first column and provides space to record your Hagen-directed extrinsic responses in the second column. The third column is my addition, prompting you to explore deeper intrinsic responses to those questions. If this level of self-reflection is new to you, this task may feel daunting as you discover, express, and write down your inner thoughts and desires. But be brave and honest. Embracing the totality of who we are can be empowering. Some of your answers may pertain to your future self – projecting and recognizing parts of yourself that you are working on, and the hopes and dreams you hold dear. Working with your 'W's can expand the work you do through affirmations and journalling.

Here is an example: Question: Where am I?

Extrinsic Answer: I am in the country, city, neighbourhood, house, room, part of the room.

Intrinsic Answer: I find myself at a crossroads, uncertain whether to assert myself and ask 'X' for what I want or retreat once more. Where am I? I am at a point of decision.

Table 12.1 Using the 'W' questions to gain insight

Question	Extrinsic Answer	Intrinsic Answer
Who am I?	Character or self.	What are my personal strengths, my personality, my values, beliefs, fears, flaws?
When is it?	Century, year, season, day, minute.	Where am I in my life journey and personal timeline?
Where am I?	Country, city, neighbourhood, house, room, area of the room.	Where am I in terms of work, study, dreams, plans? Where am I emotionally, mentally?
Who and what surrounds me?	Animate and inanimate objects that affect me.	Who are my family, friends; what are support networks, and opportunities? Are there positive or negative influences? Possibilities or fears?
What are the given circumstances?	Past and present events that shape the now.	What events – external and internal – have shaped who I am, and affect how I see my present and potential future?
What is my relationship?	In relation to total events, other characters, and to things.	What is my relationship to those in my sphere, to my environment, to my work, to study and my dreams?
What do I want?	Character's main and immediate objectives.	What do I need? What are my desires, and concrete and abstract plans?
What's in the way?	Obstacles to objectives, extrinsic or intrinsic.	What are my obstacles? Is it self, or others, commitments, responsibilities, preconceptions, behaviours?
What will I do to get what I want?	The action: physical, verbal.	What is my action plan – now, in a day, week, a month or a year?

The last 'W' of the five 'W's is the 'Why' question. Why do you act, sing, and dance? Why do you desire more of the 'It' Factor? Your core values, passions, dreams, and goals significantly influence your personal 'why'. And exploring that 'why' in public solitude excites others and captures their attention. Simon Sinek has written a bestseller exploring the power of 'why', referencing icons such as Martin Luther King and Steve Jobs, and how their 'whys' transformed their lives and the lives of those around them.[15] 'Why' shapes all of us, even when we don't realize it. Let me share my 'Why' with you. 'Why did I study this subject and write a book?' The answer consists of two parts.

Firstly, I love people, connecting with them, and making them smile. I grew up in a very creative and social household. As a little girl, I watched my mother sing and perform, and I felt the joy it brought to me and many others. She and my father dedicated their lives to loving and serving the people in their community. Their legacy shaped my core values and passions. Whether through a compliment, a helping hand, a home-cooked meal, or a song, it's a win for me. Other people's happiness is my happiness. It's just a part of my 'who'.

I love performing and have had the privilege of a professional musical theatre career in Australia and the UK. When I am in a show, my greatest desire is for the audience to have a meaningful experience and to be transformed in some way by the end. I want them to leave feeling changed and enriched.

Secondly, understanding how things work and sharing that knowledge with others is a significant motivator for me. I love witnessing those I've coached or encouraged carving their paths in this industry. When my son chose to enter the musical theatre field in Australia and began formal studies in 2014, I wanted to discover what ignited the actors I admired – the 'It' Factor that made them stand out and get hired. At a Musical Theatre Educators Alliance conference in New York in 2019, before starting my PhD, Mary Saunders-Barton, Professor Emeritus at Penn State University, asked me, 'Why? Why pursue a PhD?' My hesitant response was that I would be content if I could find just one insight to help my son thrive in an oversaturated and unpredictable profession. Mary reassured me that it was a sufficient reason. Ironically, it is David's insight into the world of theatre that continues to inspire and challenge me.

What is your Why?

Spiritual creativity

Scattered throughout the works of great theatre writers and teachers are references to the soul, spirit or inner self of an actor. As noted in Chapter 5, these texts suggest that the presence of something higher or greater than us can be at play as we open up and connect with a character or story during a performance. Several actors and creative directors confirmed this during my PhD project. While spirituality may seem less emphasized in the highly competitive landscape of the twenty-first-century theatre industry, both teachers and practitioners stressed the importance of seeking inspiration and tapping into deeper processes to connect with the inner creative state of mind.

Connecting to my higher self and spirit and acknowledging the influence of a higher power in my life is one of the personal tools I use to unlock my 'It' Factor. Regardless of one's beliefs in something divine or universal, one cannot deny the otherworldly transcendence experienced in the presence of truly great art or inspiring performances. Tapping into that vast stream of creativity and a collective or divine consciousness can unleash powerful energy.

Cameron (2020) argues that creativity is as integral to our spiritual existence as blood is to our physical body, and outlines what she refers to as a spiritual path to access that creativity, which can be initiated and practised. Four of her core principles are:

1. Creativity is the natural order of life. Life is energy: pure creative energy.
2. There is an underlying, in-dwelling creative force infuses all of life – including ourselves.
3. When we open ourselves to our creativity, we open ourselves to the creator's creativity within us and our lives.
4. We are ourselves, creations. And we, in turn, are meant to continue creativity by being creative.[16]

So, how do we put it all together – the singing, acting, physicality, and psychology? In the next chapter, I'll share some ideas on combining these tools to open up possibilities. Meanwhile, dive into your sandpit of imaginative play and start enjoying your song or script; don't worry about whether you're 'doing it right'! Take the time to explore, adding elements or swapping ideas as you go. The only rule is to let go and play.

13
PUTTING 'IT' TOGETHER: SYNERGISTIC SONG STUDY AND TOOLKIT CASE STUDIES

The previous three chapters offer numerous exercises, both old and new, that can assist in learning and layering a song or character. In this chapter, I suggest ways to incorporate some of these tools into your work. Some techniques can be used as warm-up or loosening exercises, while others will spark your imagination and help you uncover meaning as you learn the essentials of the song – the rhythm, melody, and lyrics. Others are most effective once the initial learning is complete, allowing you to freely explore available choices and instinctual pathways. Again, remember there are countless ways to implement any of the ideas presented. Please feel free to pick, choose, adapt, and play.

Incorporating tools into song study

There are many ways for actors to learn a song. Often, it involves audiation (listening to different versions), which can accelerate the essential aspects of learning the melody and rhythm; however, audiation can also reinforce bad habits. Be careful not to mindlessly mimic breath points, timbre, or accent. Make those choices your own. Frequently, the melody and lyrics are sung together as they are memorized. Uncoupling those elements and exploring them individually early in the learning process can empower the song.

Here are some alternative ideas for approaching and learning a song. Review the suggestions and include some interim steps between selecting and presenting your song. Choose your own adventure!

Consider following this order:

Know the song

- Find a safe space to work – somewhere you can move freely and make noise without the fear of being overheard.
- Explore the song's inner story: 'What is it about?' Alternatively, you might adapt its meaning to suit your desired narrative. Actively choose the story behind the lyrics.
- Draw its arc – embody the shape of the song. Does it ascend to a summit-like conclusion, resolve downward, or return to its original starting point? A song is always on a journey from somewhere

to somewhere else – emotionally and informationally. Determine its super text and where it fits into the larger narrative of the musical, or, if you are considering it out of context, decide what you want its new context to be. The song must always belong to someone, somewhere. Perhaps it is one of your 'I am' songs, one of the few that resonates deeply with a part of you and becomes an old friend you can turn to, like a favourite sweater.

- Research your character's identity. Determine who they are, who they are singing to, what they want, the present moment they inhabit, the 'moment before' that brought them here, and what they will do next. If you are embodying the character, know what you want to reveal or communicate. Can you summarize their energy, intention, or arc in just a few words?

Vision the song

- Consider the setting of your song. Be specific. Which colours stand out, what time of day is it, and how does the air feel? How far away or close are the people or objects around you?
- Tap into the atmosphere created by the music and lyrics.
- Examine the individual thoughts behind each word choice or phrase.

Breathe and actively think the song

- Notice the breath points that signal shifts in thought and narrate the story before any sound is produced.
- Examine the composer's clues in the song, including dynamics, tempo, rests, repeated patterns, melodic contour, and harmonic foundation.
- Explore the accompaniment, including its rhythmic and harmonic patterns and textures that create atmosphere or alter mood and energy, as well as the dynamic shifts, leitmotifs, and recurring themes. Play the backing track and conduct it; feel the ebb and flow, and discover the peaks and valleys, along with the calm or stormy moments.
- Immerse yourself in the song's narrative. Explore which energetic centres can be engaged as you connect to your character's journey. Do the lyrics describe your thoughts, drive your emotions, express your soul, or connect with your innermost self?
- Find the breath style and technique associated with the song's energy and narrative. Use the breath points you've discovered that connect to the changes in the lyric's thoughts and ideas and practise breathing and thinking the song as the accompaniment plays. Experiment with primal breathing and observe whether it affects bodily responses. The way you discover your thoughts will instinctively influence the impact of your breath on an audience. Experiment with your speed of inhalation, the depth of your intake, whether there is a pause or hold point before exhalation, and how you exhale.
- Envision your thoughts or the lyrics clearly in your mind as if you are speaking, impressing, or shouting aloud while producing a SOVT (Semi-Occluded Vocal Tract) sound. Lip trill the melody or use 'puffy cheeks' (as if you are playing a toy trumpet) to harness the power of your thoughts along with your torso support.

Speak the song

- 'Monologuing' is a crucial yet often overlooked step. While a well-written song enhances its power and clarity through the skilful use of melodic contour and rhythm, these elements can occasionally disrupt the flow of thoughts, lyrics, and the overall narrative. Take a few breaths and allow the thoughts related to the story, along with the visual images you've gathered, to surface before you.

- Fill your space with the people and objects you are addressing or referencing. Allow the subtextual thoughts driving your words to surface as you breathe in and recite the lines. Repeat them if they feel disconnected. Do you remember the 'and again' exercise? Articulating your subtext might help you connect with the words. Let the ideas surrounding the song bring the lyrics to life.

Physicalize the song

This next step involves exploring the character's or narrative's physicality instead of developing performance choreography for public presentation.

- Speak the lyrics and, in your own time, move around the room. If thoughts are flowing quickly or you sense urgency, let your body express that: run or walk briskly.

- Allow your physicality to adjust and express each change of thought or beat. Don't plan. Let your thoughts guide your body.

- Alternatively, adopt an outside-in approach and move your body to stimulate your thoughts as the song plays. Try combining creative twisting with your song text exploration to free you of gestural habits.

- Try moving to the accompaniment, connecting to what it communicates through metre, rhythm, range, texture, and timbre. Conduct it or dance it in whatever way you are drawn to.

Vocalize the song

- Singspiel (German for sing-play) the song. While maintaining breath work and open, resonant spaces, speak the song in the approximate melodic register. My pet name for this is 'singy-speak', or, if the tessitura is high, 'speaky-sing'. This interim step between monologuing and singing the story often helps actors find an optimal vocal tract shape and access speech-based vocal qualities.

- Sing the melody, replacing the lyrics with words and phrases related to the subtext.

- Vocalize the melody using key primal words or short phrases such as *'Don't go'* (*'Doooooon't gooooo'*), *'Come here'*, *'Love me'*, *'Yippee!'*, *'No!'* or *'Please!'*. Remember primal sounds such as wailing, whining, moaning, sobbing, chuckling, crying, and laughing can be easily accessed with a word cue for the cognitive mind to concentrate on. Afterward, check in to reflect on how your breath changed with each shift in thought or intention.

- Keep those elements of primal sound, OOPs to UBU, and breathwork that connect with your thoughts and feelings, and incorporate them into the lyrics and melody.

Sing the song

This final step naturally concludes our pull-apart work. Let me summarize some important tactics as you begin to sing the song in its entirety.

- Approach the moment with curiosity, passion, and an energetic openness to discovery. Understand the 'sandpit' you are in, including the story, background research, character, and identity.
- Easily access individual thoughts; let them trigger or tumble into one another. The breath tells that story almost simultaneously before any sound is made. The composer also provides clues through tempo, rests, and accompaniment.
- Practise different breaths linked to various stories or scenarios. Then, sing a phrase or scale using those. Breathe primally, instinctually, as the thought arises; observe how this can alter your body's response. Can this type of breath in that phrase provide your body the support it needs without disrupting your technique? How you discover the thought will influence the speed of inhalation, the depth or shallowness of your intake, whether there's a pause or holding point, and how you release the airflow.
- Work out what is your 'moment before'. Do you find it in the silence before the introduction begins, or during it?
- Now it's time to sing the song. Take your time, exploring and reflecting on each verse or chorus individually before stitching the song together. Discover the flow of thoughts and emotions that create the spine and arc of the character's journey.
- At the end of the song, remain with the story and the moment to see what arrives physically and emotionally. There is reverberation and atmosphere in the air. Allow it to exist and gradually fade away. This is your 'moment after'; it can be a powerful experience.

Case studies: A window into how the toolkit can work

As part of my PhD study, I had the privilege of working with ten talented graduates from a musical theatre tertiary institution. Over several months, I trialled the SASS! toolkit, led an interactive workshop, and later conducted private coaching sessions with graduates who worked on songs from their audition repertoire. Subsequently, I hosted masterclasses with cast members from two professional touring companies. In each scenario, the toolkit was explored, and its efficacy was observed, experienced, and assessed.

In the first workshop I held, five participants were introduced to the concept of performance synergy, and together, we tested the toolkit. To begin, the actors completed an informative questionnaire before presenting their audition cuts. Next, the group participated in a series of warm-up, loosening, and activation exercises before one-on-one coaching began. Sections of their previously performed songs were reworked using a mixture of toolkit techniques.

During the coaching, I chose to work 'in the moment' utilizing bricolage, a flexible and adaptable research methodology that addresses the needs of each participant. Bricolage:

> *… has practical application in studying complex phenomena, where researchers' interaction with their subjects, the possibility of multiple realities, and the unforeseen directions research can take are embraced by an approach to research that can follow a number of different paths, not all of which can be planned for in advance of research being conducted. This allows for greater understanding of existing phenomena and creates the possibility of addressing questions heretofore not considered.*[1]

The concept of bricolage is somewhat akin to bricklaying and parallels the layering and construction work that actors engage in while developing a believable character. At its core, it involves creating a safe space for intuitive exploration and exploring possibilities. The decisions I made regarding the choice of tactics and exercises hinged on 'the offers' each participant presented.

The pre-coaching and coaching sessions were recorded on video, with two creative directors – a stage director and a musical director – independently evaluating them. Additionally, participants shared their experiences and observations. The results were highly informative, as well as positive and encouraging.

Participants were allotted around twenty minutes. In that brief time, as we worked, significant shifts in energy and connectivity occurred. Using only four or five tools, participants discovered new ways to connect with the character and story they were conveying. Their imagined world became more expansive. As they explored atmospheric tools and psychophysical techniques, they opened up, engaged more of their intrinsic performative processes, and subliminally invited the watching audience to join them on their journey.

Below are the five songs explored on the floor and the toolkit techniques I used to open up the story and characters while discovering dynamic performance.

Song 1 – 'The Life I Never Led' from *Sister Act* (Menken and Slater, 2009)

Considered an 'I Want' song, the lyrics reveal Sister Mary Roberts' deepest desires and encompass elements of self-reflection, discovery, and longing. The story's arc is propelled by a growing sense of determination and hope. The character's self-revelation quietly transforms her, and by the song's conclusion, she experiences a greater sense of ownership over her identity.

Toolkit Techniques

Primal breath: merging thoughts and breath, increasing moment-to-moment sense of discovery.

Expanding and contracting: highlighting the character's emotional place in the text and the story. Playing with past, present, future.

Activating energetic centres: accessing power within the body, finding palpable places where thoughts reside.

Music monologue-ing: listening to the accompaniment, identifying the atmospheric and energy changes. Finding structure.

Text monologue-ing: speaking lyrics to the accompaniment. Finding space to think thoughts.

Song 2 – 'Woman' from *The Pirate Queen* (Schoenberg and Boubil, 2006)

The fiery and passionate leading lady, Grace O'Malley, is a young sixteenth-century sea-faring Irish woman who yearns to be treated as an equal. This 'I Want' song reveals her strength and desire to sail on the high seas alongside the men of her clan.

Toolkit Techniques

Finding intention: asking '*What do you want? From whom? How will you get it?*' Exploring action words (transitive verbs) for specificity and energy.

Expanding and contracting (bound and free): freeing up physicality and connecting to the imagined surroundings.

Mining the text: searching for hidden meaning and moments. Utilizing imagery to bring text to life bring text to life. What does every 'if', 'and', and 'but' say?

Qualities of movement (floating, moulding, flying): finding freedom through physicalizing the characters thoughts and dreams. Immersion.

Song 3 – 'I've Been' from *Next to Normal* (Yorkey and Kitt, 2009)

Dan, a husband and father, has doggedly supported his wife, Diana, as her bipolar disorder worsens. This song, positioned near the end of Act 1, highlights the tremendous pressure he has faced and the unravelling of his mind and emotions as he strives to keep his family together.

Toolkit Techniques

Atmospheric walks: trudging through heavy, restrictive substances, referencing the weary, unending journey the character was experiencing. Exploring physical instability and a sense of chaos found in the character's journey. Treading water, working hard to keep his head above waves, trying not to drown.

Expanding and contracting (bound versus free): encouraging the mind-body connection of thought to the character's energy, both general and specific.

Music monologue-ing: signposting the musical changes in energy and tension within the story's arc. Listening to the accompaniment helped find the atmospheric changes embedded compositionally within the song.

Activating energetic centres, including breath: feeling the energetic internal shifts inside as the story grows, breathing into the centre where the energy is bubbling or coming from.

Mining the text: highlighting the transitive verbs – the dramatic, actionable signposts within the text; colour words, adjectives and adverbs, which were analysed to find the layers of meaning. Exploring conjunctions – words that joined ideas – every 'and' and every 'but'.

Context and subtext: analysing the surrounding story and playing against the surmounting issues, and a sense of defeat. Finding the inner dialogue to assist that process.

Primal Sound: empowering timbre. Exploring sighs, moans, and wails. Bringing meaning to melismas.

Song 4 – 'How Far I'll Go' from *Moana* (Lin Manuel Miranda, 2016)

This contemporary 'I want' song occurs early in the story as Moana, the protagonist, expresses her love for the sea and yearns for adventure and discovery beyond her traditionally bound island home.

Toolkit Techniques

Atmospheric scene visualization: awakening an imagined sensate reality using all five senses.

Qualities of movement: using air (flying), water (flowing), earth (moulding), fire (radiating) to connect to the earth's energetic elements and her desires and reality.

Subtext: connecting thought and breath to the ideas beneath the text. Finding and vocalizing those.

Music monologue-ing: listening and allowing the accompaniment to evoke extrinsic images and stir intrinsic emotions.

Cross-training outside-in: dancing the story to the accompaniment. Finding physical freedom.

Song 5 – 'Safer' from *First Date the Musical* (Zachary and Weiner, 2012)

While on a first date, Casey wrestles with past issues that have hurt her. As she debates whether becoming involved again is safe, she questions the future of a potential relationship. The song is a 'What if?' song. Here, the power of the questions embedded in the lyrics creates momentum and heightens the stakes.

Toolkit Techniques

Primal breath: elucidating 'the moment before' the song begins. Establishing the subtext and physical energy at the start of the song.

Word painting: exploring alliteration, vowel colours, and qualities of consonants, aiding the discovery of lyric to express thoughts. Using weight and emphasis to colour and enliven words. Thinking fast enough.

Activating energetic centres: physicalizing thoughts moving throughout her body, 'in the moment'. Freeing up arms and torso, feeling the shifts in energy.

Outside-in: discovering the physicality of uncertainty and instability of her predicament. Connecting body to thought, finding greater physical freedom.

Experiment and explore

I hope these insights into the toolkit and its applications inspire you to experiment, explore, and engage. In the 2023 movie *Air,* which depicts the sports company *Nike* signing basketball player Michael Jordan and the creation of the iconic Air Jordan shoe, Sonny Vaccaro, a *Nike* executive, states, '*A shoe is just a shoe until someone steps into it.*'[2] This notion applies universally to any method, model, or exercise regimen. The previous chapters on the SASS! toolkit offer a collection of potentially useful concepts, but unless they are put into practice, their transformative power remains dormant.

As an audience member, there is no greater excitement than watching someone make a discovery. It's like being right there at the opening of a lost treasure chest or rounding a corner in a foreign city to find a hidden gem. Have fun, embark on an adventure, explore new things, and play. It's worth it.

PART THREE
BE

14
LIVING OUT YOUR 'IT' FACTOR: FIVE 'P'S AND ELEVEN 'C'S

What lies behind you and what lies in front of you, pales in comparison to what lies inside of you.
– Commonly attributed to Ralph Waldo Emerson.

So, there you have it – my understanding of the 'It' Factor and how it can be unlocked, encouraged or explored. Ultimately, 'It' is an individual's perception of the energetic, communicative forces that exist and are transacted in the liminal space between living beings. These forces are most often experienced 'live' as we connect and relate to others in the communal act of open sharing. The following two chapters offer encouragement and some helpful hints on how to apply this knowledge and journey forward.

First, let's quickly recap Parts 1 and 2 – what I did and learned. To start, I grounded my research in literature and historical practices. Next, experts from the world of musical theatre shared keywords indicating how and when 'It' occurs and what external factors encourage its presence. A working definition and conceptual framework for performance synergy encapsulated and expressed this new understanding. Simply put, the 'It' Factor engages many facets of an actor's thinking, being, and doing. It can be described as truthful, immersive storytelling, spontaneous, imaginative play, generous, joyous giving, and a holistic, embodied connection to others.

I designed and constructed the SASS! toolkit – Strategies for Acting Singing Synergy – and situated it in a metaphorical space I named The Sandpit of Imaginative Play. Through workshops, masterclasses, and private tuition, the 'It' Factor was safely explored 'on the floor' and 'in the moment'. Toolkit techniques and tactics were trialled and tested for their effectiveness. The results confirmed that, when these tools are applied, positive observable changes can occur to increase dynamism in an actor's performance. My studies also revealed transferable, real-world applications and opportunities to explore 'It' beyond the realm of musical theatre.

Grounding your 'It' Factor with five 'P's

So, what now? What does this mean for you, the actor, teacher or individual eager to unlock more of your personal or performative 'It' Factor? Now, it's time to put it into action and do the work, both internally and externally, to awaken or revitalize the parts of your 'who' that are hidden, neglected or forgotten.

If you want to flow in the river of vibrant, creative expression, you must practise and prepare, give yourself permission, and then let go, play, and see where it leads you. Light up, open up, and radiate your energetic whole while staying grounded and connected to the core of your existence and the source of your energy – your personhood, the place, and the people who matter, those with whom you connect.

When you have finished, return to a centred, neutral place to rest, assess, and refuel. Be attentive and nurture your 'inner personhood' and the essence of *who* you are. To assist with that part of the journey, let's explore some important 'P' words.

Purpose

Work out and walk in your life purpose. Your purpose is another way of expressing your 'why'. The reasons we do what we do are shaped by our beliefs, attitudes, and the values that undergirds them. What do you cherish? Values help clarify your 'why'. When they are evident in your vision and manifested in your life, you can withstand unemployment, lack of public recognition, relationship loss, or the daily heartaches that accompany life. In the midst of an apparent wilderness, you can flourish and continue to grow. If you haven't defined your values before, it's an intriguing and rewarding exercise. You will likely uncover some of them rooted in your character strengths (see Chapter 12). Figure 14.1 presents just a few values to contemplate.

Your values shape your goals and the strategies you employ. Keep your position and purpose in mind while doing so. The actors and creatives I interviewed are among the most authentic, humble, open-hearted, generous, joyful, and genuine individuals I have ever met. Were they completely free of concern, insecurity, or doubt? No. Despite their failings, foibles, and flaws, they cherished what they did and dedicated all their efforts to their craft, their fellow actors and creatives, the story, and those they served: the writers and the audience.

Interestingly, once you have identified your *raison d'être* or purpose for your life and work, another 'P' word comes into play – passion! Passion reinforces your values and fuels your purpose.

Figure 14.1 Personal values.

Present, presence, and presents

The word 'present' in the English language can be used in various ways. Here are three definitions derived from early French and the Latin *'present'*, meaning 'being at hand'. Two 'presents' serve as synergy-makers, while the third, although not wrong, can disrupt synergy if used without the other two. Let's address that one first.

To present – a verb – simply means to show and tell, to offer information or a story packaged within a structured format or performance. It can be funny, engaging, gripping, inspiring, entertaining or educational, to name a few. A dictionary definition includes: *'to give someone a gift or award in a formal or ceremonial way'* and *'to show or offer something for others to scrutinize or consider'*.[1]

A story or song that is 'presented' can engage an audience, but there is potential for them to remain aloof if they don't connect with the story or storyteller. For instance, consider your engagement when observing someone objectively retelling an event compared to watching them relive it while immersing themselves in the telling. Performers may 'own' their material in the 'presenter' style. However, without spontaneity or moments of discovery, their presentational approach may become representational and diminish the potential for the 'It' Factor to appear.

Representational presentation is common among novice actors and is sometimes seen in audition rooms. Their eagerness to convey the story overshadows their capacity to genuinely 'live out' the narrative. Cognitive thoughts are expressed externally but are not embodied; the audience is shown thoughts and feelings rather than witnessing the actor's discovery and experience of them. This style of presentation inhibits synergy, causing the audience to shift from attentive engagement to objective observation. In contrast, synergized actors effectively tell the story from a place of embodied, liquid knowledge without imposing external mental or physical posturing.

Some tell-tale signs of presentational performance include gestural arm movements for emphasis, directing the story toward a specific spot in the back of the performance space, and a subtle push in song delivery instead of a fluid, radiating presence that draws us in.

Second, a *present* – a noun – is an offering, an exchange between people, given with good intentions and meant to bless or enrich someone. The dictionary defines this 'present' as *'a thing given to someone as a gift'*.[2]

This type of present is transactional: someone offers it, and it is either accepted or rejected. Like our stimulus/response graph (Figure 11.1), the response to that gift creates a cycle that energizes one moment into the next. The audience perceives the 'It' Factor when they react to an actor's gift of themselves. This establishes an interactive, transactional bridge (see Chapter 4) that can occur anywhere – in an intimate setting, sharing one-on-one or during a blockbuster musical.

Gift-giving involves commitment, sacrifice, and vulnerability. Offering your audience the gift of yourself is noble and a significant part of the 'It' Factor. However, synergy can be hindered when the giver actively seeks a response from the observer – searching for acceptance, validation, or appreciation in return. Although genuine, the synergistic connection between the actor and the audience is also delicate. The gift of self must be offered with no strings attached; otherwise, the synergy bridge will collapse.

Third, to be *present* – an adjective or descriptor – means being fully available in a single moment of time and space, experiencing the essence of giving and receiving, and allowing the time, space, and narrative of that moment to inform and impact you profoundly. The definition here is: *'to be in attendance, ready, accounted for, existing or occurring in a place or thing, fully focused or involved in what one is doing or experiencing'*.[3]

Its noun counterpart, presence, captures the essence of the 'It' Factor – being fully open, engaged, and available, without any agenda or expectation, while bestowing that openness upon others. One simple way to be fully present in your real or imagined environment is to absorb it with your eyes, acknowledge it, focus on specific points within that space, and then take in the area with a natural, deep breath that engages the intercostal muscles and diaphragm. As you exhale, direct your breath into that space and toward those points. Your breath is a part of you and can facilitate your connection with the room. Connectivity begins with your gaze and your authentic, inspirational breath. Observe how dogs exemplify this with their masters.

The 'It' Factor is revealed when actors are fully present and offer themselves and their gifts as presents.

Permission

Here, I discuss two types of permission: first, allow yourself to open up and share your true self; and second, grant the audience permission to engage with you. Too many people let the fear of failure or even the fear of success limit their energetic flow. Face the possibility of momentary failure rather than the experience of deep, long-lasting regret. The very act of being on stage empowers the synergized actor to be vulnerable and subtly extends that permission to the audience to come along for the ride.

I recently watched a video that epitomizes these two forms of permission and illustrates how the 'It' Factor is released joyously. The footage is a snippet from Jacob Collier's concert at the O2 Arena in London in December 2024.

Renowned for his extraordinary musicianship and his ability to connect with audiences, Collier begins his rendition of the classic Coldplay song, 'Fix You'. As he starts to play and sing, the audience is hushed. Collier's vocals resonate with the strength and depth of the song's lyrics, which express themes of love, commitment, and connection. Instead of a sense of 'performance', there is deep immersion. It is powerful storytelling. The crowd eagerly joins Collier to sing the first chorus with him. Then, from the 15,000-strong audience, steps Chris Martin, the composer and lead singer of Coldplay, who joins Collier on stage, and they duet.

What unfolds is truly magical. Martin takes over the piano, while Collier invites the audience to sing simple yet effective chords, creating backing harmonies that drift into the atmosphere, already illuminated by the tiny lights of thousands of mobile phones. Collier deftly shapes the sound, conducting the swelling ocean of emotion in a once-in-a-lifetime moment. You can see the joy and wonder on everyone's faces, including those of Collier and Martin.

The 'It' Factor was profoundly present, as these two artists were fully 'present', humbly sharing their gifts. There was no ego, only generosity, honesty, and joy.[4] The 'It' Factor equation also involves inviting someone to participate and then guiding the way. For the audience, what began as an enjoyable observation transformed into active participation.

Permission-giving creates a metaphoric space, sets an example, comes alongside, and encourages the audience to join the party or story. This permission fosters atmosphere and energy. Remember, as a performer, you are the curator of the atmosphere. You bring it with you as you enter a room and radiate it to the person before you. Moreover, you can give us permission to join you in your story.

Play

Much has already been said about this subject. This 'P' word should roll off your tongue as easily as its cousin: fun! Remember, the goal of play is fun; the more you engage in it, the greater your capacity for discovering new experiences in the present moment, which can be the most enjoyable fun in the world. That doesn't mean it isn't hard work. Sometimes, play requires you to let go of control, step out of your comfort zone, reclaim the past or confront hidden fears. Play and adventure live in the same house. Go visit them.

Perseverance

The dictionary definition of perseverance includes *'continued steady belief or efforts, withstanding discouragement or difficulty; persistence'*.[5] Synonyms include tenacity and pertinacity. It implies a resolute and unyielding commitment to a course of action. Perseverance commonly suggests activity that is sustained over a long period. Endurance and perseverance combine to achieve success in the end. Tenacity, originally meaning glue-like adhesiveness, signifies a dogged determination to hold on.

It takes hard work and stick-ability to stay the course and accomplish goals despite setbacks or obstacles. For those in the performing arts industry, setbacks often manifest as a lack of employment opportunities. Fuel your perseverance with a healthy dose of self-belief and optimism. Determine what you need to keep moving forward. Is it positive self-talk? A reward at the end? More knowledge or wisdom from a mentor or resource? A cheer squad or just a hug?

When paired with passion, perseverance becomes a formidable weapon. In her TED talk, psychologist Angela Lee Duckworth suggests that 'grit', her new 'P' word, is a powerful blend of passion and perseverance. More important than social intelligence, attractiveness, talent, or IQ, grit is a crucial predictor of success:

> *Grit is passion and perseverance for very long-term goals. Grit is having stamina. Grit is sticking with your future, day in, day out, not just for the week, not just for the month, but for years, and working really hard to make that future a reality. Grit is living life like it's a marathon, not a sprint.*[6]

Some 'C's to enliven your performance processes

Here are some 'C' keywords that emerged from the interviews. These concepts encourage you to unlock and combine your intrinsic performative processes to reveal your personal 'It' Factor. Not surprisingly, many of these words contain 'con' or 'com' as prefixes. 'Con' means *'with'* or *'thoroughly'*, and *'com'* is defined as *'with'*, *'together'*, *'in association'* and (with intensive force) *'completely'*, Our best selves are revealed when we merge and share different facets of who we are, creating the 'greater than' aspect of synergy.

Commitment

Commitment to whatever lies before you is vital for initiating the 'greater than' process. It embodies the 'doing' aspect of an actor's work. Focus your mind and will and actively engage with the task at hand. Whether it's a movie role, a product pitch, playful dress-ups or showing genuine interest in the person before you, your focus and commitment to that moment can be transformative. Passion, focus, and commitment to what you communicate translate into exciting energies that captivate. If you remain committed, the results, though not guaranteed, could astonish you.

The next three 'Cs' create a trio that intertwines and involves cognitive decision-making.

> *Excellence is never an accident. It is always the result of high intention, sincere effort, and intelligent execution; it represents the wise choice of many alternatives – choice not chance determines your destiny.*
> (Commonly attributed to Aristotle)

Comparisons

Comparisons can have both positive and negative aspects. Elite athletes use them as performance indicators during training to reach for 'personal bests'. Similarly, like the notches on a door frame that signify the physical growth of family members, reflecting on and celebrating how far you've come can be uplifting.

However, comparing yourself to others is a habit that forms easily and is often hard to break. It begins early in life as we seek to find our place in the world; we start to understand ourselves by observing others. Our identity is shaped by recognizing our differences, which helps crystallize our individuality. Nevertheless, comparisons can be harmful if your judgement relies on another's position or status in relation to your own.

The ensuing self-judgement can take two paths. You might find yourself using others or some high standard as a measuring stick, comparing it to aspects of your life and feeling inadequate. The fear of failure or of being 'less than' is destructive. This brand of self-judgement breeds anxiety and despondency. Equally dangerous is the comparison that positions you in a stance of superiority. Thinking of yourself as 'better than' allows the ego to enter the picture. And the ego is an 'It' Factor killer. Ego is also deceptive and can serve as the armour worn by fear.

In contrast, truly successful actors are humble and approachable. I have watched film and theatre stars signing autographs at stage doors on Broadway. One who comes to mind is Hugh Jackman. The care and attention he exudes to the fans who wait patiently for a word or photograph are inspiring.

How can we break the natural tendency to judge ourselves and others? Author Faye Simpson suggests beginning a new habit to bring fresh perspective:

> *Choose a day to practice non-judgemental mind. The challenge is to not judge anyone, including yourself, all day – at home, at work, or on the street. If this is too hard, do it for an hour, and then lengthen the time gradually. Take notes in your journal when you do become judgemental … Just take a note and try again. After a period of successful non-judging, write down your new observations about people.*[7]

Confidence

Self-confidence is a cognitive process that triggers an emotional response and manifests in our will or persona. Unlike ego-driven judgement, it involves simply believing in yourself enough to 'give it a go'. This free and positive self-expression is key to unlocking 'It'. Julia Cameron succinctly states, *'All too often it is audacity and not talent that moves an artist to centre stage.'*[8] While actors and directors view high technical competencies as essential, they also recognize that the mental, emotional, and psychological factors they engage with or observe are at the heart of a synergistic performance.

Uncertainty can easily infiltrate one's thinking and undermine self-belief. Conversations with my graduate students reveal how they may be subconsciously confined by a desire for excellence. The negative self-judgement and perceived weight of expectation they face during assessments are carried into the professional arena. Auditions can transform into a form of examination accompanied by hidden agendas or an unknown measure of achievement they feel they must attain. The performer's sense of freedom and enjoyment is then impeded, which cyclically worsens the negative perception of self and ability. For some young professionals, the internal, self-defeating mind scripts: *'Do they like me*?', *'What am I doing wrong*?', *'Should I belt louder*?', and *'I must try harder!'* are common in their audition experiences.

If this resonates, remember that we are much more than our skills and performances. Conduct an internal self-check and quietly acknowledge and applaud all the facets of who you are. As a human, you are fearfully and wonderfully made, possessing purpose, power, and passion. Discover a mantra that supports your self-belief, take a deep breath, practise self-care, actively pursue your future, and summon your courage.

Courage

The virtue of courage can emerge even when self-confidence is lacking. Auditions and performances can be daunting, both mentally and emotionally. Often, our inner strength is tested. Courage was emphasized as part of our fifth performative process – our intrinsic persona (Chapter 3). It is generated from our will and fuelled by our mind or spirit. Challenges may arise both internally and externally. Courage enables us to confront perceived difficulties regardless of our fears, doubts, and concerns. Overcoming self-doubt, the thief of self-belief, is a significant hurdle for many. However, when we stand firm in our convictions – our steadfast beliefs and values – we can confront the challenges ahead, irrespective of the situational outcome.

Bravery and courage live side by side. Bravery involves taking action in spontaneous moments, often triggered instinctively. Courage, on the other hand, is the deliberate act of facing fear and choosing to move forward. Remember, everyone on the planet experiences and deals with fear. Confront that robber with courage. When you need to summon it, take a deep breath, focus and align your mind, will, and body for the task ahead, and say aloud, 'I can do this!'

Curiosity

Curiosity, often referred to as wonder or inquisitive thinking, is a personality trait that can be encouraged and ignited by specific situations. It is driven instinctively by what I affectionately call my 'back brain'. Every invention and breakthrough that has propelled our civilization forward has been fuelled by a desire to learn more. When interest is sparked, both minds and hearts become engaged. Wonder stimulates curiosity, and together, they inspire exploration and adventure.

Curiosity can be cultivated as a habit. An actor once told me that practising curiosity daily is the most important thing. We can learn something new each day and, by doing so, uncover wonder in the most fascinating and unexpected places. The more we wonder and open our minds, the richer our palette of life experience and knowledge becomes, enabling us to create compelling characters on stage.

How do you practise curiosity? Ask the 'How?', 'Why?', 'What if?' or 'I wonder … ' questions at least ten times a day. These can range from simple tasks and thoughts to deep philosophical considerations. For simpler questions, AI can be your friend. For example, did you know that, although one cubic metre of cloud weighs only half a gram, the average cumulus cloud, measuring one square kilometre, weighs about 500,000 kilograms? Thank goodness for air resistance and updraughts!

Compassion

Compassion, part of the passion family, arises from the wellspring of your emotive process. We have a family saying: 'With understanding comes compassion.' When I understand why someone makes uncomfortable choices, it becomes easier to withhold harsh judgement and find a measure of sympathy or empathy. Compassion keeps our eyes and hearts open, and the shared experience of walking alongside someone in pain enriches our lives and nourishes our souls. Your heart expands with each step you take, and a large heart is one of the most attractive forces on the planet.

Brené Brown agrees, stating,

> 'Compassion is fuelled by understanding and accepting that we're all made of strength and struggle – no one is immune to pain or suffering. Compassion is not a practice of "better than" or "I can fix you" – it's a practice based in the beauty and pain of shared humanity.'[9]

Her working definition of compassion is: *'the daily practice of recognizing and accepting our shared humanity so that we treat ourselves and others with loving-kindness and take action in the face of suffering'*.[10]

This hearkens to another golden rule, *'Do unto others as you would have them do unto you.'* Humanity is inextricably connected to one another, no matter how many desert islands we may try to escape to. The Dalai Lama writes, *'If you want others to be happy, practise compassion. If you want to be happy, practise compassion.'*[11]

Compassion begins with us. Learn to give selflessly without unintentionally imposing our personal values and beliefs. Be mindful that we often project the same judgement we apply to ourselves. Healthy self-love and compassion create space for growth, while self-condemnation quenches our inner light. Look around for someone to whom you can show compassion, even if the first place you look is in the mirror.

Choices

The small choices we make every day define our lives, for better or worse. Incremental steps ultimately lead to significant change. A single degree change in a ship's course on the ocean can result in the boat being lost at sea. Making a choice is a cognitive activity but let your head hear from your other energy centres – your heart and your soul – before making decisions that shut you down rather than open you up. Choosing to be open is challenging. Try to perform one good deed for someone else each day.

Whether it's a smile, a little time or a conversation, you can practise the giving and openness that are essential parts of the 'It' Factor.

Connection

Connection lies at the heart of the 'It' Factor; creation cannot exist without it. Watch a David Attenborough documentary about the extraordinary lengths that birds and animals go to in their courtship rituals, and you will witness another manifestation of the 'It' Factor in action!

Theatrical connections manifest in various ways: the actor engages with fellow actors, directors, the story, the audience, and the environment. Directors foster connections through their relationships with actors during auditions, rehearsals, or performances. However, actors must establish connections within their inner life first. Power is unleashed when intrinsic processes align with the task at hand promoting congruence. Reflect on your energy centres (Chapter 11). The most meaningful connections occur when these centres are all open and engaged, allowing energy to flow freely through you toward a common goal.

Vulnerability is a crucial part of connection. Producer and director Kris Stewart noted: *'Something in the human connection of vulnerability and honesty and passion that comes from the star that will make every individual member of that thousand-strong audience feel like they're the only one there in the moment with them.'*

Actor Caroline O'Connor agrees:

That essence of vulnerability is so incredibly attractive on stage, even for actors that are strong. There's something about that quality that on stage is so magnetic – when someone's really opened themselves up and being brutally honest about how they're feeling and you can feel it's honest, not play acting but actually doing it. Wow, it's so ... powerful. Mesmerising and powerful.

Psychologist and emotions researcher Susan David introduces us to the word 'sawubona', the Zulu term for hello, which reflects part of the African philosophy Ubunto: *'I am, because we are.'* Translated, sawubona means *'I see you, and by seeing you, I bring you into being.'* David asks us to question how we perceive ourselves and encourages us to connect with our inner world, building emotional agility for resilience and thriving.[12]

To practise this inner connection, take a moment to look within and take stock. Say *'Hello'* to yourself the Zulu way – sawubona – and bring yourself into being. Pause to identify if there's a part of you that is inaccessible or locked away. Practise opening up and sharing that part of yourself. For instance, if you find it challenging to be spontaneous, try improvising with words – find and articulate a subtext; or if your body is usually composed, try dancing and moving as you sing. Discover the aspects of yourself that are reclusive and bring them to light. As you engage with different parts of your intrinsic whole, this inner connection translates into an aura and transactional energy that empowers extrinsic connection and the 'It' Factor.

Competency

There is a reason why technical competency is the sixth intrinsic process I identified. Competency unlocks dynamic performance; nothing replaces 'doing the work'. Aspiration and inspiration must be outworked with perspiration.

Magic happens when actors are unconsciously competent rather than consciously competent. If you find yourself needing to focus on your singing or acting technique while performing, invest more time in embedding your skills. However, be mindful of how you practise. Practise makes permanent, not perfect, and bad habits can easily develop through repetition. When you practise, vary your approach. Explore different perspectives. Deconstruct your skills: concentrate on minutiae in one moment, then explore the overall arc and sweep of the entire song or scene the next. Practise that is overly formulaic stifles discovery and spontaneity, potentially causing you to lose the intuitive sizzle that brings the work to life.

Community

Although community isn't an inherent characteristic of an actor's performative processes, it is frequently mentioned. 'Belonging' serves as an invaluable, extrinsic asset that enables you to navigate the world, both on stage and off. Many of your most significant strengths come from your family, friends, and supporters – some are part of your inner circle, while others cheer you on from afar. They all matter. The life of an actor can be incredibly isolating. On stage, it's a collaborative effort; off stage, the responsibility rests on you. Treasure those in your tribe and community. If there is a deficiency, seek out like-minded individuals. They provide a sanctuary when you feel depleted, a trampoline to help you bounce back when you're down, a voice of reason when you need sound advice, and they will keep you humble, challenging you when you lose perspective. They are also wonderful people with whom you can practise your techniques and tactics, even if they are unaware of it.

Communion

Another word associated with 'community' is communion. Nothing is more potent than the 'common union' of hearts, minds, and intentions — when a company of people works toward a shared vision or goal, whether on stage or off. Breaking bread together, building trust with colleagues, and being vulnerable with one another enrich performances and the lives of fellow actors. However, it requires an outward-looking perspective and a dose of courage, commitment, emotional security, and maturity to achieve this. If being vulnerable or generous is something you struggle with, practise these qualities. They are traits worth developing.

We're nearly there. Let's wrap this up.

15
GIVE YOURSELF PERMISSION TO SHINE!

Be yourself, everyone else is already taken.

–Unknown
(Commonly attributed to Oscar Wilde).

We humans are truly extraordinary. There are over eight billion of us on this little blue planet, and no two are the same. Within each of us lies a unique capacity for greatness in myriad ways – we are dreamers, visionaries, storytellers, inventors, adventurers, listeners, lovers, caregivers, nurturers, pragmatists, researchers, teachers, networkers, builders, creators, curators and artists – the list goes on. On this planet, only you can be you, and only you can do you. As you explore the fundamentals of who you are, why you are here, what you believe in, and what you love to do, your 'when', 'where', 'how', and 'why' will unfold. With focused commitment and effort, you can discover that unique greatness. And it looks different for each of us.

Not everyone is destined for the stage, screen, or the fame and fortune that public accolades can sometimes bring. Those seemingly 'greater' achievements are fleeting as well. Personal fulfilment comes from living purposefully rather than seeking recognition – trite but true. When we attend to and nurture our intrinsic processes, the seeds of creativity and connectivity flourish, enriching our lives. As we extend that part of ourselves outward, we love, discovering existential meaning and our place within humanity.

My understanding of the 'It' Factor is framed through this lens: we all possess 'It'; it is part of the innate energy we call the human spirit, and it is hardwired for communication and interaction with others. For many artists, there is no other way to live – they must sing, paint, dance, construct, tell stories, design, create, play, and do. The more performers commit their inner processes to self-expression, the greater the potential for those watching to connect with them. Mirror neurons are activated, observers respond to the artist and their story, and lives are creatively enriched.

'It' is an intrinsic part of us. Yet harnessing the 'It' Factor can feel like trying to catch lightning in a bottle, as we attempt to capture the essence of something ephemeral, unpredictable, and mercurial. If we try to control 'It', it disappears. The challenge of pinning it down highlighted to me the wonder of who we are as humans, all cut from the same DNA cloth, yet extraordinarily unique, fearfully and wonderfully made. We have so much to offer each other and the world, and that's where the magic truly happens. The 'It' inside you becomes visible only when you allow it to shine, not for your ego or glory, but as a gift to those around you. There is a river within you, ready to flow. Are you ready?

Find your flow

The principles for finding flow, whether on stage or off, remain consistent. Your performative 'It' Factor is expressed as you:

- enhance your knowledge, develop skills in what you love, and push your limits, and
- discover your intrinsic motivation and mojo – they are connected to your *raison d'être,* your reason for being – your beliefs, attitudes, and values.

If you know what you want to do, let go and immerse yourself in the task. If you don't, take the time to explore until you gain clarity.

When you enter a state of flow, time may appear to stand still; you will feel relaxed yet energized, profoundly connected to the present moment yet liberated from ego or the constraints of self. But how can you achieve this state?

Reframe your fear

In this age of angst, fear surrounding performance is rampant in both work and life, particularly among those under forty. Fear manifests in many forms, including aggression, avoidance, rebellion, manipulation, and procrastination, which is my personal default.

Your limbic system, which is responsible for processing and regulating emotions, forming and storing memories, and facilitating learning, can enter a state of overdrive, leading to elevated hormone levels. A cocktail of cognitive, somatic, emotional, and behavioural responses comes into play, releasing the energy accumulated in the body and inducing stress (see Table 15.1).

Table 15.1 Elements contributing to performance anxiety

Response	Behaviour
Cognitive	Your thinking brain recognizes the danger.
Somatic	Your body's instinctive response in a panic situation is to rely on autonomic arousal which produces the 'f' responses – fight, flight, freeze, fawn (try to appease) or flop (deflate, play dead, lose all energy or desire for the task).
Emotional	Your emotional energy, or valence, gives meaning to the panic – and it can be either positive or negative.
Behavioural	You apply previously learned mechanics or routine. If your response behaviour is self-limiting or defeating, you can limit access to stored knowledge and reduce the ability to focus and perform.

Responses can be self-perpetuating; behaviours that lead to a perceived negative self-assessment foster disappointment or negative valence (emotional energy). Self-doubt drains energy, and fear can escalate sympathetic responses and adrenaline to unmanageable levels. For the 'It' Factor to flourish, these synergy blockers need to be disempowered. But finding a way out of this cycle is not as simple as saying the ubiquitous, '*Calm down and ...*', especially when a greater performance energy is required.

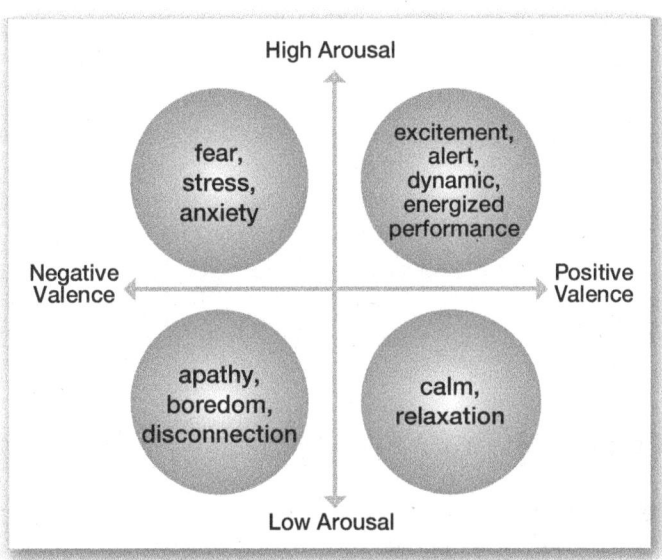

Figure 15.1 The valence/arousal matrix for optimal performance.

Research continues in the anxiety/performance space. Several studies suggest that performers can transition from high negative valence, characterized by anxiety and fear, to high positive valence, which is optimal for dynamic performance, through the power of reframing and reappraisal.[1]

Take a look at Figure 15.1. Instead of asking an anxious performer to de-escalate and change their energy level from the high/negative quadrant to the low/positive quadrant – a two-step process – and then to ramp up and find a high/positive energy for performance (a third step), research claims it is easier to move the anxious performer one step sideways from high negative to high positive. How? They can simply use self-talk to modify their perspective, reframing '*I'm scared about X*' to '*I'm excited to try X*' or something similar. Too good to be true? Well, I have experienced its efficacy; such is the power of our minds. Self-talk is a powerful tool. You have the choice to think and speak in either manner.

> *L'homme est libre au moment qu'il veut l'être.*
> (Man is free at the instant he wants to be.)
> Voltaire (1694–1778)
> Source *Brutus*, Act II, Scene I (1730)

Harness the power of your imagination and body to assist you. Pre-frame your performance by envisioning yourself confidently walking onto a stage, into a boardroom or a classroom – wherever you need to go. Picture a successful performance all the way to the end. See yourself being and feeling instead of merely doing. A disconnect between your thoughts and physicality can build up over time and rob you of confidence. Regularly practise one or more psychophysical exercises from your toolkit to maintain a strong imagination and mind–body connection. Alternatively, take a stance, hold it, and settle into it for a few minutes – try a Superman or Wonder Woman postural characterization. Some research suggests that posturing may increase testosterone (a power hormone) and decrease cortisol (a primary stress hormone).[2]

Sydney-based performance arts counsellor Sarah Marshall offers strategies for releasing the debilitating hold that hormones and fear-driven brain responses create.[3] They can be as simple as chewing gum or squeezing a stress ball with your left hand, regardless of your hand dominance. Breathwork is another effective tool. Marshall advocates box breathing, which I describe as breathing in a square (see Chapter 10). Try to 'tend and befriend' – make contact with someone you care about. It releases oxytocin, which is linked to empathy, trust, and relationships. Smile. Non-verbal communication reflects and reinforces feelings. And remember, every day is a second chance. This performance moment – be it an audition or a job interview – is just part of your life journey, not the endgame. Mentally, ease the pressure of the moment, as undue stress triggers adrenaline. While a little adrenaline is ideal for an energized performance, too much can constrict and shut down your performance.

STOP! – Surrender, Trust, Open up, Play

Several years ago, I spent time with a dear singer-musician friend who lives in Brooklyn, NY. She is talented – very talented. However, the music business, like the theatre industry, doesn't always reward talent; even the most skilled and gifted musicians may never receive 'the break' they deserve. Many strive for years, showcasing all the 'It' Factor in the world, yet still do not 'crack' it. One day, while we were chatting, we devised the mnemonic 'STOP' – what to do in difficult situations while trying to navigate seemingly unforgiving terrain. How can you avoid debilitating disappointment or burnout?

Firstly, SURRENDER. Surrender doesn't mean giving up but rather letting go. There is a difference! Don't give up on your beliefs, values or passion for they are important parts of what makes you, you. Instead, let go of what hinders your progress forward to whatever awaits.

Close your eyes and lift your hands. I lift mine high, like in a 'Stick 'em up!' movie moment. Take a breath and consciously relinquish your hold on the things outside your control – decisions, work, future events. Sometimes our hurts, fears, anxieties, limiting self-talk, and unmet expectations become a prickly blanket we wrap ourselves in to find comfort. Those things are not your friends. Let go of them. There is a greater good out there. Be brave. Surrender. Create space for new dreams, possibilities, and opportunities.

Next, TRUST. Trust that you have everything – right where you are – to meet your needs, if not your wants, and to help you take the next step on your journey. Not every step is a giant leap. Remember the tortoise? Slow and steady can win the race. Personally, I'm more of a hare; however, I don't necessarily progress any further or faster. Be kind to yourself and stop the self-judgement. Find simple, achievable ways to nurture your body, mind, heart, soul, and spirit. You have the tools: meditation, journalling, reading a book, listening to a podcast, going for a walk, dancing, singing out loud, or hitting the gym. Engage larger muscle groups; they release endorphins, which alleviate stress and pain, promote well-being, and harness adrenaline, your stress hormone, in a positive way.

Establish routines to organize your life outside of work. Check in with yourself each day. Pursue or create opportunities to express your creativity and engage in activities you enjoy, with anyone who hears or sees you.

Trust in the bigger picture. Do you have a faith? It's a powerful muscle that strengthens with exercise. Reflect on your beliefs, values, and what's important.

Then, OPEN UP. Self-belief will empower you to reach out and connect, but humility is essential. The opportunity to share ourselves with others is a gift, not a right. Remember Rodenberg's circles? As much as it is about giving, it is also about receiving with an open heart, in the present moment. Acknowledge and value your connection with others and what they give back to you. When we open up to another person, relationship, event, or experience, we become receptive to learning, discovering, growing, and more – whatever that 'more' may be. I know it's easier said than done. In a world filled with brokenness, trusting and opening up have become collateral damage in the name of self-preservation and security. But that openness is an essential part of the 'It' Factor. Find people and places where you can practise being open-hearted and open-minded.

Finally, PLAY. The 'P' represents play, not perform. Check to see if you need to make a mental shift. You are not a puppet or a performing monkey seeking work for peanuts. Don't allow the essence of who you are, your 'It' Factor, and your craft to revolve around money; instead, focus on what brings you happiness and fulfilment. Yes, you deserve fair compensation for your work, but don't let someone else's evaluation of your value determine your self-belief in your worth. Only you should retain that control.

There are many talented and trained individuals, yet few creative opportunities that offer professional pay. Many professional actors engage in flexible side hustles or offstage gigs to ensure their bills are covered. Consider exploring an alternative activity so you don't inadvertently tie your self-worth to the number of performance opportunities you receive.

Playing involves enjoying your gifts and abilities while staying curious, open, and flexible to discover and explore new opportunities as they arise. Keep an eye out for them. A common truth in the casting world is that those who are working often find more work. The 'It' Factor emerges when the need for validation through employment is removed from the equation. The 'catch-22' of needing a job to secure more work can be exhausting. Try to see the simple act of sharing your gift during an audition or interview as your job. You fulfil your role by sharing your song, story, or life with an audience of one or a few, regardless of the outcome. Viewing your work as play revitalizes it. And after you have 'played' or shone, remember to STOP again – rest and recharge.

Apply what you've learned

Create opportunities to apply your craft; plenty exist if you seek them. Graduates from any course can attest to the significant difference between cognitive and applied knowledge, something they discover when they start working in professional theatre. Recently, I managed a project – building what Australians call a 'granny flat', a secondary dwelling for a family member or someone to live independently on your property. My goodness, the learning curve was incredible! However, my biggest realization was the value of applying knowledge. The draughtsman and structural engineers knew what needed to be constructed, but the build was achieved through the experience, wisdom, and practical application of that knowledge by builders, carpenters, and specialized tradespeople. The many specific decisions required to complete the task could only be made through action, not just knowledge. Find a place where you can 'do'.

And above all, love

In the forty-two interviews I conducted, one keyword stood out above the rest: love. Interviewees expressed their love for their work and for telling stories; they cherished their connections with audiences and valued their responses, which buoyed them onward. They shared their affection for their fellow actors and the opportunities that performing provides to express themselves freely. The word 'love' conveys profundity: there is always more to discover, know, and experience. It may seem like an oversimplification to assert that a significant part of our 'It' Factor is love in action – seen, felt, and experienced – yet in many respects, it remains true.

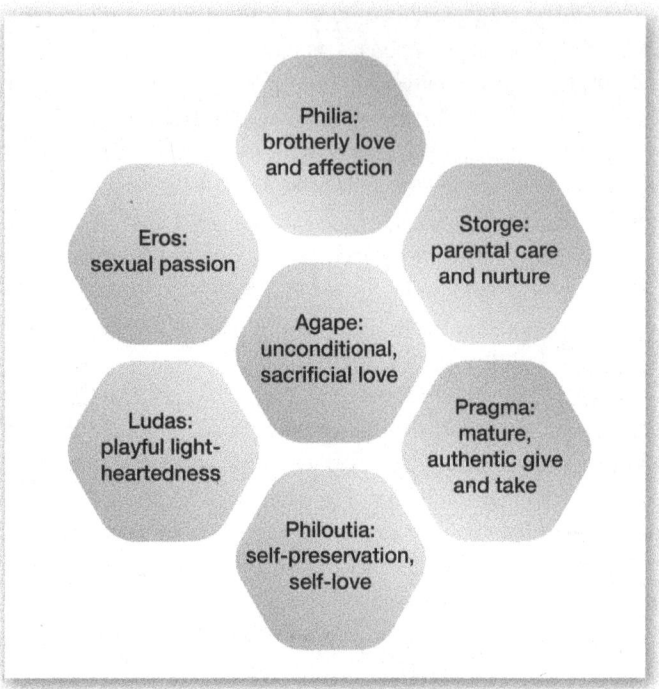

Figure 15.2 Seven Greek words for love.

What type of love are we talking about, though? The Greeks have seven distinct words for relational love (see Figure 15.2).[4] Each word plays a role in how we connect, first to ourselves, then to others, and how our 'It' Factor is unlocked and recognized. Love encompasses more than just feelings; it consists of the countless small choices and actions we make each day, week, month, and year, in different ways with different people. Unsurprisingly, many synergy-related keywords are reflected in these various forms of love.

Take a moment to consider how and to whom you can express these different forms of love, which ones come naturally to you, and whether there is some inner work that you may want to undertake to unlock other ways of expressing love. Remember, as each intrinsic process is unlocked and becomes available for use, your personal and performance 'It' Factor will grow.

One of the most powerful forms of love is 'agape'. It's a love that knows no bounds or judgement and is fully committed, present, and giving. My late golden retriever, Bailey, would pour out this unconditional love to me in bucketloads. When you looked into his eyes, you would see 'It' radiating from deep, clear, brown pools of love.

When you actively choose to love something with energy and purpose, the outcome is passion – a love that is ablaze. And that's the fire that bakes our synergistic cake, the one I discussed in Chapter 1. Passionate love acts as the oven that transforms cake batter (the separate skills and personal processes) into something far greater than the sum of its parts – a mouth-watering treat that nurtures and satisfies.

Mystery and many-sidedness

Love and mystery are closely aligned, and both serve as essential ingredients in the 'It' Factor. Ultimately, mystery remains incomprehensible; it encompasses enticing elements of curiosity, wonder, awe, and a sense of the seemingly unattainable that generates longing and desire. I am aware that, as I draw to a close, the answer to the question, *'What is "It"?* cannot be definitive. My synergy equation – shown in Figure 6.2 – remains unfinished.

In the academic writing world, we are always encouraged to conclude with 'More research is needed!' because while much can be surmised and proposed, in the world of qualitative research and philosophical thinking, nothing is ever, truly, fully known. Ironically, if my research had unravelled all the mystery surrounding the 'It' Factor rather than illuminating what 'It' might be, I would have stripped away its mystique and rendered 'It' mundane.

An ancient Indian parable, popular in Jainism, explores the mystery and concept of many-sidedness. The story involves an elephant and a small group of blind men who wish to understand what the creature is like. Each man touches a different part of the pachyderm's anatomy – a wiry tail, hard tusks, trunk-like legs, or thin, plate-like ears. Each argues that the part he feels represents the entire elephant (see Figure 15.3).[5]

Figure 15.3 Blind Men and the Elephant.
Note: Illustration from *World Stories for Children*, Ainsworth & Co. (Chicago: Ainsworth and Co., 1916), p.14. Public domain.

This parable aligns with much of what I learned about the 'It' Factor; differing perspectives may all be correct but do not necessarily present the whole picture. While acquiring new knowledge is a start, understanding this creative energy alone will not bring it into existence. Even those who ride and train elephants describe the creature differently, reflecting a multiplicity of perspectives and perceptions. I have tried to unpack the elements, substance, experiences, and contextual influences surrounding 'It'. This 'elephant' was approached directly through the workshops and toolkit application as we attempted to ride it. Those experiences 'on the floor' produced a new understanding of how the elephant – the 'It' Factor – lives and moves. Still, we may know its many sides, but we do not truly know it all.

> On a Graham Norton Show in 2023, actor Austin Butler, star of the 2022 film *Elvis*, recounted the counsel he received from visionary director Baz Luhrmann, prior to the biopic's release. Luhrmann told him, 'You can never predict the outcome, but what you can do is relish in the process.' Sage advice.
> https://www.youtube.com/watch?v=qyKA3FPcPAM

There is no singular iteration or archetype of the 'It' Factor. So many variables are at play: actors and their individual processes, which ebb and flow with their life experiences; the environment in which they perform; the shapeshifting and sometimes unpredictable nature of audiences; the quality of the work and production; and the direction. When we summon our 'It', we must remember that outcomes are often beyond our control. No matter how prepared we are, how well we 'deliver', or how 'in the moment' we can be, we may reach the final round of a lengthy audition or job interview process and still not land the role. Often, there is no rhyme or reason. It simply is.

Although we can't control the outcome, we can manage our part of the journey to wherever that outcome may lead. In 1984, as a young musical theatre actor, I left Australia for England, determined to secure my place on the West End stage. A dear friend gave me a card that read, '*It's not the end of the journey that matters, but the journey that matters in the end*.' That pithy quote has remained true through over forty-five years of ups and downs, in and out of work, study, relationships, and life. Whether the outcome is a resounding yes or no, bright lights or a flickering lamp, it's the way you 'journey' that produces the real gold. For successful working actors, their mindset enables them to thrive through audition rounds, perceived 'rejections', and whatever they do to pay the bills between theatre contracts.

It's over to you

So, after a book full of words, I have concluded that the 'It' Factor, or dynamic performance synergy, is a uniquely personal quality, inherently accessible to all who seek it wholeheartedly. 'It' involves allowing oneself to be stripped of ego and pretence, embracing openness and vulnerability, becoming fully and freely present with oneself, and joyfully offering that self to others. It's what I believe we were created to be as humans.

An old adage states, '*The greatest doors swing wide open on the smallest hinges.*' Little changes in how we approach things can lead to significant differences. Take a few deep, focused breaths. Ask curious questions. Stop and listen to those around you or take a moment to reflect within your heart and mind to gather your passion. Ultimately, you must trust yourself. Only you know you, and only you can do you, best. There are as many personalities as there are people on the planet; therefore, there are as many 'It' Factors. Yours may be the overflowing, unfettered, tomboyish Clara Bow type, or the slow-burning

Brando version. Perhaps it's more like one of our beloved British dames, Maggie Smith or Judi Dench, or as seemingly bold and laconic as Aussie Chris Hemsworth. Your 'It' may appear quiet and fragile – like a tall, tapered candle with a single beautiful flame. Or it may be a searchlight piercing the dark, or a colourful display of party lights. You know who you are, at your core.

And if you still doubt that you can find your 'It', just pause for a moment, get comfortable, close your eyes, breathe in through your nose, quieten your mind and heart, and envision yourself happy, free, and at play. Perhaps recall when you were a child in the sandpit, dressing up, singing in the shower as a teenager, or dancing to your favourite song like no one's watching. Maybe you are an adult playing with your children, watching a sunset, walking along a forest trail, or enjoying time with friends. At some point in your past, your intrinsic processes all worked harmoniously – having fun, connecting with your world without even noticing. Deep within you, aspects of your heart, soul, mind, and strength still know how to awaken, coalesce, and flow out of you.

'It' is there. Waiting to be found.

AFTERWORD

I hope you enjoyed your journey through this book and feel encouraged and inspired to ignite your 'It' and live your most free and joyful life. During the final stages of my writing, several conversations with several experienced actors – including my son David, who is currently on a national tour – inspired these closing words.

There is no substitute for the personal growth that comes through experience. If you are a newly graduated actor seeking work in this oversaturated industry, seize every opportunity to watch and learn, practise and then practise again. When you can, get 'onto the floor'. Do the work. Nothing beats the school of life, with its highs and lows, and the riches that come from 'learning by doing'. Until you've lived, loved and lost, the well of experience from which you draw will remain shallow.

David said to me, *'Tell them it's a numbers game. And that it's the reality of the industry. Tell them to audition, audition, audition.'* A working actor is not just someone who performs eight shows a week but is also one who develops or hones their craft and finds opportunities to tell stories, even in auditions. That is the primary work.

This book or any other book, or teacher, or method, is not a magic bullet that will guarantee financial success. When an audition 'no' comes your way, don't take it personally. So much is out of your control. Many hidden variables shape each 'yes' or 'no' that have nothing to do with your talent or suitability. You can be the most skilled person on the audition list and still not make the cut. Pick yourself up and move forward – your courage, authenticity and resilience are what matter.

In 2024, tennis legend Roger Federer delivered an inspiring commencement address at Dartmouth College, in Hanover, New Hampshire.[1] Some of his 'tennis lessons' are worth recounting. He talked of the broad 'talents' of discipline, patience and trusting yourself while embracing and loving the 'process'. Federer encouraged the graduates to work hard, especially when no one is watching, to amplify their game and expand their options. He then shared an axiom that is valuable for us to remember as performers. *'It's only a point,'* he said. Federer won nearly 80 per cent of the 1,526 singles matches he played during his career, yet he only won 54 per cent of the points he played. Federer stated, *'When you lose every second point on average, you learn not to dwell on every shot.'*

In this wonderful, crazy world of musical theatre, you will always lose 'points'. Federer reminds us that when you are playing a point it should be the most important thing in the world. Then, when it's won or lost, you must put it behind you and freely move on to the next 'point' and the next, with intensity, clarity, and focus.

My fervent hope is that wonderful opportunities for you to live out your 'It' Factor on stage will come your way. Regardless of wins or losses and no matter what the future may bring, you will be richer if you greet each day and each opportunity with self-belief, curiosity, an open heart and a sense of adventure.

APPENDIX

Listed below are some of the wonderful actors and creatives who generously contributed to my research and whose wisdom and perspectives are included in this book. Their professional careers have spanned over sixty-five years in Australia, Asia, the UK and the USA.

Stephen Amos is an Australian-based musical director, arranger, and orchestrator. Key credits include *West Side Story,* the 10th Anniversary production of *Les Misérables, MAMMA MIA! The Musical, War Horse, SIX! the Musical* and *Moulin Rouge!* Stephen has won two prestigious Australian Helpmann Awards for his work on *Billy Elliot* and *Matilda the Musical,* and was On Set Music Supervisor for the 2024 biopic film *Better Man.*

Geoffrey Castles is a musical director, pianist, vocal coach, and arranger, who has conducted Australian and international productions of *Miss Saigon, Mary Poppins, The Bridges of Madison County* (Australian premiere), *Aladdin,* the 25th Anniversary production of *Les Misérables, Aspects of Love, Songs for a New World,* and *Wicked.* As a coach he specializes in repertoire and audition preparation and is currently completing a Master of Fine Arts (Musical Theatre).

Alinta Chidzey is a veteran theatre and film actor, jazz vocalist, and composer, originating the role of Satine in the Australian production of *Moulin Rouge!.* Other key credits include *Chicago, West Side Story, Jesus Christ Superstar* and *Singin' in the Rain.* Alinta received theatre awards for her performances in *Chess,* and *Leader of the Pack.* She has also recorded a jazz album and released her own original material.

David Cuny is a gifted Australian actor, singer, composer and guitarist. Theatre credits include Danny Zuko in *Grease,* Corny Collins in *Hairspray,* and the Australian national tours of *Elvis: A Musical Revolution* (Elvis Alternate) and *Lord of the Rings: A Musical Tale.* His original songs can be found on Spotify and Apple Music under David Jerome.

Natalie Gilhome is a sought-after Australian-born casting director, resident director, choreographer, and producer. Her broad experience has seen her involved in productions such as *Grease, School of Rock, West Side Story, Matilda, Sunset Boulevard, Wicked, Jagged Little Pill, Groundhog Day The Musical,* and *Back to the Future.*

Simon Gleeson is an experienced actor and screen writer. He came to prominence playing Raoul in *Love Never Dies* and won a Helpmann Award for the role of Jean Valjean in *Les Misérables,* reprising his role in London in 2016. Credits include *Chess, Oklahoma!* and the UK TV shows *EastEnders* and *Kombat Opera Presents.* Simon co-wrote the 2024 Robbie Williams biopic film *Better Man.*

Joel Granger is a vibrant New Zealand-born theatre and television actor. Theatre credits include Elder McKinley in *The Book of Mormon, Hairspray, Pippin, Next to Normal, Sweeney Todd, West Side Story* and *Guys and Dolls.* TV credits include *Please Like Me, True Story with Hamish and Andy,* and the musical series *Happiness.*

Jaime Hadwen is an engaging Australian actor and cabaret artist whose theatre credits include the Australian national tours of *Muriel's Wedding* and *The Adventures of Peter Pan and Tinkerbell, Grease, Cinderella* and *Xanadu.* She presented *ONJ: The Cabaret* on Olivia Newton John in 2020.

Nancye Hayes (AM) is one of Australia's iconic treasures and a Grand Dame of theatre. An award-winning actor, dancer, singer, choreographer, and director, her career spans over six decades. Successes include *Sweet Charity, A Little Night Music, Pippin, Irene, Annie, Chicago, Sweeney Todd, Nine, Guys and Dolls,* and *42nd Street.* In 2014, Nancye was honoured as a Member of the Order of Australia (AM) for her exceptional services to the performing arts. The Hayes Theatre, a vibrant, boutique theatrical venue in Sydney, is named after her.

Georgina Hopson is a dynamic, multi award-winning Australian actor and soprano who began her career in 2015. Her versatility has opened opportunities her to create roles in shows such as *Pirates of Penzance, The Secret Garden, Ragtime, Merrily We Roll Along, My Fair Lady, Jagged little Pill, West Side Story,* the role of *Christine* in *Phantom of the Opera.* Georgina has played both Rose and Celine in the smash hit parody *Titanique.* In 2026, Georgina will be embodying the roll of Anya in the Australian national tour of *Anastasia.*

Luke Hunter is an Australian musical director and conductor of large-scale musical productions. Key credits include the Australian tours of *Beauty and the Beast, Moulin Rouge, Come From Away, Jersey Boys, The Sound of Music* and *Kinky Boots.* He is the co-creator of the popular vocal warm up app, Warm Me Up and is passionate about teaching and mentoring new talent.

Jason Langley is an award-winning theatre director, actor, dramaturg, performance Coach, and mentor whose work spans several continents. He is known for bringing fresh contemporary vision to his work. Key credits include *The Boy From Oz, Loving Repeating, Brigadoon, Here Lies Henry, Wonderful Town, The Hello Girls, Dusty, Footloose,* and *Evita.* Jason works closely with the major Australian universities directing and training young professionals.

Lucy Maunder is a beloved Australian theatre actor and cabaret artist. Her wide-ranging credits include Roxie in *Chicago,* Winfred Banks in *Mary Poppins, Fun Home, Cats, Charlie and the Chocolate Factory, Beautiful: The Carole King Musical,* and *Matilda.* Her one-woman show, *Irving Berlin: Songs in the Key of Black* has received critical acclaim; the album of the same name is available on streaming platforms.

APPENDIX

Stuart Maunder (AM) is an Australian-born opera and musical theatre director and producer with over forty years of experience. He has worked with Opera Australia, The Royal Opera (London), Scottish Opera, New Zealand Opera, Opera of South Australia and is currently the Artistic Director of the Victorian Opera. Highly skilled in directing Sondheim, Stuart is also a self-confessed Gilbert and Sullivan afficionado.

Ainsley Melham is a dynamic Australian-born actor and dancer with credits in both Australia and the US. Throughout his career, he has taken leading roles, in *Aladdin (*Australia and Broadway*)*, *Kiss of the Spider Woman, Pippin, Merrily We Roll Along, Rodgers* and *Hammerstein's Cinderella*, and *Wicked.* Most recently, Ainsley originated the role of Dwayne in *Boop! The Musical* in Chicago and on Broadway.

Sharon Millerchip is a versatile and highly awarded theatre actor, dancer, and director. Key credits include Velma Kelly and Roxie Hart in *Chicago,* Belle in *Beauty and the Beast,* Meg Giry in *Phantom of the Opera* and *Love Never Dies,* Charity in *Sweet Charity,* Red Riding Hood in *into the Woods,* Columbia in *Rocky Horror,* Caroline in *Fangirls,* Demeter in *Cats,* and Anita in *West Side Story.* Directing credits include *Strictly Ballroom, Aladdin,* and the national tours of *Six the Musical.*

Noah Mullins is an Australian-born actor and dancer whose first professional role was Riff in *West Side Story* in 2019, at age nineteen. Noah has since created the role of Mark in *Rent,* toured with *Jagged Little Pill,* and most recently embodied the character of Orpheus in the Australian production of *Hadestown.* An interview with this bright young actor can be found on the companion website.

Anna O'Byrne is a sought-after, award-winning actor, and soprano whose career has spanned musical theatre, opera, concerts, and film. She is equally at home in London's West End as in Australia. Key credits include Christine Daaé in *Phantom of the Opera,* originating that role in the sequel *Love Never Dies* (on stage and on film)*, A Little Night Music, Sweeney Todd,* Maria in *West Side Story,* Sarah in *Guys and Dolls,* Eliza in *My Fair Lady, Carousel* and *The Woman in White.* She has recorded an album, *Dream.*

Caroline O'Connor (AM) is a highly acclaimed Anglo-Australian theatre actor, singer, dancer, and recording artist with extensive credits in Australia, the UK, and Broadway. She is known for her iconic roles in *Mack and Mabel*, *Chicago, Bombshells, Gypsy, On the Town, Sweeney Todd*, *Anything Goes, Anastasia* (on Broadway)*, Hello Dolly!,* and for originating the role of 'Nini Legs in the Air' in Baz Luhrmann's 2001 movie *Moulin Rouge.* Her recordings include tributes to Piaf and Judy Garland.

Natalie O'Donnell is an highly skilled Australian actor with over twenty-five years of experience, working both national and internationally. She originated the role of Sophie in the original Australian premiere of *Mamma Mia! The Musical*, returning to the show twenty years later to play Donna. Other key musical theatre credits include*, Dear Evan Hansen, Come From Away, Next to Normal, Jerry's Girls*, and *Crazy for You.*

Tyran Parke is a celebrated and awarded Australian theatre director, actor, singer, and teacher and mentor. He has directed a diverse array of plays and musicals, both large-scale and intimate, and recent productions include *Elegies, Sunday in the Park with George,* and *Follies.* A dedicated educator, Tyran is currently the Head of Musical Theatre at the Victorian College of the Arts (Melbourne University), and the Artistic Director of the Australian Musical Theatre Festival and Clovelly Fox Production Theatre Company.

Simon Phillips is an award-winning veteran New Zealand-Australian dramaturg and director of musical theatre, opera, and plays. His work encompasses Australian premieres and national tours, US tours, and West End and Broadway productions. Key credits include *Love Never Dies, Priscilla Queen of the Desert, Muriel's Wedding, Ladies in Black,* and *Round the Twist.*

Marina Prior (AM) is considered one of Australia's leading ladies of musical theatre. Beginning in 1984 with Mabel in the national tour of *Pirates of Penzance,* she has played leading roles in *Phantom of the Opera, West Side Story, The Secret Garden, Cats, 9 to 5,* and *Kimberley Akimbo.* In 1987 she played Cosette in the original Australian production of *Les Misérables*, returning most recently to play Madame Thénardier for the World Arena Tour and in the West End. She has also recorded five albums.

Philip Quast is a beloved Australian-born theatre, film and television actor, mentor, and educator, known primarily for his work in classical plays and musical theatre. His career spanned forty-five years. To date, he is the only actor to have won the Olivier award for Best Actor three times – for the original London production of *Sunday in the Park with George, The Fix,* and *South Pacific.* Key credits include Javert in *Les Misérables, Evita, The Secret Garden, Sweeney Todd,* and *La Cage Aux Folles.*

Michael Ralph is an Australian multi award-winning choreographer, director, teacher, and performer, experienced in both large commercial and small-scale independent theatre productions, television and film, cabaret, and dance theatre. Key credits include *Elvis: A Musical Revolution, The Wedding Singer, Bring it On,* and *Dusty the Musical.* He is also a widely respected teacher for many of Australia's top performing arts tertiary and university courses.

Jemma Rix is a highly respected leading lady of musical theatre. Commencing her career in pop music, she moved into theatre in 2006 when Jemma first created the role of Elphaba in a shorter adaptation of *Wicked* for Universal Studios, Japan. This led, a year later, to her establishing this iconic role in national tours of Australia, South-east Asia, Seoul, New Zealand, clocking up over 1,000 performances. Other key credits include Elsa for Disney's *Frozen, The Wizard of Oz, Evita, Jekyll and Hyde,* and *Lord of the Rings.*

Ashleigh Rubenach is an award-winning Australian actor who has shown versatility in the diverse roles she has played. Key credits include *Anything Goes, Sweeney Todd, Muriel's Wedding, An American in Paris, Groundhog Day The Musical,* the Australian and Asian tour of *Sunset Boulevard,* and, most recently, *Back to the Future.*

Tony Sheldon is a veteran award-winning theatre actor, director, and writer with a career of over four decades. He originated and performed the role of Bernadette in *Priscilla Queen of the Desert* in Australia, New Zealand, the West End, Canada, and on Broadway receiving both Tony and Olivier nominations.

APPENDIX

Other key credits include *Torch Song Trilogy, The Producers, Dirty Rotten Scoundrels, The Witches of Eastwick, Hello Dolly!, Camelot* and *Amélie.* Tony has recorded many cast albums.

Kris Stewart is an Australian award-winning executive producer and artistic director, whose work has been seen in North America, Europe, Australia, and New Zealand. He was the founder and executive director of the New York Musical Theatre Festival (2004–2019), founder of the Sydney Fringe Festival, and artistic director of the Brisbane Powerhouse where, during his tenure, over a million tickets were sold to over 2,500 shows.

Michael Tyack is an veteran award-winning musical director, and accomplished musician who began his professional career in 1974. Key theatre credits include *The Boy From Oz, Chess, The Wizard of Oz, The Witches of Eastwick, Mary Poppins* and *Come from Away.* In 2020 he was awarded an Order of Australia for services to the Performing Arts.

NOTES

Preface

1   Patsy Rodenberg, *Presence: How to Use Positive Energy For Success in Every Situation* (London: Penguin, 2007), 10.

Chapter 1

1   Dictionary.com, Synergy, https://www.dictionary.com/browse/synergy (accessed 17 October 2025).
2   Michael Chekhov, *Lessons for the Professional Actor* (New York: Performing Arts Journal Publications, 1985), 55.
3   Alfred Korzybski, *Science and Sanity. An Introduction to Non-Aristotelian Systems and General Semantics* (The International Non-Aristotelian Library Pub. Co., 1933), 747–61.

Chapter 2

1   The monetization of social media and its effect on creativity is now a hot topic. One example is a podcast with musician Jacob Collier, who spoke to Colin and Samir. Collier talks about the shift in intention that drives the content creators for platforms like YouTube. https://www.youtube.com/watch?v=y7rvDA3MARk. Time stamp: 3:55–6:40 (accessed 16 August 2025).
2   Oxford English Dictionary, *Ethos,* https://www.oed.com/dictionary/ethos (accessed 16 August 2025).
3   Oxford English Dictionary, *Pathos,* https://www.oed.com/dictionary/pathos (accessed 16 August 2025).
4   Oxford English Dictionary, *Logos,* https://www.oed.com/dictionary/logos (accessed 16 August 2025).
5   Oxford English Dictionary, *Kairos,* https://www.oed.com/dictionary/kairos (accessed 16 August 2025).
6   The Holy Bible: 1 Corinthians 3:9, ESV.
7   Merriam-Webster Dictionary, *Charisma,* https://www.merriam-webster.com/dictionary/charisma.
8   Max Weber, *The Theory of Social and Economic Organization*. Trans. by A. M. Henderson and Talcott Parsons, Ed. (Glencos, IL: Free Press, 1947), 328, 358.
9   Jane Goodall, *Stage Presence: The Actor as Mesmerist* (London: Routledge, Taylor & Francis Group, 2008), 8.
10 Ibid., 60.
11 Rudyard Kipling, *Mrs Bathurst* (1904): Available online: http://fullreads.com/literature/mrs-bathurst/5/#google_vignette, 5.

NOTES

12 J. Roach, *It* (Ann Arbor: University of Michigan Press, 2007).
13 John Kenrick, *Musical Theatre, A History*, 2nd ed. (London: Methuen Drama, 2017), 167–74.
14 Laurence Olivier, *Great Acting Sir Laurence Olivier* (1966): Shakespeare Network. Available online: https://www.youtube.com/watch?v=SCXK26cXCa0https://www.youtube.com/watch?v=SCXK26cXCa0. Time stamp 22:00–22:20 (accessed 16 August 2025).
15 Goodall, *Stage Presence*, 33.
16 Ben Travis, *Empire's 50 Greatest Actors of All Time List* (2022): Available online: https://www.empireonline.com/movies/features/best-actors (accessed 6 March 2025).
17 Goodall, *Stage Presence*, 17.
18 Ibid., 19.
19 Roach, *It*, 28–9.
20 Ibid., 7.
21 Jersy Grotowski, *Towards a Poor Theatre* (New York: Routledge A Theatre Arts Book, 2002), 255, 256.
22 Peter Brook, *The Empty Space* (New York: Touchstone, 1968), 33.
23 E. Barba, N. Savarese, and R. Fowler, *A Dictionary of Theatre Anthropology: The Secret Art of the Performer*, 2nd ed. (New York: Routledge, 2005), 107–8.
24 Goodall, *Stage Presence*, 20.
25 J. Erickson, 'Presence', in D. Krasner and D. Z. Saltz (eds), *Staging Philosophy: Intersections of Theater, Performance, and Philosophy* (Ann Arbor: University of Michigan Press, 2006), 143.
26 Ibid., 147.
27 Mark L. Latash, *Synergy* (Oxford: Oxford University Press, 2008), 15.
28 Arthur Lessac, Keynote Address, VASTA Conference. *Voice and Speech Review*, 7, no.1: 29–33. Given on 3 August 2009. DOI: 10.1080/23268263.2011.10739516
29 Lessac, Keynote Address, 31.
30 Erica Fischer-Lichte, 'Introduction: Transformative Aesthetics – Reflections on the Metamorphic Power of Art', in E. Fischer-Lichte and B. Wihstutz (eds), *Transformative Aesthetics* (New York: Routledge, 2018), 1–25.

Chapter 3

1 *The Sound of Music*, directed by Robert Wise (Los Angeles: 20th Century Fox, 1965).
2 Figure 3.1. Performance artistry word map is adapted from 'Exploring Musical Theatre Synergy: Accessing Seven Performative Processes,' by J. Cuny, 2022, *Studies in Musical Theatre,* 16(2): 133–50. https://doi.org/10.1386/smt_00094_1.
3 Gerd Gigerenzer, *The Intelligence of Intuition* (Cambridge: Cambridge University Press, 2023), viii.
4 Nelson Mandela, *Long Walk to Freedom: The Autobiography of Nelson Mandela* (London: Hachette UK, 1995), 403.
5 Lorna Marshall, *The Body Speaks* (New York: St Martin's Griffin, 2008), 92.
6 To further explore the role of chakras and the energetic body, please refer to Judith Carman's journal article, 'Yoga and Singing: Natural Partners', *Journal of Singing: The Official Journal of the National Association of Teachers of Singing*, 60, no. 5 (2004): 433–41., and Mark Moliterno's article in *Journal of Singing* 65, no.1, (2008): 45.

Chapter 4

1. Charles Riborg Mann and George Ransom Twiss, *Physics* (New York: Scott, Foresman and Company, 1910), 235.
2. Uta Hagen, *A Challenge for the Actor* (New York: Scribner, 1991), 21.
3. Chekhov, *Lessons*, 97–100.

Chapter 5

1. Brené Brown, *Daring Greatly: How the Courage to Be Vulnerable Transforms the Way We Live, Love, Parent, and Lead* (New York: Gotham Books, 2012), 18.

Chapter 6

1. You can see the video of that moment on YouTube. https://www.youtube.com/watch?v=9wQ-GYnKPYM (accessed 16 August 2025).
2. Robin Nelson, *Practice as Research in the Arts: Principles, Protocols, Pedagogies, Resistances* (London: Palgrave Macmillan, 2013). DOI: 10.1057/9781137282910.
3. Zachary Dunbar, 'Practice as Research in Musical Theatre: Reviewing the Situation'. *Studies in Musical Theatre*, 2, no. 1 (2014).
4. J. R. R. Tolkien, *The Tolkien Reader* (New York: Ballantine Books, 1966), 21.
5. Michael Chekhov, *To the Actor: On the Technique of Acting* (New York: Harper and Row [1953] 2014), 19–20.
6. W. Passow, and R. Strauss, 'The Analysis of Theatrical Performance: The State of the Art'. *Poetics Today*, 2, no. 3 (1981): 237–54.
7. Modern research into empathetic response is ongoing. For more information, see E. Bilevicius, T. A. Kolesar, S. D. Smith, P. D. Trapnell and J. Kornelsen, 'Trait Emotional Empathy and Resting-State Functional Connectivity in Default Mode, Salience, and Central Executive Networks', *Brain Sciences* 8, no. 7 (2018): 128, and V. Gallese, 'Visions of the Body: Embodied Simulation and Aesthetic Experience', *Aisthesis: Pratiche, linguaggi e saperi dell'estetico* 10, no. 1 (2017): 41.
8. Millie Taylor explores this concept in her book, *Musical Theatre, Realism and Entertainment* (New York: Ashgate, 2016).
9. S. M. Jaeger, 'Embodiment and Presence', in D. Krasner and D. Z. Saltz (eds), *Staging Philosophy: Intersections of Theater, Performance, and Philosophy* (Ann Arbor: University of Ann Arbor Press, 2006), 122–41.
10. While not one of the original interviewees for my PhD, David Cuny has been performing consistently in musical theatre since 2018, meeting the criteria set for an 'experienced performer'.
11. J. F. Sherman, *A Strange Proximity: Stage Presence, Failure, and the Ethics of Attention* (New York: Routledge, 2016), 40.
12. A. Macaulay, *Don't Tell Me, Show Me: Directors Talk About Acting* (Sydney: Currency Press, 2003), 9.
13. Ibid., 179.
14. Grotowski, *Towards a Poor Theatre*, 38.
15. This interview is an insight into the mind of a dedicated actor, SAG-AFTRA Foundation (2019, January 12). *Conversations with Bradley Cooper*.

16. G. E. Schwartz, 'From Parapsychology to Postmaterialist Psychology: The Emerging Integrative Science of Consciousness, Spirit, and Soul'. *The Journal of Parapsychology*, 76 (2012): 50.
17. Ulrich Weger, and J. Wagemann, 'The Behavioral, Experiential and Conceptual Dimensions of Psychological Phenomena: Body, Soul and Spirit'. *New Ideas in Psychology*, 39 (2015): 24.
18. J. Carman, 'Yoga and Singing: Natural Partners'. *Journal of Singing: The Official Journal of the National Association of Teachers of Singing*, 60, no. 5 (2004): 433.
19. J. J. Loizzo, 'The Subtle Body: An Interoceptive Map of Central Nervous System Function and Meditative Mind-brain-body Integration'. *Annals of the New York Academy of Sciences*, 1373, no. 1 (2016): 78–95.
20. Konstantin Stanislavski, *An Actor's Work*. (Abingdon: Routledge, [1948] 2017); J. Benedetti, Stanislavski: *His Life and Art: A Biography* (London: Methuen, 1999).
21. Konstantin Stanislavski, *An Actor Prepares*, trans. E. Reynolds Hapgood (New York: Routledge, 1980), 37.
22. Ibid., 304.
23. Jerry Daboo, 'Michael Chekhov and the Embodied Imagination: Higher Self and Non-self'. *Studies in Theatre and Performance* 27, no. 3 (2007): 261–73, 269.
24. Marshall, *The Body Speaks*, 141.
25. N. Strohminger, J. Knobe, and G. Newman, 'The True Self: A Psychological Concept Distinct from the Self'. *Perspectives on Psychological Science*, 12, no. 4 (2017): 551–60. Also refer to U. Weger, T. Sparby and F. Edelhäuser, 'Dualistic and Trichotomic Approaches in Psychological Enquiry. The Question About Body, Soul, and Spirit'. *European Psychologist*, 26, no. 2 (2021): 85–95, 86.
26. M. Csikszentmihalyi, *Flow: The Psychology of Optimal Experience* (New York: Harper, 1990).

Chapter 7

1. Sanford Meisner, *Sanford Meisner on Acting* (Vintage Books, 1987).
2. Dictionary.com. 'Charisma', https://www.dictionary.com/browse/charisma (accessed 17 August 2025).
3. C. L. Palmer, and R. Peterson, 'Physical Attractiveness, Halo Effects, and Social Joining'. *Social Science Quarterly* 102, no.1 (2021): 552.

Chapter 8

1. J. F. Sherman, *A Strange Proximity, 17*.
2. 'Hugh Jackman Recalls The First Time He Ever Met Dame Judi Dench'. The Graham Norton Show, February 18, 2023 https://www.youtube.com/watch?v=N6tXjhtl3Go (accessed 17 August 2025).
3. Fred Luthens et al., *Psychological Capital: Developing the Human Competitive Edge* (Oxford: Oxford University Press, 2006).
4. A. Newman et al., 'Psychological Capital'. *Journal of Organizational Behavior* 35, no.1, Special Issue: The IRIOP Annual Review Issue (2014): 120–38.
5. Csikszentmihalyi, *Flow* 74.
6. Matteo Bonfitto, *The Kinetics of the Invisible: Acting Processes in Peter Brook's Theatre* (Lausanne: Peter Lang Edition, 2016), 74–9.
7. Csikszentmihalyi, *Flow, 212*.

Chapter 9

1. Lenard Petit, *The Michael Chekhov Handbook: For the Actor* (London: Routledge, 2010), 14–17.

Chapter 10

1. Rodenberg, *Presence*, 76.
2. Janice Chapman, *Singing and Teaching Singing: A Holistic Approach to Classical Voice*, 3rd ed. (London: Plural Publishing, 2017), 47.
3. Antonin Artaud: *The Theatre and its Double*, Trans. Mary Caroline Richards (New York: Grove Press, 1958), 260.
4. Petit, *The Michael Chekhov Handbook*, 39.
5. Chekhov, *On the Technique of Acting*, 41.
6. Ibid., 45–8.
7. Ira Seidenstein, *The Clown Secret*. (Milton Keynes: Lightning Source UK Ltd, 2018), 95-9.
8. Chekhov, *Lessons for the Professional Actor*, 28-32, 37, 38.
9. Accent Method was designed by Professor Sven Smith as a holistic therapeutic regime to coordinate breathing, articulation, and resonance. In recent years, Janice Chapman and Dr Ron Morris have adapted it to provide singers and teachers with a tool to enhance breath management and vocal strength.
10. Ron Morris and Linda Hutchinson, *If in Doubt, Breathe Out: Breathing and Support for Singing* (Oxford: Compton Publishing, 2017).

Chapter 11

1. Chekhov, *To the Actor*, 174.
2. The author of this quote is unknown, although it aligns with Frankl's determinist teachings, found in his book, *Man's Search for Meaning*.
3. Dr Seuss, *Oh, the Thinks You Can Think!* (New York: Random House, 1975).
4. Viola Spolin, *Improvization for the Theater*, 3rd ed. (Chicago: Northwestern University, 1999).
5. Larry Moss, *The Intent to Live* (New York: Bantam Books, 2005).
6. Bella Merlin, *The Complete Stanislavsky Toolkit* (London: Nick Hern, 2014), 24.
7. https://www.pnas.org/doi/epdf/10.1073/pnas.1702247114 (accessed 19 August 2025).
8. Brené Brown, *Atlas of the Heart* (London: Penguin Random, 2021).
9. Chekhov, *On the Technique of Acting*, 15–36.
10. M. Chekhov, 'Love in Our Theatre: Art or Profession?', in M. Chekhov and C. Leonard (eds), *To the Director and Playwright* (New York: Limelight Editions, 1984), 14–26.
11. Stephen Sondheim, *Sooner or Later* (Milwaukee, WI: Hal Leonard, 1990), digital score.
12. Declan Donnellan, *The Actor and the Target* (London: Nick Hern Books, 2005)

NOTES

13 The NMCA – The National Michael Chekhov Association – has helpful material including a Chart of Inspired Acting created by Chekhov for Mala Powers at https://www.chekhov.net (accessed 19 August 2025). There are also archives from his teaching in 1935 at Dartington Hall, England, available at *Michael Chekhov: The Actor is the Theatre*. These can be viewed at: https://collections.uwindsor.ca/chekhov/1935 (accessed 19 August 2025).

14 Lin-Manuel Miranda, *How Far I'll Go* (Milwaukee, WI: Hal Leonard, 2016), digital score.

15 Tracey Moore and Allison Bergman, *Acting the Song*: *Performance Skills for the Music Theatre* (New York: Allworth Press, 2016), 21.

16 Dane Chalfin, 'Primal Sound for Singers Introduced'. *Voice Council*. Available online: https://www.youtube.com/watch?v=QkatmC5lRFg (accessed 8 March 2025).

17 Jo Estill, *Voice Craft. A User's Guide to Voice Quality. Level One: Primer of Compulsory Figures* (Pittsburg: Estill Voice Training Systems, 1996).

18 Alan Menken and Glenn Slater, *The Life I Never Led* (Milwaukee, WI: Hal Leonard, 2011), digital score.

19 David Craig, *A Study Guide on Singing Onstage* (New York: Applause Publications, 1990), 30.

Chapter 12

1 Chekhov, *To the Actor*, 2.
2 Ibid.
3 Stephen Wangh, *An Acrobat of the Heart: A Physical Approach to Acting Inspired by the work of Jerzy Grotowski* (New York: Vintage Books, 2000), 11–18.
4 Fay Simpson, *The Lucid Body: A Guide for the Physical Actor* (New York: Allworth Press, 2020).
5 Ibid., 11.
6 Ibid., 31.
7 Chekhov, *On the Technique of Acting*, 44.
8 Jean Newlove and John Dalby, *Laban for All* (New York: Routledge), 129–40.
9 Chekhov, 2014.
10 Chekhov, *To the Actor*, 58–9.
11 Petit, 2010, 41.
12 Simpson, *The Lucid Body*, 20.
13 Uta Hagen with Haskel Frankel, *Respect for Acting* (New York: Macmillan, 1973).
14 Pip McKay, *The Eight principles of Achievement, Love and Happiness: How to Get What You Want and Enjoy the Process*. (Manly, NSW: Evolve Now! Mind Institute Pty Ltd, 2015).
15 Simon Sinek, *Start With Why: How Great Leaders Inspire Everyone to Take Action* (UK, Penguin Random House, 2009).
16 Julia Cameron, *The Artist's Way* (London: Profile Books, 2020), Kindle edition, 3.

Chapter 13

1 David Wicks, 'Bricoleur', *Encyclopedia of Case Study Research* Vols. 1–2, edited by A. J. Mills, G. Durepos and E. Wiebe. (Thousand Oaks, CA: SAGE Publications, Inc, 2010).

2   As seen in the movie *Air,* Director: Ben Affleck, Screenplay Alex Convery, Distributed by Amazon. Com MGM Studios, Warner Bros Pictures, 2023.

Chapter 14

1   Oxford Dictionary online.
2   Oxford Dictionary online.
3   Oxford Dictionary online.
4   You can see this performance at: https://www.youtube.com/watch?v=TwC0Db7oerM (accessed 19 August 2025).
5   Collins English Dictionary – Complete & Unabridged 2012 Digital Edition (London: HarperCollins Publishers, 2012).
6   Angela Lee Duckworth, *Grit: The Power of Passion and Perseverance.* https://www.ted.com/talks/angela_lee_duckworth_grit_the_power_of_passion_and_perseverance/transcript?subtitle=en (accessed 19 August 2025).
7   Simpson, *The Lucid Body,* 6.
8   Cameron, *The Artist's Way,* Kindle edition, 33–4.
9   Brown, *Atlas of the Heart*, 118.
10 Ibid.
11 This quote from His Holiness, the Dalai Lama, was originally reported in *India Today,* on 30 September 2021. A transcription of this article is available online at https://www.dalailama.com/messages/transcripts-and-interviews/the-purpose-of-life-is-to-be-happy (accessed 10 March 2025).
12 Susan David expands on this theme in her insightful book *Emotional Agility: Get Unstuck, Embrace Change and Thrive in Work and Life* (Wayne, NJ: Avery Publishing Group, 2016).

Chapter 15

1   Amy Cuddy's research and her iconic TED talk has triggered ongoing conjecture and research into hormone levels achieved through this technique. However, many actors affirm the positive psychophysical effects of power posing. For information on Cuddy's original research visit: https://www.ted.com/talks/amy_cuddy_your_body_language_may_shape_who_you_are (accessed 10 March 2025).
2   Sarah has shared her techniques personally in conversation and in workshops. She can be contacted via https://performingartscounselling.com.au (accessed 19 August 2025).
3   Eight Greek words used to describe aspects of love can be found in Dictionary.com. Available online: https://www.dictionary.com/e/greek-words-for-love (accessed 8 March 2025).
4   T. Bahadur, 'The Blind Men and the Elephant'. *On Art and Aesthetics* (2016). Available online: https://onartandaesthetics.com/2016/07/03/the-blind-men-and-the-elephant (accessed 27 March 2025).

Afterword

1   2024 Commencement Address by Roger Federer at Dartmouth. You can view online: https://www.youtube.com/watch?v=pqWUuYTcG-o (accessed 1 April 2025).

BIBLIOGRAPHY

Arlen, Harold, and E. Y. Harburg. *Over the Rainbow*. 1939.
Artaud, A. *The Theatre and its Double*, trans. Mary Caroline Richards. New York: Grove Press, 1958.
Auden, W. H. *The Age of Anxiety: A Baroque Eclogue*. New York: Random House, 1947.
Bahadur, T. 'The Blind Men and the Elephant'. *On Art and Aesthetics*. 2016. Available online: https://onartandaesthetics.com/2016/07/03/the-blind-men-and-the-elephant (accessed 27 March 2025).
Balk, H. W. *Performing Power: A New Approach for the Singer Actor*. Minneapolis: University of Minnesota Press, 1985.
Balk, H. W. *The Radiant Performer: The Spiral Path to Performing Power*. Minneapolis: University of Minnesota Press, 1991.
Barba, E., N. Savarese and R. Fowler. *A Dictionary of Theatre Anthropology: The Secret Art of the Performer*. 2nd edn. New York: Routledge, 2005.
Bartholomew, D. J. *Measuring Intelligence: Facts and Fallacies*. Cambridge: Cambridge University Press, 2004. https://doi.org/10.1017/CBO9780511490019.
Benedetti, J. *Stanislavski: His Life and Art*: *A Biography*. London: Methuen, 1999.
Berry, Cicely. *Voice and the Actor*. Edinburgh: Harrap, 1973.
Bilevicius, E., T. A. Kolesar, S. D. Smith, P. D. Trapnell and J. Kornelsen. 'Trait Emotional Empathy and Resting State Functional Connectivity in Default Mode, Salience, and Central Executive Networks'. *Brain Sciences* 8, no. 7 (2018): 128. http://dx.doi.org/10.3390/brainsci8070128.
Bonfitto, Mateo. *The Kinetics of the Invisible: Acting Processes in Peter Brooks Theatre*. Lausanne: Peter Lang Edition, 2016.
Brook, Peter. *The Empty Space*. New York: Touchstone, 1968.
Brown, Brené. *Atlas of the Heart: Mapping Meaningful Connection and the Language of Human Experience*. London: Penguin Random House, 2021.
Brown, Brené. *Daring Greatly: How the Courage to Be Vulnerable Transforms the Way We Live, Love, Parent, and Lead*. New York: Gotham Books, 2012.
Cameron, Julia. *The Artist's Way: A Spiritual Path to Higher Creativity*. London: Profile Books, 2020, Kindle edition.
Carman, J. 'Yoga and Singing: Natural Partners'. *Journal of Singing: The Official Journal of the National Association of Teachers of Singing*, 60, no. 5 (2004): 433–41.
Chalfin, Dane. 'Primal Sound for Singers Introduced'. *Voice Council*. Available online: https://www.youtube.com/watch?v=QkatmC5lRFg (accessed 8 March 2025).
Chapman, Janice. *Singing and Teaching Singing; A Holistic Approach to Classical Voice*. 3rd edn. San Diego: Plural Publishing, 2017.
Chekhov, Michael. 'Love in Our Theatre: Art or Profession?', in *To the Director and Playwright*, edited by M. Chekhov and C. Leonard, 14–26. New York: Limelight Editions, 1984.
Chekhov, Michael. *Lessons for the Professional Actor*. New York: Performing Arts Journal Publications, 1985.
Chekhov, Michael. *On the Technique of Acting*. New York: Harper Collins, 1993.
Chekhov, Michael. *To the Actor: On the Technique of Acting*. New York: Harper and Row [1953] 2014.
Chubbuck, Ivana. *The Power of the Actor: The Chubbuck Technique*. New York: Avery, 2004.
Collins English Dictionary – Complete & Unabridged 2012 Digital Edition, HarperCollins Publishers, 2012.
Craig, David. *On Singing On Stage* (rev ed.). New York: Applause Publications, 1990.

Cramer, Lyn. *Creating Musical Theatre: Conversations with Broadway Directors and Choreographers*. London: Bloomsbury, 2013.
Csikszentmihalyi, Mihalyi. *Flow: The Psychology of Optimal Experience*. New York: Harper, 1990.
Csikszentmihalyi, Mihalyi. *Creativity: Flow and the Psychology of Discovery and Invention*. New York: Harper Perennial, 1996.
Cuny, Jacqui. 'Exploring Musical Theatre Synergy: Accessing Seven Performative Processes'. *Studies in Musical Theatre*, 16, no. 2 (2022): 150. https://doi.org/10.1386/smt_00094_1.
Cuny, Jacqueline. Musical Theatre Performance Synergy: Exploring Elements, Constructs, and Practice. Doctoral Thesis, Griffith University, Qld, 2022.
Daboo, Jerry. 'Michael Chekhov and the Embodied Imagination: Higher Self and Non-self'. *Studies in Theatre and Performance* 27, no. 3 (2007): 261–73, 269.
David, Susan. *Emotional Agility: Get Unstuck, Embrace Change and Thrive in Work and Life*. London: Penguin Life, 2016.
Da Vinci, Leonardo. *Notebooks*. Edited by Irma A. Richter. Oxford: Oxford University Press, 1980.
Dictionary.com. 'Charisma', https://www.dictionary.com/browse/charisma (accessed 19 August 2025).
Dictionary.com. 'Synergy', https://www.dictionary.com/browse/synergy (accessed 17 October 2025).
Donnellan, Declan. *The Actor and the Target*. London: Nick Hern Books, 2005.
Duckworth, Angela Lee. *Grit: The Power of Passion and Perseverance*. Available online: https://www.ted.com/talks/angela_lee_duckworth_grit_the_power_of_passion_and_perseverance/transcript (accessed 19 August 2025).
Dunbar, Zachary. 'Practice as Research in Musical Theatre: Reviewing the Situation'. *Studies in Musical Theatre*, 2, no.1 (2014): 64.
Erickson, Jon. 'Presence', in *Staging Philosophy: Intersections of Theater, Performance, and Philosophy*, edited by D. Krasner and D. Z. Saltz Michigan: University of Michigan Press, 2006. https://doi.org/10.3998/mpub.147168.
Estill, Jo. *Voice Craft. A User's Guide to Voice Quality. Level One: Primer of Compulsory Figures*. Estill Voice Training Systems, 1996.
Fischer-Lichte, Erica. 'Introduction: Transformative Aesthetics – Reflections on the Metamorphic Power of Art', in *Transformative Aesthetics*, edited by E. Fischer-Lichte and B. Wihstutz, 1–25. New York: Routledge, 2018.
Flacks, Niki. *Acting with Passion: A Performer's Guide to Emotions on Cue*. London: Bloomsbury Methuen Drama, 2015.
Gallese, V. 'Visions of the Body. Embodied Simulation and Aesthetic Experience'. *Aisthesis*: *Pratiche, linguaggi e saperi dell'estetico* 10, no.1 (2017): 41. Available online: https://go.gale.com/ps/i.do?p=AONE&u=griffith&id=GALE%7CA533409544&v=2.1&it=r&sid=summon&asid=0d870b44 (accessed 19 August 2025).
Gigerenzer, Gerd. *The Intelligence of Intuition* (Cambridge: Cambridge University Press, 2023).
Goleman, Daniel. *Emotional Intelligence: Why It Can Matter More Than IQ*. London: Bloomsbury, 2021.
Goodall, Jane. *Stage Presence: The Actor as Mesmerist*. ProQuest Ebook Central: Routledge, 2008.
Grotowski, Jerzy. *Towards a Poor Theatre*. New York: Routledge, A Theatre Arts Book, 2002.
Hagen, Uta. *A Challenge for the Actor*. New York: Scribner, 1991.
Hagen, Uta, with Frankel, H. *Respect for Acting*. New York: Macmillan, 1973.
Jaeger, S. M. 'Embodiment and Presence', in *Staging Philosophy: Intersections of Theater, Performance, and Philosophy* edited by D. Krasner and D. Z. Saltz, 122–41. Ann Arbor: University of Michigan Press, 2006.
Kenrick, John. *Musical Theatre, A History*. 2nd edn. London: Methuen Drama, 2017, 167–74.
Kipling, Rudyard. *Mrs Bathurst*. Available online: http://fullreads.com/literature/mrs-bathurst/5/#google_vignette 1904 (accessed 6 March 2025).
Korzybski, A. (1933), *Science and Sanity. An Introduction to Non-Aristotelian Systems and General Semantics*. The International Non-Aristotelian Library Pub. Co. 747–61.
Latash, M. L. *Synergy*. Oxford: Oxford University Press, 2008.
Lessac, Andre. Keynote Address, VASTA Conference, August 3, 2009, *Voice and Speech Review*, 7 no.1 (2013): 29–33. http://dx.doi.org/10.1080/23268263.2011.10739516.
Linklater, Kristin. *Freeing the Natural Voice: Imagery and Art in the Practice of Voice and Language* (revised and expanded). Hollywood, CA: Drama Publishers, Quite Specific Media, 2006.

BIBLIOGRAPHY

Loizzo, J. J. 'The Subtle Body: An Interoceptive Map of Central Nervous System Function and Meditative Mind-brain-body Integration', *Annals of the New York Academy of Sciences* 1373, no.1 (2016): 78–95. https://doi.org/10.1111/nyas.13065.

Luthans, Fred, C. M. Youssef, and B. J. Avolio. *Psychological Capital: Developing the Human Competitive Edge*. Oxford: Oxford University Press, 2006.

Macaulay, A. *Don't Tell Me, Show Me: Directors Talk About Acting*. Sydney: Currency Press, 2003.

Mandela, Nelson. *Long Walk to Freedom: The Autobiography of Nelson Mandela*. London: Hachette UK, 1995.

Mann, Charles Riborg, and George Ransom Twiss. *Physics*. New York: Scott, Foresman and Company, 1910.

Marshall, Lorna. *The Body Speaks: Performance and Physical Expression*. London: Methuen Drama, 2008.

Mayer, John. 'The Age of Worry.' *Born and Raised*. Columbia Records, 2012. Audio recording.

McKay, Pip. *The Eight Principles of Achievement, Love and Happiness: How to Get What You Want and Enjoy the Process*. Manly, NSW: Evolve Now! Mind Institute Pty Ltd, 2015.

Meisner, Sanford. *Sanford Meisner on Acting*. New York: Vintage Books, 1987.

Menken, Alan and Glenn Slater. *The Life I Never Led*. Milwaukee, WI: Hal Leonard, 2011. Digital score.

Merriam-Webster.com Dictionary, s.v. "charisma," https://www.merriam-webster.com/dictionary/charisma (accessed October 17, 2025).

Merlin, Bella. *The Complete Stanislavsky Toolkit*. London: Nick Hern Books, 2007.

Miller, M. T. *On Stage Blog: A Professor's Recipe to Electric Musical Theatre Presence. The Acting Life*. 29 October 2019. Available online: https://www.onstageblog.com/columns/2015/10/29/a-professors-recipe-to-electric-musical-theatre-stage-presence (accessed 27 March 2025).

Miranda, Lin-Manuel. *How Far I'll Go*. Milwaukee, WI: Hal Leonard, 2016. Digital score.

Moliterno, Mark. 'YogaVoice: Balancing the Physical Instrument', *Journal of Singing* 65, no.1 (2008): 45. https://go.gale.com/ps/i.do?p=AONE&u=griffith&id=GALE%7CA187562366&v=2.1&it=r&sid=summon&asid=6f2de6d6 (accessed 19 August 2025).

Moore, Tracey and Allison Bergman. *Acting the Song: Performance Skills for the Music Theatre*. New York: Allworth Press, 2016.

Morris, Ron and Linda Hutchinson. *If in Doubt, Breathe Out: Breathing and Support for Singing*. Oxford: Compton Publishing, 2017.

Moss, Larry. *The Intent to Live*. New York: Bantam Books, 2005.

Nelson, Robin. *Practice as Research in the Arts: Principles, Protocols, Pedagogies, Resistances*. London: Palgrave Macmillan, 2013. https://doi.org/10.1057/9781137282829.

Newlove, Jean and John Dalby, *Laban for All*. New York: Routledge, 2004.

Newman, A., D. Ucbasaran, F. Zhu and G. Hirst. 'Psychological Capital'. *Journal of Organizational Behavior* 35, no.1, Special Issue: The IRIOP Annual Review Issue (2014): 120–38.

Olivier, Laurence. *Great Acting Sir Laurence Olivier* (1966): Shakespeare Network. Available online: https://www.youtube.com/watch?v=SCXK26cXCa0https://www.youtube.com/watch?v=SCXK26cXCa0. Time stamp: 22mins:20secs (accessed 6 March 2025).

Palmer, C. L. and R. Peterson. 'Physical Attractiveness, Halo Effects, and Social Joining'. *Social Science Quarterly*, 102, no. 1 (2021): 552.

Passow, W. and R. Strauss. 'The Analysis of Theatrical Performance: The State of the Art'. *Poetics Today* 2, no. 3 (1981): 237–54.

Petit, Lenard. The Michael Chekhov Handbook: For the Actor. London: Routledge, 2010.

Petit, Lenard. Lenard Petit on Michael Chekhov's 5 Guiding Principles for Actors. (2022) [Video]. YouTube. Available online: https://www.youtube.com/watch?v=PufzXM820w4 (accessed 19 August 2025).

Roach, Joseph. *It*. Ann Arbor: University of Michigan Press, 2007.

Rodenberg, Patsy. *The Right to Speak: Working with the Voice*. 2nd edn. London: Methuen Drama, 2015.

Rodenberg, Patsy. *Presence: How to Use Positive Energy For Success in Every Situation*. London: Penguin, 2007.

Rodgers, Alan Zachary and Michael Weiner. *Safer*. Milwaukee, WI: Hal Leonard, 2013. Digital score.

SAG-AFTRA Foundation. *Conversations with Bradley Cooper*. YouTube. 12 January 2019. Available online: https://www.youtube.com/watch?v=5uvvQmdDEPo&t=2686s (accessed 19 August 2025).

Schönberg, Claude-Michel and Alain Boublil. *Woman*. Milwaukee, WI: Hal Leonard, 2007. Digital score.

Schwartz, G. E. 'From Parapsychology to Postmaterialist Psychology: The Emerging Integrative Science of Consciousness, Spirit, and Soul'. *The Journal of Parapsychology*, 76 (2012): 49–51.
Seidenstein, Ira. The *Clown Secret*. Milton Keynes: Lightning Source UK Ltd, 2018.
Seuss, Dr. *Oh, the Thinks You Can Think!* New York: Random House, 1975.
Sherman, Jon F. *A Strange Proximity: Stage Presence, Failure, and the Ethics of Attention*. New York: Routledge, 2016.
Simpson, Fay. *The Lucid Body: A Guide for the Physical Actor*. New York: Allworth Press, 2020.
Sinek, Simon. *Start With Why: How Great Leaders Inspire Everyone to Take Action*. UK, Penguin Random House, 2009.
Sondheim, Stephen. *Sooner or Later*. Milwaukee, WI: Hal Leonard, 1990. Digital score.
Spolin, Viola. *Improvisation for the Theater*, 3rd ed. Chicago: Northwestern University, 1999.
Stanislavski, Konstantin. *An Actor's Work*. Abingdon: Routledge, [1948] 2017.
Stanislavski, Konstantin. *An Actor Prepares*, trans. E. Reynolds Hapgood. London: Methuen,1980.
Stevens, A. *The Handbook of Jungian Psychology: Theory Practice, and Applications*. London: Routledge, 2006.
Stevenson, A. (ed.) Synergy. *Oxford Dictionary of English*, 3rd ed. 2015. DOI: https://doi.org/10.1093/acref/9780199571123.001.0001.
Taylor, Millie. *Musical Theatre, Realism and Entertainment*. New York: Ashgate, 2012.
Taylor, Millie. 'Integration and Distance in Musical Theatre: The case of Sweeney Todd'. *Contemporary Theatre Review*, 19, no.1 (2009): 74–86.
The English Dictionary (Lexico, 2022). Available online: https://www.lexico.com/en/definition/synergy (accessed 19 August 2025).
The Holy Bible, English Standard Version.
Tolkein, J. R. R. *The Tolkein Reader*. New York: Ballantine Books, 1966.
Travis, Ben. 'Empire's 50 Greatest Actors of All Time List', 2022. Available online: https://www.empireonline.com/movies/features/best-actors (accessed 6 March 2025).
Verne, Jules. *The Mysterious Island*, trans W. H. G. Kingston. New York: Signet Classics, 2004.
Wangh, Stephen. *An Acrobat of the Heart: A Physical Approach to Acting Inspired by the work of Jerzy Grotowski*. New York: Vintage Books, 2000.
Weber, Max. *The Theory of Social and Economic Organization*, trans. A. M. Henderson, T. Parsons, ed. Talcott: Free Press of Glencoe Collier-Macmillan Limited, 1947.
Weger, U., T. Sparby and F. Edelhäuser. 'Dualistic and Trichotomic Approaches in Psychological Enquiry. The Question About Body, Soul, and Spirit'. *European Psychologist*, 26, no. 2 (2021): 85–95. https://doi.org/10.1027/1016-9040/a000427.
Weger, U. W. and J. Wagermann. 'The Behavioral, Experiential and Conceptual Dimensions of Psychological Phenomena: Body Soul and Spirit'. *New Ideas in Psychology* 39 (2015): 23–33. https://doi.org/10.1016/j.newideapsych.2015.07.002.
Wicks, David. 'Bricoleur', *Encyclopedia of Case Study Research* Vols. 1–2, edited by A. J. Mills, G. Durepos and E. Wiebe. Thousand Oaks, CA: SAGE Publications, Inc, 2010. https://doi.org.10.4135/9781412957397.
Wise, Robert, director. *The Sound of Music*. Produced by Robert Wise. Screenplay by Ernest Lehman. Music by Richard Rodgers and Oscar Hammerstein II. 20th Century Fox, 1965.
Wood Brooks, Alison. 'Get Excited: Reappraising Pre-performance Anxiety as Excitement'. *Journal of Experimental Psychology: General*, 143, no. 3 (2014): 1144–58. https://doi.org/10.1037/a0035325.
Yorkey, Brian and Tom Kitt. *I've Been*. Milwaukee, WI: Hal Leonard, 2009. Digital score.
Zinder, David. *Body Voice Imagination: ImageWork Training and the Chekhov Technique*. Theatre Arts Book, Abingdon, Oxon: Routledge, 2009.

GRATITUDE

The world of musical theatre can be both a lens through which we view the world and a mirror through which we see ourselves. That is certainly true for me. I have learned so much about dynamic performance and myself.

Thankfully, many individuals have walked part or all of this journey of discovery with me. 'Acknowledgements' seems such an inadequate word to express the profound gratitude I feel for the many folk who offered me their wisdom, expertise, guidance, love, and support to bring this book to fruition.

My eight-and-a-half-year project began humbly as a master's degree exploration into the world of musical theatre tertiary training. A doctoral thesis on the power of performance synergy followed, and now, this book. Several wonderful souls guided me on my initial academic pathway. I am especially indebted to my former principal supervisor and mentor, Associate Professor Irene Bartlett, for her tireless support and wisdom as we ploughed the road towards my PhD. Her wholehearted encouragement spurred me on as I tried to capture the 'It' Factor's ephemerality.

A heartfelt thank you to the many talented actors and creatives – including my PhD research participants – who gave freely of their time and shared generously during the interviews. It is your wisdom, experience and stories that I endeavour to tell. Thank you, too, to the workshop participants and private students over the years who have been my 'synergy guinea pigs' as new ideas and techniques for my toolkit were developed often 'in the moment'.

I am so grateful to the editorial staff at Bloomsbury Publishing. In particular, my deepest thanks to my commissioning editor, Dom O'Hanlon; you believed in this rookie writer and championed my work. Thank you too to his assistant, Mark Jones, for your patience and support.

My life is filled with dear friends who cheered me on me through this time: Associate Professor Dr Kate Simpson, whose practical knowledge, advice and patience were a rock I could cling to; Jason Langley and Tyran Parke, two inspirational directors and fellow thespians who believe in me more than I do myself sometimes; Philip Quast, an inspirational and a supportive friend; and, most especially, my dear friend Bill Nielson, the creative soul who gave Syd Synergy and friends their life and assisted me greatly recording my voice and composing the soundscapes for the companion website recordings.

A huge thank you to two gifted actors, Chelsea Dawson, and my son, David, and to videographer Jerry Guan who willingly helped to bring the toolkit warmup exercises for the companion website to life. And to beautiful Natalie Lynch who helped design the cover and designed and formatted the book's tables and figures. Other dear friends have assisted, reading chapters and providing much needed perspective. Still others have joined me in copious cups of coffee and let me rave on passionately. You know who you are and are all part of the reason this book is in your hands.

A heartfelt thank you to my family. To my late parents, who were guiding lights and foundational in my career; they were extraordinary examples of 'being present' – giving and sharing life with others. To my mother, Rosemary, who lit up a room and a stage with her stage presence and introduced me to her passion for musical theatre and performing at an early age. To my two sons, Nic and David, who have supported and championed me – you are an unending source of encouragement. You keep me honest and inspire me to discover the magic in every day and every performance. To David, particularly, who is currently practising what I am endeavouring to preach in this crazy business – keep radiating your love for storytelling, keep making bold, generous choices, and never lose your sense of joy, imagination, curiosity and wonder. Watching you grow in skill and passion was the catalyst for my journey back into academia. You have worked and trained hard. Continue to curate 'It' well.

Finally, to my God and my Lord, the source of 'It'. The creative life force and power in me. You are. With all of me, thank You.

INDEX

Page numbers in italics refer to tables and figures

acting 20, *23*, 25, 51, 55, 57, 60–1, 70, 80, 82, *105*, *111*, 116, 118, 153, 155, 185
    tools 137–14
actions (actioning) 16, 42, 52, 61, *98*, *111*, 112, 119, 122, 130, 139, 140, 142, 145, 158, *163*, 172, 192
actor(s)
    role in 'It' Factor 39, 48, *49*
    personal methods 57, 104–7, *105*
affirmations 59, 135, 161–2
Amos, Stephen 28, 32, 52–3, 84–5, 92, 108
anxiety
    emotional responses 161, 182
    behavioural responses 94
    performance 33, 95, 159, *188*, 189
archetypes (Pip McKay) 160
Aristotle, *Rhetoric* 11
    modes of persuasion 11
atmosphere 40, 42, 47–8, 58–9, 74, 80, 87, *110*, 112, *120*, 130, 137, 144, 147–8, 150, 154, 158, 168, 170–1
atmospheric walks 116, 132, 144, 172–3, 180
attitude(s) *22*
    mental 29, 97, 112
    vowels *120*, 134
attraction (see also charm, beauty) 14, 17, 35, 45, 85
audience (observer) 11
    empathy 67–8
    role of 19, 28, 40, 41–4, 48, 65–6, 69–75, 80, 82, 109, 179–80
audition 27, 30, 33, 42, 44–5, 97, 107, 183, 196
authenticity (see also truth) 23, *24*, 36, 67–8, 74, 124, 196

ball work *120*, 129, 141, 154, 156, 190
beauty 8, 13, 14, 35, 71, 83, 85–6, 160
Being, Ways of 54, *65*, 110, *110–11*
belief 64, 95, 97
    self 95–96, 97, *98*
body-centring (*see also* grounding) 155–7
body language 14, 34

Bow, Clara, The It Girl 13–14, 90, 126
bravery *23*, 28, 44, *49*, 55, 68, 74, *110*, 160, 183
breath 16, 54, 56–7, *61*, *105*, 107-8, 111, 149, 180
breathing 118–19, 120, 122
    Accent Method 132
    breathing in a square 124,
    intercostal diaphragmatic 124–5
    primal *110*, 125–7
    rhythmic 123
    SPLAT (Singers Please Loosen Abdominal Tension) 125
    squat 123,
    and song study 168
    and stretching 121–2
    Swiss Army Knife 133
bricolage 170–1
bridge-building (see also transactions)
    synergistic, interactive 28, 66, 68, 71, 89, 112, 142
    actor-driven 71–2, *72*, 80, 139
    audience-driven 73–4,
Broadway musicals 14–15
Brook, Peter 16, 99
Brown, Brené 54, 143, 184

Cameron, Julia 25, 71, 162, 165, 183,
Castles, Geoffrey 59–60
chakras 36, 76, 155
Chalfin, Dane 149
Chapman, Janice *110*, 125, 149
character 21, *23*, 27–8, 67, 86, 106–7, 146, 158, *163*, 178
    traits 32, 83, 160
characterisation 33, 48, 60, *61*, 104–5, 139, 140–1
    embodiment 34, 37, 52, 53–4, 58, 64, 69, 150, 159, 168, 171
charisma, charismatic 12, 15, 21, *22*, 35, 83–5, 88
Chekhov, Michael 6, 47, 58, 66, 76, *105*, 108, *110*, *111*, 130, 137, 144–6, 154–5, 164
    Five guiding principles for actors 115–16
    psychophysical exercises 158–9
Chidzey, Alinta 27, 45, 69, *105*

choices 53, 58, 70, 90, *105*, 107–8, 112, 126, 139, *140*, 158, 167, 184
cognition
    Ideational 21–2, *24*, 27, 51–2, 64–5, 139, 148
    Intuitive 21, 23, 29, 51–2, 64, *65*, 140, 149
Collier, Jacob 180,
Come From Away 48, 87,
comparisons 182
commitment 51, 71, 107, *110*, 145, 179, 180–2, 186–7
communion 186
community 87, 161, 186
compassion 32, 184
competency (*see also* technical competencies) 186
conceptual framework 5, 21, 79–80, *81*, 177
confidence 14, *22–3*, *24*, 27–8, 29, 31–2, 36, 45, 55, 83–4, 97, 111, 137, 160,182–3, 189
connection(s) *20*, 82, 90, 105, 119, 129, 132, 153, 185
    to self (grounding) 127–30
    transactional 39–49 *49*, 67, 112, 161,
courage *20, 24* 33, 74, 95, 97, 183, 186
creative directors (*see also* directors) 22–3, 26, 30–1, 36, 42, 45, 89, 95, *108*, 114
    techniques 51, *61*, 107–9
Creative Twisting exercise *120*, 130–1, 169,
Creativity 3, 64, 71, 77, 98, 115, 116, 131, 164–5
crossing the threshold exercise 135–6
Csikszentmihalyi, Mihalyi 78, 98–9
Cuny, David 69, 164, 196,
curiosity 20, 33, 52, 61, 70, *70*, 110, 170, 183–4, 193

dance (*see also* physical competency) 9, 44, 57, 97, 111, 118
David, Susan 185,
determination (*see also* grit) 156, 181
directors (*see also* creative directors)
    methods 29, 32, 33, 34, 47, 52, 56–60, *61*, 71–2, 84
discovery 4–6, 36, *49*, 59–60, 68–71, 86, *105*, 110–11, 149, 170, 174, 179
Doing, Ways of 57, *61*, *64*, 110, *111*
Donnellan, Declan *110*, 145

ease *49*, 68, 80, 86, 104, *105*, *110*, 127
efficacy 97, 170,
ego 28, 29, 36, 56, 76, 95, 144,
    no *23*, 36, 68, 77, 80, 180, 182
    higher 76, 144,
emotion(s) 11, 17, *20*, 31, 35–6, 40, 42, 47–8, 59, *61*, 66–7, 98, *105, 111*, 116, 119
    breath 56, 124–6, 142
    exercises and 128, 131, 137, 139, 141, 144, 148, 149–50
    memory 37, 142–3
    negative 97
    thought and 120
emotive (emotio) processes 21, *23*, *24*, 31, 111, 142, 150
empathy 4, 11, *23*, 31, 41, 67–8, 109, 138, 142, 184, 190
empowerment *22*, 31, 35, *111*
energetic centres 76,*111*, 115–16, 135, 138, 143, 145, 155, *156*, 168, 171, 173–4
energy (*see also* synergy) 4, 6, 9, 11, 17, 19–20, *22*, 26, 35–6, 45, 49, 59, 71, 73
    circles of 82, 84
    exercises 135, 150, 155, 158, 161–2
    radiant 66,
    spirit 75
    types 82–86, 107–8, 188
engaged neutral *120*, 127–8
engagement 6, 43, 51, *70*, 78, 84, 88–9, 145, 179
ensemble (*see also* teamwork) 61, 87–8, 90
    role in synergy 59, 83
environment(space and time) 109, 112–13, 138, 145, 180
    influences 95, 97
    and synergy 44, 48, 97, 116, 127
essence, *24*, 32, 45, 64, 77–8, 82, 103, 115, 149, 161, 178–9, 191
etymology, use of in synergy 58, *105*, *139*
expanding and contracting 158, 717–2
expectation(s)
    audience 46, 79, 88,
    others 33, 44, 78, 94
    self 180, 190
exploration (*see also* discovery) 37, 113–16
    personal 160

failure 27, 33, 180
fear 33, 95–6, 182, 188
fearlessness 27–8, 45, *110*
five W's (*see* W questions)
flow 22, 24, 30, 37, 49, 51, 54, 64, 70, 78, 83, 98–9, 110, 137, 154–5, 157, 188
focus *22–4*, 28, 40, 44, 51, 53, 55, 59, 69, 83, 89, 90, 96, *98*, *105*, *108*, 110, 115, 134
    and readiness *120,* 134–6
forgive(ness) 160
fourth wall 42
freedom 10, 22, *22–3*, 25, 29, 30, 31, *49*, 55, 57, 61, 78, 87, 97, *108*, 111, 114–16, 119, 140, 160, 172–4

generosity (generous) *23–4*, 31, 36, 46, *49*, 71, 74, 75, 78, 84, *111*, 180
gift-giving *24*, 36, 40, 44, 97, 179, 187, 190–1

INDEX

Gigerenzer, Gerd 29
Gilhome, Natalie 29–30, 34, 59, 60, 69, 77, 84
Gleeson, Simon 27–8, 33, 46, 58, 93, *105*, 118
Glyn, Elinor 13–14
Goodall, Jane 12–13, 15–16
Granger, Joel 28, 30, 32, 34, 43, 58, 74, 85, *105*
gratitude 160, 162,
grit (*see also* determination) 181
Grotowski, Jerzy 16, 74–5, 154
grounding
 'It' Factor 177–8
 self 127–30

Hadwen, Jaime 29, 35, 68–9, *105*
Hagen, Uta 42, 137, 139, 162–3
halo effect 85–6
hard work 37, 51, 53, *61*, 90, 94, *110*
Hayes, Nancye 26, 31, 43, 55–6
heat 25
Hope Efficacy Resilience Optimism (HERO) 97
higher self (*see also* true self) 77, 144, 164
history
 of 'It' 9–15
 of presence 15–17
honesty (*see also* authenticity) 23, *24*, 40–1, *61*, 67, 82, *111*, 119, 160, 180, 185
hope 97, 139, 163
Hopson, Georgina 28, 31, 35, 44, 52–60, 67–8, 75, *105*
humility (humble), *23*, 75, 160, 178, 182, 186, 191
humour *24*, 28
Hunter, Luke 27, 30–2, 34, 42, 45, 54, 55, 57, 60, 68, 72–3, 93, 108

ideational cognition 22, *24*, 27–8, 139–40, 148–9
identity 21, 32, 71, 78, 96–7, 168, 170
imagination 17, *20*, 25, 39, 41, *61*, 70, *70*, 140, *110*, 112, 115–16, 145, 149, 189
 atmosphere 47, 132, 138
 discovery 69–70, 140–1, 151
 instinct 140, 149
 physicalisation 145, 151, 154, 156–8
 senses/visualization 135–6, 138, 141–2, 147, 189
imaginative play 30, 35, 46, 51, 57, 119, *120*, 121–2, 124, 127, 129–31
imaginative vocalising 132–4
immersion 22–3, *24*, 27–8, 53, 71, 74, 78, 87, *98*, 104, *110*, 115, 172, 180
improvisation (improvising) 22, 106, 112, 130, 132, 139
 Seidenstein, Ira 130–1, 141, 143, 149, 151, 157
 Spolin, Viola *110*, 141

individual(ity) 12, *20*, 32, 35, 76, 79–80, 99, 108, 114, 150
inspiration 6, *20*, 22, 76, 86, *110*, 164, 186
 breathing 122, 125, 129
instinct(ual) 16, 20, 30, 53–4, 61, *108*, 140–1, 149
 breath (primal) 120, 125–6
instinctual response (*see also* intuitive cognition) 23, 29, 37, 46, 47, 52–4, 56, 58, 70, *110*, 130–1, 149
intention 20, 33, 55–6, *61*, 95, 104, *110–11*, 119, *120*, 126, 129, 139, 147, 149, 157, 168, 172, 182
interactions (*see also* connections) 39, 48, *49*, 67, 73–4, *98*, 112, 129
intrinsic
 performative processes 21–36, 41, 46, 48, 51, *61*, 64, 68, 108–11, *163*, 171, 181, 185, 187, 195
 persona (*see also* persona processes) 67, 74, 82, 86, 90, 150, 183
intuitive cognition 21, *23*, *24*, 29–30, 37, 51, 64, *65*, 67, 92–3, *110*, 140–142, 149–50,
'It' movie 13–14
'It' Factor
 biblical understanding 12
 concept of 11, 187
 conceptual framework of 5, 80–1
 definition in musical theatre 6, 79–80
 general understanding 19
 history of 11–15
 other names 4
 perception of in life 5, 45–6
 personal 4, 13, 17, 181
 terminology 13–14
 theory 15–17
'It' Girl see under Bow, Clara

Jackman, Hugh 96, 182
journaling 143, 160, 162, 163, 190
joy 23, *24*, 31, 36, 46, *49*, 55, 68, 74–5, 78, 90, 104, 107, *111*, 180
judgement
 non-182, 190
 self- *98*, 182–3, 184, 190

kairos 12, 82,
keywords 5, *20*, 22–3, 32, 103–4, 107–9, *110–11*
kind(ness) *23*, 32, 78, 160, 184, 190
Kipling, Rudyard 13
knowledge (*see also* liquid knowledge) 9, 43, 51, 52–54, 71, *98*, 146, 159, 188, 191
Korzybski, Alfred 6–7
Kosky, Barry 70,

Laban, Rudolf *111*, 137
 Eight Efforts 157

Langley, Jason 28, 52, 56, 60, 86, 108
light 6, *24,* 25–6, 135, 144, 184
liquid knowledge 63, 64–6, *65,* 109, 179
love 107,*111,* 136, 144, 160, 184, 188, 192
    part of synergy 75
    Greek understanding of *192*
lyrics 30, 33, 53, 69, 86–7, 114, 126, 139, 141, 148–51, 156–8, 167–9, 171

magic 5, 13, 25, 27, 63, 69, 70, 82, 107, 186–7
magnetism 13, *22–3, 24,* 26, 82, 83–4, 185
many-sidedness 193
Marshall, Lorna, *The Body Speaks,* 34, 77, 79
Maunder, Lucy 59, 61, *105*
Maunder, Stuart 26, 27, 30, 34, 52, 55, 57, 60, 67, 90
Melham, Ainsley 26, 28, 30, 32–3, 43, 45, 53–4, 55, 58, 104, *105,* 106
meditation *105, 111, 120,*135, 160, 162, 190
Meisner, Sanford 82, 105, 106,110, 129, 137, 138
methods 35, 51–2, 57–60, *61,* 105–107, 137, 139, 147, 153
Millerchip, Sharon 31, 33, 37, 43, 46, 52–3, 54, 56, 59, 60–1, 68, 71–3, 92, *105,* 106–7, 109
mirror neurons 67, 187
Moana (musical) 147–8, 173
moment before 118, 135, 139, 168, 170, 174
monologue 139, 151,169, 171
motivation 98, 107–8, 188
movement 26–7
Mullins, Noah 199
music
    role in synergy 29, 39, 52, *61,* 79, 82, 86, 89, *98*
    tools *110,* 115, 139, 149, 150–1, 158, 171–3
musical directors 22–3, 32, 55, 60, 68, 73, 125,148
musical theatre, history of 9–15
mystery 70–1, 193–4

nature (natural ability) 23, 90–4
Nelson, Robin 64
Nothing exercise (see also Seidenstein) 131, 141
nurture (developed skills) 90–4, 178, 187, 190, *192*

observer (*see* audience)
O'Byrne, Anna 25, 26, 32
O'Connor, Caroline 32, 43, 55, 58, 107, 185
O'Donnell, Natalie 26, 27, 58–9, 69, 84, *105*
Olivier, Laurence 13, 15, 36
OOPs to UBU continuum 148, 169
opening up 119, 123, 190–1
opportunity 16, 46, 91,160, 191, 196
optimism 97, 181
ownership *20, 23,* 31, 40, *49,* 59, 80, *111*

Parke, Tyran 26, 32, 34–5, 59–60, 94, *108*
partner, partnering work *120,* 129, 130, 141, 156
passion *23–4,* 36, 40, *49,* 71, 75, 78, 80, 107, *111,* 115, 139, 150, 170, 178, 181, 183–4, 190, 192, 194
Performance Quotient (PQ) 36–7, 68, 71, 85, 97, 103, 110
performance synergy 4, 5, 6, 20–1, 35, 36, 63, 70, 77, 79–83, 86, 87–94, *110–11,* 194
performative processes 21–3, 25, 35–6, 44, 46, 48, 51, 55, *61, 65,* 67, 73, 80, *108,* 111, 117, 119, 137, 142, 154, *155,* 181
permission 22, 25, 42, 63, 92, 94–5, 106, 178,180, 187
perseverance (*see also* tenacity) 160, 181
persona *20,* 21, 25, 54, 55, 67, 77, *111,* 119, 162, 182–3
    processes 21, *23, 24,* 32, 40, 45, 48, 61, 64, *65,* 74, 144, 150, 155
personality (*see* persona)
Phillips, Simon 30–2, 55, 56, 71, 108, 145
physical(ity)
    embodiment 22, *23–4,* 34-7, 39–40, 48, 51, 54–6, 65, *108,* 115–16, 151
    exercises 118–19, 122, 127–36, 137–52
    freedom 61, 80, 87, 110,
    space 59, 114, 144
    tools 56, 59, 113, 118, 153–9, 169, 146
    and synergy *20,* 61
play *22–3, 24,* 30, 35–7, 40, 45, 51, 57, *61,* 70, 95, 105, 108, 112, 121, 134–7, 177, 181, 154, 181, 190
Prior, Marina 26–8, 31–3, 44, 46–7, 54–5, 58, 68, 74, 92, *105,* 106
positive psychological outlook (PsyCap) 19, 97, 99, 153, 160
power (*see also* energy) 13, *23, 24,* 36, 47, *49,* 54–5, 83–4, 112, 118, 134, 143–5,153, 164, 171, 174, 183, 185, 189
presence 4, 6, 11–13, 15–17, *20, 22,* 28, 34–5, 39, 42, 44–5, 67, 69, 74, 82, 98, *111,* 144, 179–80
present (verb) 179
present (noun) 179
primal breath 56, *110,* 116, *120,* 125–7, 143, 168, 171, 174
primal sound *110,* 116, 134, 149–50, 154, 169, 173
Psychological Capital (PsyCap) 97–9, 160
psychological gesture 159
psychophysical
    Chekhov 130, 132, 141, 158–9
    connection 112

INDEX

embodiment 104, 108, 115, 145–6
   exercises 47, 58, 66, *105*, *110*, 144, 189
puppet play 128
purpose 75, 88, 96, 139, 178, 183, 192

Quast, Philip 44, 54, 56–8, 59, 69, 73, 82, *105*

radiance 13, 25–6, 45, 58, 66, 71, 91, 115, *120*, 135, 144, 162
Ralph, Michael 25–6, 30, 34–5, 42, 57, 70, 83, 85–6, 95, 108
rehearsal and 'It' 28, 30–1, 34, 36, 42, 44, 46, 52, 58–61, 97, 103, 106–7
resilience 97 185, 196
resonance 132,
response (responding) *81*, 140, *140*
rituals 59
Rix, Jemma 27, 45, 68, 75, *105*
Rodenberg, Patsy 58, *111,* 122
   energy circles of presence 82, 84, 190
Rubenach, Ashleigh 44, *105*

sacrifice 179,
Sandpit of Imaginative Play 103, 113–15, *114*, 154, 177
   structure – macro and micro *114*
   use of 115–16, 165
SASS! Toolkit – Strategies for Acting Singing Synergy
   background 103–4,109–12, *110–11*, 177
   contents *111, 112*, 115–16, 153
saw and seesaw exercise 130
sawubona 185
Seidenstein, Ira *110–11,* 137
   Creative Twist exercise 130
   Nothing exercise 131
self-awareness 24, 36, 40, 84, 160
self-belief *23*, 27–8, 95–6, 97, *110*, 160, 181, 183, 190–1
sensate experience (*see also* senses) 21, *22*, 25, 64–5, 137
senses (sensate) 20, 21, *22*, 25–7, 37, 41, 48, *110*, 122, 135, 142, 161
   five sense stimulation 80, 142, 147, 158, 173
   memory 138, 142–3
   perception 142–3
   tools 138, 147–8
sex appeal 83, 85
Sheldon, Tony 25, 58, 92, *105*
Sherman, Jon 70, 93
Simpson, Fay 155, 160, 182
spontaneity 20, 30, 68–9, *105*, 119, 126, 131
stage presence (*see also* presence) 16–17
STOP (Surrender, Open up Trust, Play) 190–1

study
   text 51, 109, *110*
   song 137, 167–74
soul 74–5, 6
SOVT (Semi-Occluded Vocal Tract exercises) 133–4
space (*see also* environment) 113
specificity *20*
spirit (higher self) 74–5, 77–8
spiritual creativity 164
spontaneity 68–69, *70,* 71, 80, 119, 126, 131, 179, 186
stage 44, 46–7
Stanislavski, Konstantin 42, 58, 76, 137, 139, 142–3, 144,162
   exercises for character building 143
Stewart, Kris 34, 45, 56, 72, 185
stimulus 126, 140, *140*, 141,179
story 3, 14, *23*, 28, 33, 37, 40, 48, 52, 54, 61, 67, 71, 72, 74, 80, 87, *105*, 109, *111*, 112, 114–15, 124–6, 131, 148, 162, 167, 168, 170–1, 179
strategies 5, 51, 103, 117, 178
   stretching 121–3
subtext 53, 58, *105*, *110*, *120*, 126, 134, 139, 141, 143, 159, 169, 173, 174, 185
surrender 31, 77, 190–1
Syd Synergy 7, 24
synergy 6, 19, 61, 91–4
   blockers 7, 162, 179, 188
   definition of 4, 37, 79–80
   equation 61, *64*
   origins 11–12
   qualities of *20*
synergy types 82–90
   audience-driven 88
   ensemble 83, 88
   false 89–90
   genre-driven 88
   performance 4, 5–6, 21, 35, 70, 79–83, 82–3, 177
   personal 51, 80–2, 88
   story-driven 87

talent *23*, 74, 88, 90, 92, 181, 183, 196
teamwork (*see also* ensemble) 17, *120*, 160
technical competencies (skill) 22–4, 33–4, 36
technique (*see also* technical competencies and toolkit) 9, 15, 16, *20*, 30, 92, *105*, 116, 118,146,147, 186
   integration 35, 55, 57–61
temperament 32
tenacity (*see also* perseverance and resilience) 181
text 11, 52, 59, 61, 67, 114, 126, 149, 156
   contributing factor to synergy *23*, 28–9, 30, 39, 51, 86

mining of 33, 52–3, 58, *105*, *108*, *110*, 139–41, 149, 156–7, 172–3
super text 168,
thinking (*see also* ideational and intuitive cognition) 56, 76, *105*, 139, 156, 183
and synergy 23, 28–29, 141
Thinking, Ways of 49, 51, 52–4, 60, *61*, 64, *65*, 69, 110, *110–11*
time 9, 12, 27, 39, 44–8, 56, 67, 68, 71, 78, 80, 98, 112–13, 123, 141–2, 179, 188
Tina: The Tina Turner Musical 48
toolkit tools and techniques 5, 104, *110–11*, *112*, 171–4
 acting 137–146
 application 170–4
 musical 146–51
 physical 153–9
 psychological 160–5
 singing 146–51
 whole-self activation 117–36
training 16, 34 , 60, 64, 112, 116, 153
 cross 116, 137, 147, 173
 formative 51, 91–3
 methods 51–2, 57–8, 146
transaction(al) (*see also* connections) 39, 72, 74, 79, 179, 185
 bridge building 66, 71, 72–3, *72*, 80
 interactions 39–44, 48, *49*, 74, *98*, 109, 112
 Stanislavkian graph 140
true self 74, 77, 180
trust 19, *22–3*, 30, 31, 35, 43, 66–8, 74, 95, 99, *105*, 160, 186, 190, 194
 and the audience 43–4, 67–8
truth(ful) 11, *22*, 25, 44, 61, 66–8, 71, 75, 77–8, 125, 139

acting *24*, 29, 49, 65, 67–8, 73, 87, 106, 138, 147, 177
Tyack, Michael 34, 73, 126

valence/arousal matrix *189*
validation 3, 71, 179
values 11, 78, 95–7, 163, 164, 178, *178*, 183, 184, 188, 190
 production 82, 89
VIA character strengths 160
visualization 59, 97, 104–5, *111*, 173, 138
visualize 59, 105, 107, *111*, 123–5, 127–9, 133–5, 141, 144–8, 156–7, 161
vowels exercises *120*, 133–4, 139, 148
vulnerability 16, *24, 49*, 74–5, 63, 68, 74, 90, *111*, 112, 179, 185, 194,

'W' Questions (who, what, when, where, why, whether) 20, 37, 41, 80, 115, 128, 162–4, 184, 187
Wangh, Stephen 154
warm-ups (*see also* whole-self activation) 58–9, *105*, 177–19, *120*, 122, 154
 acting 130–2
 singing (vocalising)132–4,169–70
 physical 127–30, 169
 psychological 135–6
 theatre performance 119
whole-self activation (*see also* war-up) 117–136
why (*see also* W questions) 115, 126, 178
work (*see also* story) 49, 71, 86–7

yoga (yogic)
 breathing *120*, 122, 124
 exercises 56–7, 118
 thinking 36, 76, *156*

ABOUT THE AUTHOR

Jacqui Hall Cuny is a passionate musical theatre researcher, pedagogue, creative director and performer with forty-five years of professional experience in Australia and overseas.

A graduate of the Queensland Conservatorium and University of Queensland, Jacqui toured Australia with major commercial musicals in the 1980s before moving to England to further her career. There she performed in productions in Manchester, Birmingham, and London's West End before returning to Australia in 1989. Since that time, Jacqui has continued performing and teaching, completing a Master's in Voice Pedagogy and a PhD in Music, which explored the elements and constructs of musical theatre performance synergy. She performs, teaches, lectures at conferences, and runs musical theatre performance workshops in Australia and internationally. She maintains strong affiliations with the staff of Australia's top tertiary musical theatre courses and currently coaches some of Australia's professional actors.

Her joy is empowering singing actors as they move forward in their careers. For more information visit jacquihallcuny.com.